THE AMERICA OF TODAY

T0382623

THE AMERICA OF TODAY

BEING LECTURES DELIVERED AT THE
LOCAL LECTURES SUMMER MEETING
OF THE UNIVERSITY OF CAMBRIDGE
1918

EDITED BY

GAILLARD LAPSLEY, M.A.
PH.D. (HARVARD)
FELLOW AND LECTURER OF TRINITY COLLEGE

CAMBRIDGE
AT THE UNIVERSITY PRESS
1919

CAMBRIDGE
UNIVERSITY PRESS

University Printing House, Cambridge CB2 8BS, United Kingdom

Cambridge University Press is part of the University of Cambridge.

It furthers the University's mission by disseminating knowledge in the pursuit of education, learning and research at the highest international levels of excellence.

www.cambridge.org
Information on this title: www.cambridge.org/9781107544635

© Cambridge University Press 1919

First published 1919
First paperback edition 2015

A catalogue record for this publication is available from the British Library

ISBN 978-1-107-54463-5 Paperback

PREFACE

THE lectures here brought together in permanent form have been chosen with a special object in view. A large, and happily an increasing number of English people are interesting themselves in American affairs and American activities. But one knows from the questions frequently put to one, that they are sometimes puzzled by references to things which in America are assumed—often gratuitously enough—to be matters of common knowledge. It is hoped that this book will help to overcome these difficulties and make the movement of American life a little more intelligible to busy English readers.

The Cambridge Summer Meeting was held last August and the discourses addressed to it, therefore, were read or spoken under the shadow of the war. No attempt has been made to adjust the printed lectures to the bewildering changes which have taken place in the past nine months; they are offered to the public as they were delivered to the audience for which they were prepared. This has led to the retention of a certain number of apparently repetitious or contradictory passages. There is, however, a great advantage in seeing the same group of facts from varying points of view and in different contexts. As regards contradictions they will be found to be apparent rather than real. American life is so complex and the American background so various that the most cautious generalization may often be supplemented by a statement which appears to contradict it. Turning from facts to judgments it is perhaps needless to say that each writer is alone responsible for such theories or opinions as may be expressed in his contribution. It is thought, however, that the book has a certain unity which one would scarcely have expected to find in a group of essays composed independently by people for the most part unacquainted with one another.

The heavy pressure of college work which has been almost uninterrupted since the armistice has occasioned a delay in the appearance of this volume which no one regrets more than the editor. He is under the greatest obligation to the Syndics of the Press for their sympathetic patience and to the Rev. Dr Cranage without whose generous and skilful help he could not have completed the work at this time.

GAILLARD LAPSLEY.

Trinity College,
Cambridge.
April 1919.

CONTENTS

INTRODUCTION

WHEN President Wilson issued the 'strict account-ability' note in February 1915 people in England began to ask each other 'What will America do?' 'What does America think?' These questions may be thought to have received a pretty conclusive answer on 5 April 1917. But even then the declaration of war with Germany by the United States government might be taken as the act of the government alone, leaving the original questions open. There would be some show of reason in this, for those who put the question 'What does America think?' ought to be ready to say what they mean by America. It would be fair to ask them whether they are prepared to attribute a common mind to a mixed population of upwards of a hundred millions of persons spread over the better part of a continent. The problem stated in this way becomes formidable and it is worth attending to a little because any estimate that the friends of America in this and other countries may form of its share in the present war and the future community of nations will depend upon its solution. A brief discussion of this problem, accordingly, may constitute a fitting intro-duction to a volume which tries to illustrate to English readers the organization and movement of the national life of America at this moment.

To speak of American national life is to presume the existence of an American nation in whatever sense the word may be taken. The inhabitants may of course be regarded as a people in the political sense of the term. They are united for a common political purpose, they are agreed upon the form of a government, its ends and methods. After any political strife the defeated minority acquiesces in the will of its opponents and adapts itself with tolerable loyalty. There is a reasonable diffusion of information and the knowledge required to make use of it. In short the conditions requisite for the formation of a public opinion upon a given question are present and upon the most urgent of contemporary questions, at least, there can be little doubt that such a public opinion has been formed. That does not, however, take us very far. Much the same judgment might, in the first year of the war, have been passed on the Russian empire or Austria-Hungary to neither of which events allow us to impute a common mind or continuing purpose. The question is of something deeper and more abiding than a public opinion upon an immediate issue however far-reaching and important that issue may be. It is a question of a common mind and a common will that shall be coherent, continuous and self-consistent. Such a common mind you will expect to find in a nation as contrasted with a people or a race using the term in a biological sense. The word may be taken to imply the result of the play of a good many forces, some physical as common blood or descent, some social as manners and customs, and some moral as language, tradition, religion, the sense of a common history and a common destiny.

Can the American people be described as a nation in this sense? At first it seems impossible to return anything but a negative answer to the question so put. For one thing the structure of the continent and the nature of its settlement appear to condemn the American people to regionalism. The Alleghanies drawing a barrier from the St Lawrence almost to the Gulf define the Atlantic coast as a unity, just as on the other side of the continent the Sierras guard a region which describes itself as the coast and resents, very properly, being called western. Between these extremes you must reckon with the basin of the Mississippi and its great tributaries, the regions that look toward the Gulf, the prairies rising slowly to the foot of the Rockies and between them and the Sierras, a more or less desert region rich in minerals and toward the south in grazing lands. Such environment has had its natural effect upon the economic life of the people. The east is largely industrial, the south is preoccupied with cotton, the middle region thinks of maize and wheat, until as you go further west the interest changes to timber, mining and cattle-raising; and finally the life of the Pacific coast is almost self-contained. To these centrifugal forces must be added the great diversity of races which compose the population. This has been the case, of course, from the very beginning. From the Kaatskills to Los Angeles, from Sault Ste Marie to New Orleans you may trace on the map the races that helped to plant a European population in the new world. Dutch ancestors are still invoked in New York, French Law prevails in Louisiana and the English spoken in California is enriched with an infusion of Spanish[1]. Since the last decades of the nineteenth century the stream of immigration has poured ceaselessly into American ports. The newcomers have mostly left homes in south-eastern Europe, though we have received many Germans and Scandinavians and a fair scattering of other races and nationalities. They have been needed and turned to useful ends, but economic exploitation of the new material has outstripped the moral and social processes of absorption. Great cities like New York and Chicago appear to a native American as wholly cosmopolitan. The newcomers have accepted exile without getting as far as repatriation in a new fatherland. The returning exile indeed, asks in his bewilderment to be shown the English quarter. Milwaukee used to be reckoned the third largest German city in the world. In the north-west there were regions where candidates for political office found it desirable to make their campaigning speeches in one or other of the Scandinavian languages. In San Francisco, before the fire at least, very nearly half the population, which then amounted to some four hundred thousand, were of foreign birth. I have never seen a census of newspapers published

[1] It might be added that the German spoken in Pennsylvania is considerably diluted with English.

in the United States in other languages than English, but it must exist and would make instructive reading. The population has nearly doubled in the course of a generation and immigration has contributed very substantially to that result.

But race, environment and economic interest do not exhaust the elements of diversity with which we have to reckon. Political decentralization reinforces, though it does not coincide with these. The states and the great municipalities make a claim upon individual pride, loyalty and sense of duty which is readily admitted. So readily, indeed, that there is often little of these qualities left with which to satisfy more remote but equally legitimate claims. In Wheeling, Boisé City or El Paso the activities of Washington are obscure, those of London, Paris or Petrograd almost fabulous. But this point is so admirably elucidated in Lord Eustace Percy's lectures which follow that it need not be further laboured here.

A consideration of the same order, however, may detain us for a moment. A federal government and particularly one resting on so wide a territorial basis as that of the United States, must depend for its success in a very large degree upon its power to appeal to the imagination of its citizens. Their response to such an appeal will depend again upon their resources of imagination whether temperamental or cultivated. Now it is futile to attribute a common temperament to a population composed of such various and confused elements. What then is left? Beside the flag there is no visible symbol to arouse and attract the imagination of simple folk and help them to conceive themselves as members of a whole larger than the one immediately visible to them. Presidents come and go and with the help of their caricaturists try to transform themselves into the political entities which Mr Graham Wallas considers so important. Sometimes like Mr Roosevelt they succeed without returning to the White House. While they are there the conditions of presidential government require them to double the rôle of chief magistrate and party-leader. As party-feeling is deep and strong in America the chief magistrate tends to fall into the background unless the president happens to be in his second term and without ambition or hope of re-election. Clearly it is the chief magistrate who would have the best, perhaps the only chance of arousing the popular imagination; but in this he is hampered by his political connexions.

Then the historic principles of the two great American parties involve what appear to be inharmonious, perhaps even irreconcilable, theories of the state. To English ears the names democrat and republican may sound either meaningless or indistinguishable. Certainly they do not suggest any important or even intelligible differences of political opinion. The names, indeed, are the not very happy results of a series of political accidents. The republicans were whigs before they broke with their friends in the south and before that again they were federalists and when they were called federalists the ancestors of the present democrats called themselves republicans. These two parties have divided on many issues, some of which today are dead and others sleeping, the construction of the constitution, national banking, protective tariffs and so on. But beneath or behind all these, they have held views of the nature of the state and the consequent function of government which came to the surface and found clear expression when the present constitution was framed and adopted. Ten years of confederation had reduced the independent colonies to a state of disorder and impotence that cried out for remedy. Hamilton and his friends suggested a remedy in a series of essays which, under the title of *The Federalist*, has become a classical text of political theory. Jefferson and his supporters met the federalist views with a vigorous opposition which, though both parties agreed to the compromise of the present constitution, is alive and operative today. I have not the pretension of analysing the two views in as many paragraphs, but some general indication of their nature is indispensable. The federalists sought to secure the liberty and well-being of the individual as citizen. They thought of him and provided for him in that capacity. It would not perhaps be fantastic to say that their attitude toward the individual was that of the common law because they were concerned to construct an organism which should function permanently, adapting itself therefore to new conditions and securing in its own health and welfare that of the individuals who for the moment composed it. They dreaded administrative oppression and inefficient government. If they did not actually dread the immediate expression of the will of the majority, they certainly did not trust it. The scheme of government which they devised and succeeded in setting up was based on the principle of the separation of powers secured by a system of checks and balances and strong government departments. It was objected to this plan that it tended to thwart the expression or at least the realization of the popular will. This is probably true, though the admission ought to be qualified by some discussion of what is meant by the popular will. The federalists trusted the government and thought that a considerable measure of initiative and leadership should be allowed it in order to meet new conditions as they arose and deal with emergencies that could not have been foreseen. To this end they advocated what is called a loose construction of the constitution. Jefferson and his friends on the other hand began with the individual and proceeded from him to the minimum amount of government necessary to secure for him the opportunity of developing himself without molestation either from other individuals or from the state. They had a robust faith in the American citizen and reckoned on the good will and equal worth if not equal ability of all citizens. These they considered were self-reliant and resourceful and if they were left free to work out their own destinies the state would prosper. The functions of a government constructed upon such a faith was to keep its hands off and to follow the lead given by the democracy. It is not surprising, therefore, that in proportion as the republicans of those days trusted the people they distrusted government activity and desired to restrict it as much as possible. One way of doing this was to make the written constitution fairly explicit and then insist upon a strict construction of it. This policy, with all that it implies, has been consistently pursued by the party—at present called democratic—which has maintained the Jeffersonian tradition.

For our purposes the point to be noticed is this—a republican administration would probably think it its duty to give the country a lead, to shape and inform, if not actually to evoke, public opinion. It would try, in short, to make the people conscious of a common purpose and a common mind. No such course, on the other hand, would be open to a democratic administration. It would no doubt have to take measures to educate and enlighten individual opinions throughout the country, but it would then have to wait until the majority had spoken or intimated its will. The case, of course, is never as simple as this, nor is the contrast as sharp. It is important, however, to get the general tendencies and guiding principles clearly stated.

Now it might be thought that despite the elusiveness of a federal government and the small appeal it seems able to make to the loyal citizen of any one of the states, despite the divergent views of the two parties with regard to the nature of the state and its relation to the individual, the idea of America as a nation with a history and a destiny would still have been able to impose and develop itself in favourable conditions. The existence of such conditions, one assumes, would depend in a great degree upon the general system of education and the character of the prevailing forms of religion. By these means more than by any others each generation could learn to handle life imaginatively and get some grasp of ideas. But in this respect the American system of education in spite of its many and striking merits appears to be defective. It is regional, concrete and secular. These are defects of its qualities but from our point they are none the less defects. The schools are provided by the states and the towns to which they are a just source of pride and satisfaction. But the tax-payer thinks of them in connexion with his state or his municipality and compares them and their achievements in wholesome rivalry with the schools of neighbouring communities. Then the tendency of education, up to the university stage at least, is toward the practical and the concrete. This is very natural where most if not all of the boys and girls are being trained to earn their livings. The best evidence that it is felt as a shortcoming by the people concerned is to be found in the deliberate attempts made to cultivate patriotism by ceremonies in connexion with the national flag and the study of what is called 'civics.' In the universities, where of course a considerable freedom of choice is left to the undergraduates, economics is the only theoretical study that attracts considerable numbers. I am speaking of the average man or woman in the state universities, not of the better sort whom the philosophers and mathematicians attract readily enough. The higher secondary schools indeed furnish the exact opposite of the conditions described by Maurice Barrès, in his picture in *Les Déracinés* of the students of a French provincial *lycée* uprooted and detached by the study of philosophy Finally all public education has had to be secularized. There are pretty obvious reasons for this, but the effect upon the national temper and habit of mind is still unfortunate. If we turn to examine the prevailing character of religion in America, one generalization appears to be safe In so far as the religion is American it is subjective and individualistic. The protestant tradition in that respect is very strong. This is perhaps the only part of the religious system held by a majority of the original settlers that remains general and vigorous today. Calvinist theories of church and state have vanished and Calvinist theology is not general. Church government tends to be congregational, though to this there are many striking exceptions, notably the large and influential Methodist connexion. But personal religion remains among all who bear the American tradition, a personal and not a corporate life, and the notion of a nation state involving alike the destinies of the individual and the community has little help to gain from this quarter. The churches that understand and cultivate the corporate idea are exotic. I use the word with all respect and gratitude. The United States would be at a loss to discharge the task that has fallen to their lot without the loyal and generous help they have received from the Roman church. But the Roman church remains the church of Rome and its strength in America is among men and women of foreign birth or extraction. The Protestant Episcopal church though influential in the large towns and cities is relatively very small in numbers. Christian Science undoubtedly exercises a very important moral force but it is doubtful to what extent, if any, it influences people in their way of conceiving the state.

I have touched a few salient points only, and on them very briefly, but I have said enough perhaps to make a stranger to the country feel that if these are really the prevailing conditions it would be idle to look for a common purpose or the abiding common mind upon which the existence of a common purpose depends. It is, of course, easily understood that upon a given issue a public opinion would be formed and expressed. Upon an issue so universal in its importance as the present war that could scarcely fail to be the case. But it is another and a very weighty question to know whether the public opinion as to the existence and force of which evidence is daily accumulating is really the considered expression of a common mind and therefore continuous and consistent with the decisions which the country has taken at earlier crises in its history. In spite of the case I have tried to state for the antecedent improbability of this, I believe that it is so and that for reasons which may now be brought together in a summary fashion.

In the first place history and science have transcended many though not all of the obstacles to unity to which attention has been called in the preceding pages. Take for example the development of communications and the movements of population. The great pioneer movement, what is called the winning of the west, was, in general, an achievement carried through by men of English blood and colonial descent. There were Indians to be pushed back, Frenchmen and Spaniards to be absorbed, but if we except Louisiana and parts of the south-west where the Spanish influence was strong, the political societies from the Alleghanies to the Pacific were founded by men from the original colonies from which they received their moral and political traditions and their forms of government. In many cases they had already a respectable accumulation of history before they were called upon to undertake the business of making Americans out of almost any material that came to hand. The movement westward was slow because the struggle with nature was hard, but though there was not much communication, at first at least between the pioneers and the homes they had left, the population of the country was continuous in texture and quality. Then, after two generations of hardship and isolation the railways came to lead the movement of population and eventually for all effective purposes of human intercourse, to reduce the continent to an ideal area probably smaller than that of the original colonies. The advantages of this were quickly felt but some consequences very embarrassing to the federal idea have not yet quite found their place. These Mr Kennedy has discussed in his lecture that follows and it may suffice to allude to one aspect of them here. In many material respects we find ourselves in America, whether we like it or not, living the life of a single national community. Labour, capital, business and in some degree opinion, are organized upon what is called a 'nation-wide' basis. You may pass from New York to San Francisco, a distance of some 3000 miles, in four days and as many nights—faster, it may be, now—and Californians, at least, used to complain that that was twenty-four hours longer than was necessary. The New York Stock Exchange before the war at any rate was the scene of operations that were initiated at many and distant points in the country and executed, thanks to the telegraph and telephone, on the same day. The more important firms of stock-brokers have private wires connecting them with groups of distant customers. The scale of production has become so great as to unite whole regions in a common interest irrespective of state or party attachments. In the case of such commodities as cotton, Indian corn and wheat, indeed, these interests permeate the entire country. The expansion of the American population from sea to sea has thus been followed by a process of concentration that has in many ways produced truly national conditions presenting at the same time difficulties and problems demanding, it would seem, a national solution. Perhaps the best illustrations of this are to be found in the legislation by which the federal government was authorised to exercise some control over the railways and those combinations of capital loosely called trusts. Mr Kennedy has discussed the nature and working of the Interstate Commerce Act of 1887 and the Sherman Act of 1890 and I need do no more than refer to what he has written. But I may mention, by way of further illustration, certain other problems that appear to insist upon a national solution. At present the separate states determine the qualification for the franchise, the conditions upon which divorce is granted, the regulation of the liquor trade, and question of capital punishment[1]. The irregularities not to say the scandals which have arisen out of this state of things are well known. One state at least allows no divorce, in several the process is accomplished with Mosaic simplicity and despatch, you have only to establish a domicile by six months' residence and take certain easy and appointed steps. Again certain states prohibit

[1] These words were written in September 1918.

absolutely or relatively the sale of alcohol, or leave the
question to local option, while in others there is little or no
control of the trade. For a long time the state of Louisiana
harboured a lottery that 'operated' over the entire country.
Some states have admitted women to the franchise, others
have withheld it in practice, though not in theory, from the
negro. The list could be lengthened, but the point is clear
enough. The advocates of 'causes' that are supported by a
good deal of organization are tending to give up the old
state campaigns and to try the formidable adventure of a
constitutional amendment. If they succeed they will by so
much have advanced the process of concentration of national
life. Finally there is a tremendous force working consciously
or unconsciously in this direction, in the newspaper and
periodical press. In a great many ways this is obvious and
requires no comment. But there is one aspect of it that is
not at once apparent. The unifying force of the American
press consists, I venture to think, less in the way in which
it selects and accents the news of the day, or in the editorial
views which it expresses than in the fashion in which it
contrives to feed the imagination and the humour of the
country. It may be admitted that the diet is meagre and not
always digestible but the uniform movement (it can scarcely be
called the growth) of the language, apart from local differences
of pronunciation and idiom, is evidence to the point. I may
just mention two illustrative instances. It is twenty years ago or
more that Mr Peter Dunn began to write, for a Chicago daily
paper, articles in which in the character of an Irish bar-tender
he commented on events of local and sometimes of national
interest. The opinions of 'Mr Dooley' were reprinted and
welcomed up and down the country—I don't know on what
scale Mr Dunn wasn't syndicated and circulated but there
were years when the whole country rocked with laughter
over his shrewd satire and free whimsical humour. To take
another instance, there is a large group of daily papers
owned by Mr W. R. Hearst and published simultaneously

in most of the great cities of America. These devote a good deal of space every day to a series of rough cuts representing the adventures of fantastic characters who have become better known to large numbers of Americans than many public men. One pair of such characters was devised long ago in San Francisco, where Mr Hearst discovered and annexed their inventor. Since then English-speaking Americans have known and laughed in common over 'Jeff and Mutt,' to whom you would be safe in alluding in a company where Dogberry or Sam Weller were as unknown as Hammurabai.

Under the play of such forces the process of concentration has been going on for a generation or more. It has had to compete, of course, with the great annual influx of foreigners and with the conditions of regionalism to which attention has already been called. We may ask therefore whether this process of concentration has been alone enough to create or make possible the growth of a national mind and purpose. The answer I think must be in the negative. The process of concentration has not been a material thing alone and it could never have been accomplished without the cooperation of a moral or spiritual force. Such a force has been at work since the beginning of our independent history, though it did not originate then. The American people began their independent life with a tradition and a purpose which is hard to define though it may be illustrated both with reference to its content and its working.

Anyone who wishes to understand the ideals and purposes that have animated and united Americans from the beginning will do well to attend to the history and spirit of the common law. Dr Hazeltine has discussed this subject in a later part of this book and I have already alluded to it in connexion with the Hamiltonian theory, but I may be allowed to touch on one or two relevant points here. Historically the system of the common law was one of the earliest and strongest forces that made for the growth of English national life and English character. It is perhaps the greatest differentia between the development of England and the rest of Europe, and its influence in the long run has been toward that ordered liberty in which freedom and authority, in external life at least, are harmonized. It has known how to adjust itself to the life and growth of the community, though the process has sometimes needed strong external stimulus, as for example in the seventeenth century. It has sought to secure justice and liberty and to perpetuate them, and not seldom the individual has had to suffer in the interests of the community present and to come. On the other hand the common law has never taken an inquisitorial attitude toward the individual—its machinery was there for him to put in motion if he had need and could bring his case within the scope of any of the established remedies. On the other hand the law would regard him as a legal person having rights and obligations but as no more. There lies the true reconciliation of the apparently divergent views of the two great American parties which in effect seek the same goal by different paths. The spirit of the common law expressed in the Jeffersonian theory its attitude toward the individual, it would seek to secure his rights and not to interfere with his personal liberty. On the other hand it regarded itself as a living organism which must grow with the growth of the community and consider, in speaking its judgments, that it is not merely doing justice between man and man but extending or restricting the application of principles in a way that may affect unborn men and unheard of interests. Hard cases, it is said, make bad law, and where the interests of the living body of the law and the litigant were in conflict it has been the litigant who suffered. This enlightened self-regard had its share no doubt in shaping the Hamiltonian view of the state in its relation to the individual. Moreover the common law was a birthright of English-speaking men and the measure of the trust which Americans of all parties have felt and still feel in it, is the fact that they have been content to leave the last word in constitutional matters—and many political ones as well—with the judiciary.

Now, the ideal of the rule of law, the sense of public justice, order and equality of treatment which the common law implies, while excluding certain forms of government does not necessarily require for its realization any particular political or constitutional machinery. When the American revolution came to be associated with the forms of self-government and the notion of liberty as an end, the idea that has directed and still directs the course of American history was formulated. That idea constitutes the true unity of the American people and the strangers who have cast in their lot with America. It has led them by paths they little expected to tread, but the guidance has never been in doubt.

With Washington's warning against entangling alliances in mind America turned away from Europe to tend the guarded flame of freedom and self-government that appeared to be extinguished everywhere else. The European reaction after 1815, the Holy Alliance and the colonial policy attributed to Russia set American nerves on edge and President Monroe's message to congress in 1823 committed the country at once to a policy and a belief. The policy was the exclusion of European interposition or colonization on the American continents, and the belief, sound enough at that time, was that Europe was reactionary and dynastic. Trade with Latin America, which would have come to an end with the restoration of the rebellious colonies to Spain, was a factor, but on that we need not dwell. The point I wish to make is that in 1823 the country knew and spoke its mind. It would work independently of older societies which, as it thought, neither sympathized with nor understood the great end it had to pursue. We were content to turn our backs on Europe and concern ourselves with the task in hand—reserving comment on transatlantic affairs to Elijah Pogrom. Dickens and Mrs Trollope told us that we were provincial.

This being true we were angry in proportion. We may have been ludicrous but we were grimly in earnest. Behind us, though shut out now by our own act, was autocracy and reaction, in front of us the wilderness to be cleared and settled. To this end there was a common mind and purpose, but on the point of method there was serious disagreement. No one could be quite comfortable about slavery and the question arose in connexion with every new movement westward. But slavery was not the cause of the bitter tragedy of the civil war nor the true issue that was decided in those dark years. That was rather the assertion of the unity of the American people, their common mind and common purpose. No doubt from a strictly legal and constitutional point of view the southern states were right, as from a like point of view Charles I was right and that in each case constitutes the very essence of the tragedy. In 1865 the American people took up its task again conscious of the purpose that had steadily animated it. In the south there was mourning for an old order that had passed away beyond the hope of recall. In the north a feeling that the old isolation had better be continued. But there could be no further question of separation. There was no longer any doubt that behind the political union of sovereign states lay the moral unity of a people with a common task to perform and a common will to perform it.

Thus upon the generation that followed the civil war the events of material nationalization, the sort of concentration that I have tried to describe, came in numbers and rapidity that threatened to sweep them off their feet. But the changed conditions brought the national existence that had been asserted in the civil war into a strong light. Then, as the century waned, adventures in the Atlantic and Pacific left America with dependencies upon its hands that were not states nor territories and could probably never become either. Washington's warning was recalled, imperialism was denounced in certain quarters and the supreme court turned some extremely awkward corners in constitutional law. But the invisible barrier of the Monroe doctrine still stretched across the Atlantic, effectually hiding from American eyes the political movement in western Europe. School histories dwelt on British tyranny, children remembered George III and Lord North after they had forgotten their dates, and Irish-American opinion helped to give something contemporary to an ancient evil. A large Jewish element in the population spread a horror of Russian autocracy. Americans tended to confound all kinds of monarchy, to regard the house of lords as the instrument of an ancient and exclusive aristocracy and to interpret the English establishment in terms of the Holy Synod. Then in August 1914 the world came to an end. The catastrophe found America bewildered and uninformed, clutching with desperate resolve at the high purpose to which it had long ago committed itself and for which it had suffered and fought. Only quite gradually it came to see what the Atlantic barrier had hidden so long, and understand that isolation was no longer necessary because England and France and Italy had long been working, each according to its own genius, for the same end as America. Once that was grasped it became clear that the country had reached another great turning point. And so the dominant idea that turned America toward isolation in 1823 and cast it into civil strife in 1861, led it back in 1917 into the community of free peoples fighting for a common end.

ENGLISH INFLUENCE ON AMERICAN IDEALS OF JUSTICE AND LIBERTY

H. D. HAZELTINE, LL.B., Litt.D.

ENGLISH INFLUENCE ON AMERICAN IDEALS OF JUSTICE AND LIBERTY

I

UNITY in ideals is one of the most striking of all the characteristics of the world alliance now opposed to the autocratic states of Central Europe. The many scattered communities of this alliance possess social, economic, political, religious, and legal systems widely divergent one from another both in historical development and in general character; and yet all of these communities are animated by the same ideals. Of these common ideals, justice and liberty are the two which fill the largest place in the thoughts and hearts of men; they are the chief intellectual and emotional forces which are moving the allied peoples towards victory. But how varied are the constitutional and legal institutions by which liberty and justice are now safeguarded in the different political units of the alliance! The historical explanation of the existence of unity in ideals, amid this amazing diversity in national institutions, will constitute in the future one of the most absorbing and fruitful of all studies. Only by comparing many separate developments in all parts of the world shall we finally understand the vast processes of history which lie behind the war and which have united the allied communities in their firm determination that justice and liberty shall be preserved as the permanent possessions of mankind and that they shall be the governing factors in international as well as in national life.

I propose to deal in my lecture with one special aspect of this course of world history. The question which I ask you to consider is this: What influence has England exercised upon the growth of America's ideals of justice and liberty and their embodiment in her laws and institutions? What processes of history have led to the union of England and America as the joint guardians of legal ideals now common to both countries? Inasmuch as my inquiry is thus limited to constitutional and legal evolution, I shall not consider liberty and justice in their purely social, economic, political, and religious aspects. Nor shall I be concerned with the ideals of democracy, individualism, equality, and nationalism. All of these features of American idealism are intimately related to my theme, and in a comprehensive survey they would require careful consideration. But the scope of my lecture, restricted as it is to the embodiment of liberty and justice in constitutions and laws, permits me to refer to these wider characteristics of American life only as the environment in which constitutional liberty and legal justice have been evolved.

II

It will help us to understand the nature and scope of English influence on the American development if we focus our attention for a moment upon the English conception of law as the realization or embodiment of the ideals of justice and liberty which have animated the nation. For many centuries law has played a masterful part in the life of the English people. Out of the disruptive conditions and tendencies of feudalism England emerged at last as a consolidated and unified national state. Of all the present states of Europe she was the first to express the consciousness of national solidarity in strong central institutions and in a common law. During this formative epoch of their evolution as a political community the English people were imbued with a strong legal spirit, which gave to their institutions the legal character which distinguished them from the institutions of other countries. The absolutism of the Norman and Angevin kings was at length checked and controlled by law. The underlying and permanent significance of Magna Carta is that it expresses and enforces the idea that the king is below and not above the fundamental law of the realm; and from this point of view we may look upon the Great Charter as the turning-point in English constitutional development from an unlimited to a limited monarchy. The notion that the kingship is based upon and subject to law, despite temporary reactions and reversions to absolutism, has ever since remained one of the dominating features of the English constitution. The work of the seven centuries since 1215 has been to develop, from age to age, the necessary machinery for making this fundamental principle effective in the life of the nation; and at the present time the principle is safeguarded not only by law in the narrower sense, but by the conventions or customs of the constitution which, in the final analysis, rest also upon legal sanctions. The centralization of the judicature and the growth of common law and equity were likewise an expression of the English legal spirit; while the development of parliamentary legislation, based finally upon the doctrine of parliament's legal sovereignty, strengthened still further the legal character of all the institutions of the state and of all the fundamental rights of the subject in respect to his person and property. The principle of the rule of law has thus permeated for many centuries the whole fabric of English social and political life. The evolution and the application of this doctrine constitute one of the permanent contributions of the English people to civilization.

The development of English law as the governing factor in the public and private life of the nation has resulted in the firm establishment of the principle that justice and liberty are far more effectively safeguarded by judicial procedure than by the mere declaration of these fundamental rights of man in constitutional documents. No other aspect of their history represents in more striking fashion the practical character of the English people. English legislators and judges have always devoted far more attention to the working out of the machinery for the enforcement of rights than to the elaboration of legal theory. This tendency of the law-making and law-enforcing institutions of the state has given to English jurisprudence one of its chief characteristics, for in its realism, its close attention to the enforcement of legal sanctions, it stands in sharp contrast with the more theoretical jurisprudence of continental countries. In England the fundamental notion has been and still is that justice and liberty rest upon the foundation of an enlightened, upright, and independent judicature capable of enforcing civil and political rights by ordered processes and practices. This aspect of the English common law is especially striking in the domain of its constitutional and criminal branches, but it is likewise noticeable in the branches of private law. The English, unlike the French people, have never issued mere declarations of the rights of man. The great constitutional documents of the common law, from Magna Carta to the present day, have dealt chiefly with the actual processes, constitutional and legal, whereby public and private rights are enforced; and the importance of judicial precedents, as safeguards of justice and liberty, shows also the vital significance of procedure in the English system. The history of the jury as judges of fact in both criminal and civil cases illustrates in another way this same tendency of English jurisprudence to insist on the necessity of machinery. But perhaps the most striking single instance of English realism in law is furnished by the place which the writ of *habeas corpus* has occupied in the whole evolution of justice and liberty. As a protection of individual liberty this process of the courts has been of far more effectiveness than any number of declarations of the abstract rights of man. More than any other people of Europe the English have proceeded upon the assumption that "justice" and "liberty" are but high-sounding phrases, bereft of practical meaning, unless they are assured of realization by means of a stable and effective procedure enforced by all the power of the community. Hence we find that in England the ideals of justice and liberty animating the people have been worked into the whole fabric of actual government. The ideals have been transformed into realities.

I have thought it important to emphasize this leading feature of the evolution of English common law in order that I may explain with more effect the nature of the influence which English ideals of justice and liberty have exerted upon America. The Americans have derived their ideals from England; and in its broadest aspect English influence consists in the extension to America of the common law as a system of rules and processes whereby justice and liberty are assured to the people. American jurisprudence, resting as it does upon English foundations, has thus assumed a practical character no less pronounced than that of the jurisprudence of England. The main outlines of this historical development, whereby the English conception of law has been transferred to America, constitute the theme of my lecture.

III

The North American colonies of England in the seventeenth century were very different in many respects from the mother country. The seventeenth century is the American Anglo-Saxon age. Planted in a vast wilderness inhabited by wild Indian tribes the colonies were, in contrast with England, social and political communities of a primitive character. From the very beginning of their history the colonies possessed certain institutions and legal features based on the English model, but in general they developed, in the environment of the new world, many characteristics which marked them off as communities of an older type than contemporary England. No feature of colonial life illustrates this backwardness in more striking manner than the nature of the courts and of the law. The courts were composed of laymen and administered a popular law suited to colonial conditions. Apart from certain English features which were introduced in accordance with charter provisions that colonial law should conform as nearly as possible to the law of England, the legal systems of the colonies embodied native American elements founded largely on colonial customs and the ingenuity of colonial

legislators and judges, while in the Puritan communities of
New England the Word of God was adopted as the foundation
of the law.

The gradual evolution of the colonies brought about during
the eighteenth century a marked change in the tendency of
legal growth. With their expansion as social and economic
communities the older system of popular courts and popular
law failed to meet the altered conditions of life. The result
was a more rapid adoption of English common law and equity
and of English judicial processes. By the close of the colonial
period the legal system of each one of the provinces was based
in large measure upon that of the mother country. Many
of the judges were still laymen; but in the course of the
eighteenth century a colonial bar, based on the English model,
had developed in each separate province. The influence of
the legal profession operated, in combination with other
factors, in the direction of a fuller reception of the technical
system of English justice. Many of the colonial lawyers received their training in the English universities and Inns of
Court. The spread to the colonies of English law treatises
and collections of statutes and cases also furthered the influence of the legal system of the mother country.

From the very beginning of effective colonization in the
early seventeenth century Englishmen in America claimed
that they were entitled to all the constitutional rights of
Englishmen at home. They based this claim on their status
as subjects of the crown and also on the provisions of the
colonial charters, which formed the earliest American constitutions. They regarded the English common law—more
particularly that part of it which secured the rights and
liberties of the subject—as their own birthright; and they
strenuously insisted upon its principles and processes as their
protection against the encroachments of arbitrary power on
the part of imperial and colonial authorities.

This early appeal of the colonists to the constitutional
aspect of the common law is one of the striking features of

American legal history. Many of the provisions of Magna Carta were embodied in colonial legislation; and, in course of time, the seventeenth century struggle between king and parliament was reflected in the colonies by the incorporation of the Bill of Rights and other great constitutional documents in their own written law. The processes of the colonial courts likewise illustrate this early insistence upon the constitutional safeguards of English justice and liberty. Trial by jury, the writ of *habeas corpus*, and other features of English procedure were adopted by the colonies as integral parts of their own judicial processes. They viewed this machinery of the courts as necessary for the protection and preservation of their rights.

By the close of the colonial era the English conception of law as the embodiment of the ideals of justice and liberty had been adopted by each one of the American communities, even by the Puritan colonies with their theocratic tendencies and their strong emphasis upon the binding authority of the Word of God; and in the colonies, as in England itself, stress was laid upon judicial procedure as the chief instrument for making abstract rights the realities of life. This incorporation of the English conception of law into colonial thought and practice constitutes one of the most fundamental of all the influences of England upon America. Despite a wide divergence in institutional development, a divergence which began in early colonial times and has reached its culmination in the present differences between the English and the American constitutions, this underlying notion of justice and liberty as ideals worked into the practical processes of the courts has always formed a vital feature of American jurisprudence.

IV

During the revolutionary epoch (1760–1789) the American constitution, based upon the institutions which had taken form in the course of the colonial era, developed further upon its own lines. Important features derived from England were retained and embodied in the framework of government, but in general the constitution continued to display, in its main characteristics of growth, marked differences from the contemporary constitution of England. The general tendency of development was more and more in the direction of the federal system, which was definitely established in 1789. This system owed more to the American processes of growth in the colonial and revolutionary periods than to the tendencies which were shaping the English constitution during the same centuries.

I must not pause to consider in detail the features which distinguish the American revolutionary institutions from those of the mother country, and I mention the institutional tendency to divergence only in order to be able to emphasize a fundamental difference between the growth of institutions and the growth of law. In contrast with the constitution the law of the revolutionary times retained its English character. Despite the revolution the colonies as they grew into independent states not only preserved but further developed their legal systems of English derivation. The Anglo-American common law possessed by each one of the states was a system of public as well as of private law, and many of the principles of English constitutional law survived the stirring times of the revolution. These English principles were retained, not through the fortunes of chance or the inertia of tradition: they were retained because the colonists jealously claimed them as their own and as the main safeguard of their liberties. During the long years of controversy with the mother country, before the outbreak of war in 1775, the colonists appealed to "the rights of Englishmen" as the foundation and justification of their cause. They based their arguments not alone on the law of nature; they maintained even more strenuously that their rights were founded upon the English common law as the embodiment of the ideals of justice and liberty which they, as Englishmen, had inherited from the home country. Not only the controversial literature but the state papers of the time prove that the colonists clung to the common law as the highest expression of their ideals —ideals safeguarded by constitutional and legal machinery, which was both English and American because it had been evolved out of the common past of the realm and the colonies.

The English conception of law as the embodiment of the ideals of justice and liberty thus played a leading rôle in the American revolution. Preserved and strengthened by the revolution, this fundamental idea has ever since continued to shape the constitutional and legal evolution of the republic.

V

Lord Bryce, in his *American Commonwealth*[1], has described the American federal union as "a Commonwealth of commonwealths, a Republic of republics, a State which, while one, is nevertheless composed of other States even more essential to its existence than it is to theirs." In our study of the period of independence I shall ask you to hold this description of the political nature of the United States in mind, for it expresses very clearly the duality in institutions and laws incident to American federalism.

There are at the present time forty-eight separate states in the American union, each one of which has its own written constitution and its own system of public and private law. The original states on the Atlantic seaboard, the little republics which declared their independence in 1776, are the oldest of all the American commonwealths, for they are the direct descendants of the thirteen English colonies. They are indeed the colonies in their free and independent form as states, and their constitutional and legal systems have been derived by historical processes from the colonial and revolutionary epochs. The newer states have been formed in response to social, economic, political, and territorial expansion in the period of American independence. Their institutional and legal systems are also based upon pre-revolutionary

[1] Vol. I, 1910, p. 15.

evolution, for, as each new state has been added to the union, it has adopted a political framework and a body of laws derived from the older commonwealths.

I shall not attempt to analyze, from the point of view of their historical evolution, the legislative, executive, and judicial institutions of these forty-eight states. Broadly speaking it may be said that their present structure and spirit are due in part to the influence of English models and in part to the political and legal genius of the American people. An examination of the legal systems of the states proves, in a similar way, that they are based partly on English law and partly on rules and principles which have been evolved, in the course of the centuries, within the American environment. In Louisiana the legal system is founded on the civil law, which was carried to this region in the periods when it formed a part of the colonial dominions of France and of Spain. But in all of the other states the fundamental characteristics of the law are based upon the English common law as it was adopted and adapted by the English colonies before the revolution and further developed by each separate commonwealth in the national era. The existence of these state systems of Anglo-American law has always constituted one of the leading cohesive forces in the social and political life of the republic; for, although each one of these systems differs in certain particulars from the others, they all embody nevertheless many fundamental common elements derived from the common law of England. Amid the many forces which have tended to separatism in the American system of states the common law has always acted as a unifying and consolidating influence; and even in Louisiana the common law has modified the civil law in harmony with the general trend of evolution.

The main result of this whole process of legal development is that all of the separate state systems of law are now permeated by English legal principles. Throughout the union the fundamental English conception of law as the embodiment of the ideals of justice and liberty is also the American conception, and in America as in England stress is laid upon the vital importance of judicial process in the enforcement of rights. If time were at our disposal, I should ask you to consider in detail the working out of this fundamental conception of Anglo-American jurisprudence in the substantive law and the judicial procedure of each one of the states. I must, however, content myself with a reference to one special aspect of American state law.

Each of the written state constitutions embodies, as one of its chief features, a code of fundamental rights known as the "bill of rights," in analogy to the English Bill of Rights of 1689. This bill of rights of the state constitutions is perhaps the oldest feature of American law, for it is based on all the preceding ages of English and American history. It is derived, by successive stages of evolution, from Magna Carta itself and from the other great documents and precedents of English and American justice and liberty down to the Declaration of Independence. The bill of rights of the American state constitutions, grounded as it is upon the medieval and modern common law of England, represents therefore one of the most fundamental of all the influences which the mother country has exercised upon the life and thought of America. Time has not lessened, it has increased, this vast power of the English ideals of right and freedom. The present-day vitality of forty-eight state bills of rights is indeed one of the most important of all the forces which have brought the United States into the war beside Britain. The fact that the American bill of rights is of English derivation explains in a striking way the historical background of the common ideals which now animate both of the great Anglo-Saxon nations. These ideals embodied in the state bills of rights are not merely of historical interest; they are living forces in our own day, guiding and directing Britain and America in their work of eliminating autocracy and militarism from the world and of substituting everywhere the principles of justice and liberty.

VI

The written federal constitution, no less than the written constitutions of the separate states, bears in many of its features the impress of English influence. The framers of the constitution were no doubt guided in part by French political thought. The most striking single instance of French influence is to be found in the adoption of the principle that the federal legislature, executive, and judicature are three co-ordinate and independent powers of government: this feature of the constitution, so unlike the English doctrine of the supreme or sovereign power of parliament, is derived from Montesquieu. The great source, however, from which the fathers of the constitution drew their inspiration was the English political theory of the seventeenth century. From Sydney, Locke, Milton, and the Whig revolutionists they obtained the doctrines of the law of nature and natural rights, the social and political contract, and popular sovereignty. But although the inspiration and many of the political notions of the fathers were derived from English thinkers, the institutions and law of the federal constitution were based in large measure on the actual institutions and laws of England and the colonies.

The origin of the federal legislative, executive, and judicial institutions in the institutional history of England and the colonies is an important aspect of American constitutional history closely related to my main theme. But I must not pause to consider this subject further, for I am chiefly concerned to trace English influence upon the legal as distinct from the institutional provisions of the federal instrument. This influence was profound. Incorporated in the original instrument of 1789 or in the amendments are many of the principles and processes of English liberty and justice, which had long formed vital parts of the common law either in its English or in its colonial form. This indebtedness of the fundamental law of the union to the fundamental law of

England is one of the closest of all the historical ties between the two countries. If we remember at the same time, as I have already endeavoured to explain, that the constitutional law of each one of the separate states is similarly indebted to English law, we shall grasp more clearly the full scope of English influence upon the legal ideals of the American Republic.

The preamble of the constitution of the United States sets forth the lofty ideals of the American people in these words: "We, the people of the United States, in order to form a more perfect union, establish justice, insure domestic tranquility, provide for the common defence, promote the general welfare, and secure the blessings of liberty to ourselves and our posterity, do ordain and establish this Constitution for the United States of America." Justice and liberty are thus enshrined in the first sentence of the constitution as two of its main objects; and in the articles which follow the preamble these purposes are safeguarded by various provisions. Thus, the constitution provides for taxation by the legislature only, trial by jury in criminal cases, and the privilege of the writ of *habeas corpus*. Furthermore, the constitution prohibits bills of attainder, *ex-post facto* laws, laws impairing the obligation of contracts, and laws imposing religious tests. These and other provisions of the instrument of 1789, provisions derived in large measure from English and colonial precedents, form a body of constitutional guaranties of liberty and justice, the importance of which in the life of a free people it is difficult to over-estimate.

The federal instrument of 1789 contained, however, no formal "bill of rights" similar to the one included in all the state constitutions. The people viewed this omission as a danger to their liberties, and in response to their persistent demands the first ten amendments were added in 1791 to the original document. These ten amendments constitute the federal "bill of rights." In certain of their fundamental characteristics we may regard the thirteenth, fourteenth, and fifteenth amendments as later additions to it.

The federal bill of rights, like that of the state constitutions, is based, in some of its most important provisions, on the constitutional law of England. Especially striking is the influence of Magna Carta, the Bill of Rights of 1689, and other great documents and precedents of the common law. The amendments deserve full and careful study from this point of view of their English origin; but in today's lecture I shall confine my attention to two or three of their provisions.

One particular aspect of English influence is deserving of special notice. The fifth amendment (1791) declares that "no person shall be deprived of life, liberty, or property without due process of law; nor shall private property be taken for public use without just compensation." In the fourteenth amendment (1868) it is also declared that "no State shall make or enforce any law which shall abridge the privileges or immunities of citizens of the United States; nor shall any State deprive any person of life, liberty, or property without due process of law; nor deny to any person within its jurisdiction the equal protection of the laws." The prohibition of the fifth amendment is a check on the federal or central government, while that of the fourteenth amendment is a check on the state governments. Owing to the duality of government inherent in American federalism, this double check—one upon the federal and one upon the state government—ensures to all individuals the protection of their rights to life, liberty, and property by the forms and processes of law as against arbitrary and tyrannical action on the part of either federal or state authorities. The law rules and is supreme.

These "due process of law" clauses of the constitution are derived from the thirty-ninth chapter of Magna Carta. By a long process of historical development this part of Magna Carta has been worked into the very essence of American constitutional law[1]. But in America the principle embodied

[1] Lord Coke regarded the words *per legem terrae* of chapter thirty-nine as equivalent to "by due process of law," and the American courts have always followed his view. See McKechnie, *Magna Carta*, 2nd ed., p. 381; *Twining* v. *New Jersey* (1908), 211 U.S. 78, 100, 28 Sup. Ct. 14.

in the Great Charter has been given an even wider application than it has received in England. Whereas in England the principle operates as a check only on the executive and judicature and not on the legislature, in America it acts as a limitation of legislative no less than of executive and judicial action. Herein lies one of the fundamental differences between the English unwritten and the American written constitution. In America, in contrast with England, the legislature is not the legal sovereign and it cannot of itself alone alter the fundamental law of the land embodied in the federal written constitution.

Viewed in respect to their main purpose and scope, the "due process of law" clauses ensure the rule of law throughout the republic. The rule of law, as opposed to the rule of arbitrary power, lies at the very root of American institutions, both state and federal. The English conception of law as the embodiment of justice and liberty is thus a fundamental characteristic of the whole body of American public law. The actual working of this great principle of government and law in America presents certain features of contrast with its actual working in England. This contrast is due to fundamental differences between the English limited monarchy and the American federal republic. But the point which I wish to emphasize, and it is an important point in our present study, is that, despite these differences between the governmental forms of the two countries, the same fundamental doctrine of the rule of law, the same basic notion of law as the realization of the ideals of justice and liberty, prevails in America as it does in England. It prevails in America because the Americans have adopted it from England. It is one of the most vital of all the English influences upon American political life.

There is one other special feature of the federal bill of rights which I must not fail to mention. In the first amendment to the constitution it is declared that "Congress shall make no law respecting an establishment of religion, or prohibiting the free exercise thereof." State constitutions also embody this principle of religious liberty and the separation of church and state. Thus, for example, it is provided in the New York state constitution that "the free exercise and enjoyment of religious profession and worship, without discrimination or preference, shall forever be allowed in this state to all mankind." This embodiment of the principle of religious liberty in American public law is due to English influence.

The growth of the English ideal of religious liberty, safeguarded by Magna Carta and other provisions of the English law, exercised a profound influence upon colonial America, and shaped the evolution of constitutions and laws in the era of independence. One stream of English influence flowed to America with the Pilgrim founders of the colony of Plymouth, another with the liberal English catholics who established the colony of Maryland. Religious liberty took root in other parts of colonial America, but in Plymouth and Maryland it was one of the predominant characteristics of law and government. From these two centres the ideals spread to other regions, and in the course of time it was worked into the whole fabric of American institutions.

The history of the Pilgrims stands in marked contrast with that of the Puritans. The Puritan colonies of New England were theocracies in which there flourished the spirit of intolerance in religion and of opposition to the separation of church and state. The Pilgrim colony of Plymouth, founded upon the Mayflower Compact, was a community in which there were established the ideals of separation between church and state, religious freedom, and just and equal laws. The Puritan colony of Massachusetts ultimately absorbed the little Pilgrim community, but it did not obliterate the Pilgrim notions of law and government. These notions persisted and constantly widened the sphere of their influence, until they permeated the life of the American people and embodied themselves in the institutional and legal system of the United States. Nor, in tracing English influence upon the growth of

religious liberty in America, should we overlook the contribution of the English tolerant catholics who founded the
colony of Maryland. Lord Acton, in his *History of Freedom*[1],
declares that "the Catholic emigrants [to Maryland] established, for the first time in modern history, a government in
which religion was free, and with it the germ of that religious
liberty which now prevails in America." The influence of
the liberal institutions of Maryland upon American history
has been indeed profound. I shall not attempt to apportion
to Plymouth and Maryland the share which each contributed
to the common stock of American ideals. In its own way and
in its own time each one of these two English colonies
established in America the foundations of religious freedom;
and upon these foundations the constitutional and legal safeguards of today have been reared.

I shall touch but lightly upon the vast subject of slavery in
its relation to the American ideals of justice and liberty, only
reminding you that the abolitionists and the pro-slavery party
held diametrically opposite views as to the nature of human
liberty. The abolitionists maintained that liberty was the
birthright of all men equally, while the defenders of slavery
asserted that liberty was the possession of those alone who
were fitted for it and that the black men were fitted only for
complete subjection. There was an irreconcilable difference
between these two theories of liberty. Lincoln's position was
that there should be adherence to the teaching of the Declaration of Independence that all men are created equal. "They
who deny freedom to others," he asserted, "deserve it not
for themselves, and under a just God cannot long retain it[2]."
The fundamental idea which guided Lincoln's thought and
action was that slavery and freedom cannot permanently exist
side by side in modern civilized societies. Applying this
universal doctrine to American conditions, he maintained
that the union could not permanently endure so long as half

[1] P. 187.
[2] See Merriam, *History of American Political Theories*, 1910, p. 224.

2—2

of it held to freedom and half to slavery. Lincoln's aim, and the true issue of the civil war, was the preservation of the union. The victory of the north settled this question once and for all, and it settled at the same time the issue between the parties of slavery and of freedom. The principle of the president's Proclamation of Emancipation was embodied, after the close of hostilities, in the thirteenth, fourteenth, and fifteenth amendments to the federal constitution. By means of these additions to the fundamental law of the republic the ideals of justice and of civil and religious liberty inherited by the Americans from England have received a far-reaching extension of their application. The constitutional and legal safeguards and guaranties by which these ideals are carried out in practice now protect the black as well as the white population of the whole country.

VII

I have now directed your attention to the incorporation of English ideals of justice and liberty in the constitutional and legal system of the United States. It remains for me to point out that during the era of independence these English-American ideals have exerted a world-wide influence. Their application has been extended from the internal or national life of America to the life of other communities, and of that vaster society of states bound together by international law and morality.

In the first place, American principles of liberty and justice have spread to many parts of the world by the influences of literature and of social and political intercourse. The ideals as embodied in American law and government have served as an exemplar and have thus affected the evolution of foreign political societies. This voluntary adoption of American legal ideals has been a potent factor in the life of the world, a factor comparable in its scope and effect to the wide influence of British parliamentary institutions.

The American ideal of liberty profoundly influenced

France. The American revolutionary ideas spread to France and formed an important factor in the growth of the French revolutionary movement which ended in the dominance of the notions of "liberty, equality, and fraternity." But, as Lord Acton reminds us in his *Lectures on the French Revolution*[1], the influence of America was more in the direction of presenting to the French people the model of revolution accompanied by ordered government than in the direction of shaping French institutions themselves.

Both the American and the French Revolutions affected the Spanish and Portuguese colonies in the new world. The ideal of liberty spread to Latin America and helped to transform the colonies into independent states. If American and French notions of liberty have not become as firmly planted in Latin America as in the United States and in France, this is partly due to the heritage of long centuries of autocratic rule during the colonial epoch. But the alignment of Latin America on the side of free nations in the present war indicates that in this part of the world as in others the vestiges of autocracy derived from earlier times are doomed to disappear. The Latin American republics will take their place in the future organization of the world as liberty-loving and justice-loving states. This consummation of Latin American evolution will be due in no small degree to the influence of the ideal of liberty established in the English North American colonies and fostered ever since in the federal republic.

There are still other striking illustrations of the part which American ideals of liberty and justice have played in the history of foreign countries, but I must pass on to consider the second main aspect of the influence of these ideals on the world. In the era of independence the American republic has itself extended the application of these principles from her own internal or national life to the broader field of her international relations. In the study of this wider development I shall once more take the preamble to the federal

[1] Pp. 35–38.

constitution of 1789 as the starting-point. As you will recall, the preamble declares that justice and liberty are two of the main ideals or objects of the constitution.

"To 'establish justice,'" remarks Story, the distinguished American jurist, "must forever be one of the great ends of every wise government; and even in arbitrary governments it must, to a great extent, be practised, at least in respect to private persons, as the only security against rebellion, private vengeance, and popular cruelty. But in a free government it lies at the very basis of all its institutions.... No one can doubt, therefore, that the establishment of justice must be one main object of all our State governments. Why, then, may it be asked, should it form so prominent a motive in the establishment of the national government ?[1]"

Mr Justice Story finds the answer to this question in the inability of each separate state government to ensure justice to the other states of the union and their citizens and to foreign states and their citizens. This conclusion is founded upon the conditions which prevailed in the time of the loose confederation of states formed under the stress of the revolution; for, in the period of the confederation, the central government was on the whole weak and ineffectual, in comparison with the power of the individual states. Owing to this experience under the Articles of Confederation the framers of the federal constitution determined to give the central government greater power. One of the ideals which guided the work of the framers was that by means of a strong central government justice might be established and maintained not only in the separate states, but also throughout the entire union and in the still wider field of international relations.

This ideal of international justice which inspired the framers, and which they embodied in the constitution, is expressed in striking terms by one of the ablest of the Chief Justices of the United States.

---

[1] *Commentaries on the Constitution of the United States*, 5th ed., vol. I, p. 365.

"Prior [to the establishment of the Federal Constitution],"
remarks Mr Chief Justice Jay in the case of *Chisholm* v. *Georgia*[1],
"the United States had, by taking a place among the nations of
the earth, become amenable to the laws of nations; and it was their
interest as well as their duty to provide that those [international]
laws should be respected and obeyed. In their national character
and capacity, the United States were responsible to foreign
nations for the conduct of each separate State relative to the laws
of nations and the performance of treaties; and there the in-
expediency of referring all such questions to State courts...be-
came apparent. While all the States were bound to protect each,
and the citizens of each, it was highly proper and reasonable that
they should be in a capacity [by means of a central government],
not only to cause justice to be done to each and the citizens of
each, but also to cause justice to be done by each and the citizens
of each; and that, not by violence and force, but in a stable,
sedate, and regular course of judicial procedure."

The fundamental notion underlying these words of Jay is
that of interstate and international justice safeguarded by law
and judicial processes. This is the ideal which the framers
inserted in the federal constitution, where it has served ever
since as a guide to American international policy. The ideal
was not invented by the framers. In its origin it goes back
to the old English and English colonial principles of the rule
of law, and of law as the realization of justice protected and
enforced by judicial machinery. The striking thing—and
this is the point which I would emphasize—is that this ideal,
founded upon English and American evolution, was incorporated in the fundamental law of the republic as the constitutional basis of its policy in respect to legal relations with
foreign states.

The preamble likewise declares liberty to be one of the
main objects of the American people in ordaining and establishing the federal constitution. The actual words of the
preamble refer only to the liberties of the American people
themselves: the object of the people is to "secure the blessings
of liberty to ourselves and our posterity," the blessings of the

[1] 2 Dall. 419, 474; Story, *op. cit.*, vol. I, p. 370, n. I.

liberty which was traced back through colonial and English history to Magna Carta. But the ideal of liberty, thus placed in the first words of the constitution, has always occupied a prominent place in the foreign policy of the United States. Like the ideal of justice, liberty has inspired American statesmen not only in the realm of national policy and national legislation, but also in the sphere of international relations and of international morality and law.

I should like to mention certain of the main features of this tendency of the American government to further the cause of justice and liberty in the world.

The American foreign policy known as the Monroe Doctrine has proved to be a powerful factor in the preservation and development of free institutions in the new world. In its earlier history the Monroe Doctrine saved North America as well as South America from the ambitious designs of the autocracies of the Holy Alliance, and gave the states of the western hemisphere free scope for the development of their own systems of justice and liberty, unfettered by European interference. In the future the doctrine of President Monroe may well enter upon a still wider sphere of usefulness. If applied, as has been suggested by certain leading publicists, to the lands of the South Pacific and the East, it would serve as a barrier to shield these regions from future aggression on the part of Germany or of any other autocratic state.

The freedom of the seas has always been a cardinal feature of American foreign policy. By her firm adherence to this great principle America has contributed in no small measure to the growth of international justice and liberty. America's entry into the present war was largely occasioned by her determination that this principle of maritime freedom should be respected by Germany and her allies.

America has played a prominent part in the formulation of conventionary international law and in the establishment of machinery for the settlement of international disputes by peaceful means. Her policy has furthered the development of the principle and process of arbitration and the setting up of international courts of justice. The recent pronouncement by President Wilson in favour of the formation of a League of Nations is but a more extended application of the well-established American policy in respect to international justice and liberty, an application deemed by the President to be necessary for the preservation of the future peace and civilization of the world. The fundamental notion which underlies this plan of international organization is that all the states of the world, large and small alike, shall be safe-guarded in the possession of their own national systems of justice and liberty and that in international relations these two ideals shall also serve as the inspiration of laws and of the machinery to enforce them.

Perhaps the greatest of all America's contributions to the spread of the ideals of justice and liberty throughout the world consists in her active armed participation in the present war on land, at sea, and in the air. These ideals of America, which are at the same time the ideals of all the allied states in their struggle with autocracy and militarism, have been admirably expressed by President Wilson in state papers and public speeches. Of all his utterances I wish to single out the concluding sentences of the Second Inaugural Address, de-livered shortly before the American declaration of war. "The shadows that now lie dark upon our path," said the President, "will soon be dispelled. We shall walk with light all about us if we be but true to ourselves—to ourselves as we have wished to be known in the counsels of the world, in the thought of all those who love liberty, justice, and right exalted[1]." In these words, a prophecy of America's momentous decision to throw her full strength into the world struggle, we see the true spirit of the American people: for them the war is a necessary struggle by force for the preservation and the spread of their national and international ideals of "liberty, justice, and right exalted."

[1] *America and Freedom: being the Statements of President Wilson on the War* (with a preface by Viscount Grey), 1917, p. 44.

VIII

These, then, are the two main aspects of the history of American influence upon the spread of principles of justice and liberty throughout the world: the diffusion of these American principles to other lands, and their embodiment in American international policy. In these two ways America's influence upon world evolution has been far-reaching and profound. But although this influence has spread outwards from America and although it constitutes one of her greatest contributions to civilization, it is nevertheless an influence which, both in its origins and in its growth, owes much to the mother country. England's share in this whole development consists of two contributions of fundamental importance.

England's first contribution was made in American colonial days. The extension of English ideals of liberty and justice to the colonies, and their incorporation in law and procedure, served not only as the foundation of American national development, but also as the basis of America's influence on other countries and on international relations. Transformed in many ways by historical processes within the environment of the new world, these ideals have always preserved the essential characteristics derived from the mother country. America's influence upon the world has been an Anglo-American influence. If in today's lecture I emphasize the significance of the English spirit in this influence, I do not forget, nor will you forget, that the Americans have contributed to the spread of Anglo-American principles and processes of freedom and right their own political and legal genius. But, fixing our gaze on the English strains in American influence on the world, we may not unjustly claim that the ideas which have proceeded from the United States to France, Latin America, and other lands, and also certain vital features of the international policy of the United States, have been based in large measure on the heritage from the mother country. If, for example, we examine the American project for a League of Nations, we find that the underlying conception is English in its origins. In its insistence on the rule of law and on the necessity of safeguarding international freedom and justice by the machinery of an international executive and judicature, President Wilson's plan is based on all preceding centuries of English and Anglo-American history. Stress is laid not so much on the fundamental rights of man and of nations as on the protection of those rights by institutions and procedure. Like the great constitutional documents of English and American history, the project of a League of Nations expresses the main English conception of law as the practical realization of liberty and justice in institutional processes.

England's second contribution to the world-wide spread of American ideals has been made during the period of independence. English progress towards a fuller realization of the ideals common to England and America has influenced American life and thought; and through this influence England has played a rôle in the evolution of America's notions and practices and in their extension beyond her own frontiers. Through their active cooperation in international affairs the two Anglo-Saxon nations have also influenced each other in many ways. Despite periods of conflict and tension, the two countries have in general worked together for the furtherance of peace and of justice and freedom in the world. Not the least of these joint contributions of the two countries has been the peaceful settlement of their own disputes for over a century. To the growth of international law and the setting up of international judicial machinery they have both contributed in no small degree. If we survey the whole history of international relations during the hundred and fifty years of America's separate political existence, we shall find that on most questions of policy which have involved the ideals common to both countries, they have acted together in the interest of human progress.

There are many historical proofs of English influence on American policy to further the cause of liberty and justice throughout the world, but I shall mention only two or three of them. England's aloofness from the designs of the Holy Alliance both in the old and in the new world led to Canning's suggestion for a joint, or at least a simultaneous, declaration by the United States and Great Britain of their hostility to the threatened intervention of autocracy in Latin America. Although this joint declaration was never made, Britain's attitude helped to crystallize American opinion and to shape the policy announced by President Monroe in 1823. Similarly, since England's abandonment of her policy of impressment of American seamen, both countries have resolutely maintained, by united action, the principle of the freedom of the seas. England's support of this principle, so vital to international intercourse, has acted as a powerful factor in the growth of the American policy to insist that all maritime powers shall respect the seas as the open highways of the world. Likewise the two countries have worked in harmony in the great work of establishing the machinery of international arbitration, and English influence has contributed not a little to the placing of arbitral justice in the forefront of America's plan for world peace. Finally, I may remind you that Britain's example during the first years of the present war—the example of a great country fighting for justice and liberty under the rule of law—powerfully influenced America in the formation of her resolve to throw all the weight of her numbers and resources into the struggle. This is not the least—indeed it is one of the greatest—of all English influences upon the development of America as a land of high national and international ideals.

The present union of England and America in this world-conflict of opposite ideals is thus based upon long centuries of historical development. These centuries are the prophecy of the future. The world's national and international institutions and laws are even now, in the midst of war, undergoing vast processes of transformation; and in the after-war period these processes will continue. In this work of re-shaping constitutions and laws England and America, as two of the chief guardians of civilization, are destined to play a rôle of commanding influence. That influence will be directed towards securing the world's permanent peace by the destruction of arbitrary political and military power and by the firm establishment of liberty and justice under the rule of law. In the attainment of this high purpose, upon which the future welfare and happiness of mankind are dependent, the statesmen of both countries, acting in unison, will receive their greatest inspiration from the ideals which animate the English and American peoples alike and which are embodied in the principles and procedure of their common law.

STATE AND MUNICIPAL GOVERN-
MENT IN THE UNITED STATES

LORD EUSTACE PERCY, M.A.

STATE AND MUNICIPAL GOVERN-
MENT IN THE UNITED STATES[1]

WHEN I was asked to deliver two lectures in this course on some subject connected with the United States, I felt that I could not do better than give some slight sketch of government in the states and municipalities, because the part they play both in constitutional development and in social reform seems to be too little understood on this side of the Atlantic.

The place of the state governments in American political life is particularly important. These forty-eight governments are not local authorities charged with certain restricted and delegated powers. They are sovereign bodies, the centres of traditions and loyalties deeply rooted in the soil of American history, and they are, indeed, in large measure the independent and supreme agencies for the formulation and execution of those social policies which constitute the main interest and activity of modern politics. As the economic and social life of the United States becomes more closely knit, the federal government is indeed assuming an ever increasing responsibility for the whole range of economic and industrial problems. But this tendency has not yet proceeded far enough fundamentally to change the outlook of the average American voter. State politics still remain today the centre of those reform movements and party struggles through which the

[1] The two lectures reproduced in this and the following chapter were delivered without written notes, and they appear here in a somewhat expanded form. It will be observed that some of the references and quotations in them are later than the date of the lectures. I must apologize, especially to any of my American friends who may read these lectures, for the incompleteness of my treatment of the subject and for any possible inaccuracies. My only excuse is the pressure of other work under which these lectures were prepared.—E. P.

average voter of a democracy realises his part in the responsibilities of self-government. It is in state politics that he receives his training in active citizenship. In other words, the position and character of the American democracy as a member of the Family of Nations grow directly out of the activities of the American citizen in the affairs of his state.

And what is true of the state governments is also, in large measure, true of the municipalities. No sphere of government touches more immediately the problems of ignorance and poverty which are the material of the social reform movement. In the affairs of great municipalities like New York, Cleveland, and Chicago, many of the ablest and most active citizens in the United States find the centre and incentive of their public work, while not a few of the most prominent figures in national politics have made their first name in municipal administration. No study can therefore be more important than that of the development of state and municipal government in the United States.

In the present lecture we shall consider some of the features of the recent constitutional history of the states and municipalities. We shall then be in a position in the next lecture to study the more interesting social reform movements which have marked the last two decades. Constitutions and forms of government are means to an end, and the incentive to constitutional changes is commonly the desire of the people for social and economic reforms. This has been emphatically the case in the United States, but nevertheless an understanding of the nature of these constitutional controversies is an essential preliminary to the study of political movements of more immediate human interest.

At the outset, it is essential to avoid the mistake of considering the states and municipalities as so many water-tight compartments. Their nature and their affairs cannot be understood except in relation to the federal government and the nation as a whole. Information as to the American constitution can readily be obtained. But, leaving aside for a moment the legal machinery of the constitution, it is important to realize that, in actual practice, the connecting link between municipal, state, and federal government is represented, not by the judges of the supreme court or by the established organs of legislation and administration, but by the average citizen and voter himself. The unity of the United States resides and is embodied, not in the president or in congress or in the supreme court, but in Jones and Smith who are, at one and the same time, citizens of Atlanta, citizens of Georgia, and citizens of the United States.

Now, most of the problems of constitutional government in the United States grow out of this concentration of various responsibilities in the persons of Jones and Smith. The politics of the United States developed early into a two-party system, and it early became the aim of each party to organize the average voter in all his activities from the election of county or municipal officers right up to the election of the president himself. The two parties—Republican and Democratic—have aimed at electing party candidates for all these offices by the carefully organized vote of the members of the party. This involved the most comprehensive organization in every sphere, from the local to the national. Such organization can only be built up by one method. The tendency naturally is for the local party organizer in the county or the city ward to secure the support of the voter for the local party candidate by satisfying local interests and demands. He then delivers the support thus gained to the state organizers for use in electing state officers or the members of the state legislature. The state organizers in their turn must confirm the support of the voters by satisfying such of their interests and demands as apply to the large sphere of state government. They then deliver this vote to the national party managers for use in the congressional and presidential campaigns. Indeed, these gradations in the scale of party organization are more elaborate than here outlined, and include a variety of local interests and local predilections of which only a party organizer himself could give an adequate idea. At each stage the party candidates must be most carefully selected; competing candidates must be "choked off"; and any split in the party, even in the smallest local politics, must be prevented, lest such a split should extend itself gradually into the wider spheres of state and national politics.

It is obvious that in the course of these successive deliveries of blocks of votes the actual connexion between the opinions of the voter and the policies in favour of which he casts his vote becomes fainter and fainter, and at each successive stage the party managers are more and more free to formulate policies and nominate candidates at their discretion, uncontrolled by any clear expression of the views of the average elector. The whole constitutional history of the United States from early days has therefore largely centred round the recurring efforts of the voters, at moments of social crisis when they have become conscious of desires hitherto unexpressed, to devise more representative methods of nominating party candidates and formulating party policies. Up to a few years ago, these functions were universally performed by the party convention. The party convention system originally represented a revolt from the former method of nominating candidates, commonly known as the "caucus." The convention nominally secures a democratic representation of the rank and file of the party for the purpose of nominating the party candidates and drawing up the party "platform." But in the course of the last fifty years the convention system itself had, in the view of many Americans, hardened into a close corporation of party managers and their adherents hardly more representative than the old caucus. Consequently, in the last two decades a new revolt has grown up against what Senator Beveridge, in his speech as Chairman of the Convention of the Progressive Party in 1912, called "the hidden government."

This revolt has been intensified by the fact that in the course of the rapid economic development of the country—a development due largely to the pioneer efforts of the railways and other great corporations whose success and prosperity depended in a peculiar degree upon the legislation and administration of the state governments—such corporations came to exert an undue degree of influence and power in the management of the parties. This tendency culminated in a situation in some states, such as New Hampshire and California, where the railways—the Boston and Maine in the former case, and the Southern Pacific in the latter—came really to control the party "machine" and were felt to be the real governing force in the state.

Before proceeding to give an account of the revolt against these conditions, we have to consider one or two other features of state government intimately connected with the reform movement. The defects in the machinery of representation which we have sketched above are to a certain extent common to all democratic nations, though they have been intensified in the United States by the size of the country and the sub-division of government involved in the federal system. Other defects in the state governments arise out of factors more or less peculiar to the United States.

The constitutions of the original thirteen states were evolved to a large extent out of the forms of government under which they lived in the colonial period. They were consequently not at first modelled so closely as the federal constitution upon the strict theory of a definite division of powers between executive, legislature, and judiciary. The precedent of the federal constitution has, however, had a powerful effect upon the constitution of these original thirteen states as time has gone on and has more or less determined the constitutions of the thirty-five additional states established since the union. Generally speaking, it may be said that all state constitutions are now based upon a more or less strict division of powers between the governor, as the chief executive, and a two-chamber legislature, elected by manhood, and in many cases by universal, suffrage. In two respects, however, these constitutions differ materially from the federal constitution, especially in the case of the newer states. In the first place, while under the federal constitution the president has the appointment of his cabinet and of all executive and judicial officers—subject indeed to the consent and confirmation of the United States Senate, but on his own initiative and at his own choice—in the states a large number of the executive officers, including the governor's immediate cabinet, are elected by popular vote, and in many—though by no means in all—states, the state judges are also elected often for brief terms of office. In the second place, though the part played by the United States Congress in controlling the internal organization of the executive departments through a minute earmarking of appropriations has often been criticized by American writers and public men as a serious flaw in the efficiency of the federal government, the interference of the state legislatures with executive functions has been carried to a much greater extreme. The lack of a properly unified budget system, either in the state or the federal government, is partly responsible for this confusion of executive and legislative functions, but, in addition to this, in the states the legislatures have, from early days, tended to create, by statute, boards, commissions, or departments responsible for the administration of particular pieces of legislation. This multiplication of executive bodies has grown to such a point in recent years that, to take one instance, the state of Illinois, in enacting an administrative code in 1917, was able to abolish more than fifty separate administrative agencies and to consolidate them into nine main departments. In another middle western state, Kansas, the governor, in his annual message for 1917, described the existing condition of the state administration in the following language:

Kansas has admittedly outgrown our present system of government. It is a hodge-podge; a patch-work; antiquated, cumbersome, wasteful, inefficient, entirely out of keeping with the more scientific systems of business now employed by private concerns and many other states. A multiplicity of boards, commissions, bureaux and departments duplicate the work of one another, divide responsibility which should be concentrated, and by interfering with one another often retard the public business.

These two defects in the state governments have combined, in the opinion of many Americans, to sap the sense of executive responsibility, to create political friction between the governor and his cabinet, to make the arts of politics, rather than administrative ability, the qualification for executive office, and to render the administration of public business so intricate and confused as to preclude any real control over it by the governor. The number of names necessarily appearing on an election "ticket" precludes the exercise by the voter of any real judgment on the qualifications of candidates. The difficulty of compiling any sort of coherent "ticket" gives to the party "machines" at once a justification for their existence and an opportunity for undesirable manipulation[1]. The election of judges and state officers has been felt, moreover, under the old defective machinery of party politics, to endanger the position of just those officials whose independence is most essential to good government, by bringing them under the control of the party machine and of the "interests" which have been suspected of exercising too much influence over that machine.

One final word must be said. The main obstacle to a rapid adjustment of government to the new needs of a developing society has been felt throughout the United States to lie in the system of fixed constitutions on which both the state and federal governments have been based. Every state government, as well as the federal government, is carried on under a constitution limiting the powers not only of the executive

---

[1] A few years ago the "blanket-ballot" presented to the voters at elections in Philadelphia contained some 400 names, the various party "tickets" being arranged in parallel columns. The result of this is shown by a recent article in the *Philadelphia Public Ledger*, complaining that voters have no sort of information about the candidates for whom they vote, and urging the formation of a Voters' League like that already existing in Chicago, for the purpose of informing the public, on a nonpartizan basis, as to the character and record of candidates for office.

but of the legislature, and the function of interpreting the constitution is confided to the judiciary. The courts thus have the duty of pronouncing whether a given statute passed by the legislature is, or is not, in accordance with the constitution, and therefore, whether it is valid and has the force of law. The federal constitution can, in practice, only be altered by a vote of a two-thirds majority of the United States Senate and House of Representatives subsequently ratified by a vote of three-fourths of the state legislatures of the country. The state constitutions can also only be altered by a similar elaborate machinery. A constitutional amendment, after passage by the state legislature, has to be submitted to a referendum of the whole electorate. Another method of revising state constitutions is however provided for by the periodical summoning of constitutional conventions charged with the duty of reconsidering and redrafting the constitution as a whole. The recommendations of such conventions have, however, equally to be submitted to a referendum of the electorate and the difficulty of carrying through any radical revision is shown by recent experience in the state of New York. At the state elections in 1915, a new constitution drafted by a constitutional convention and embodying many reforms in the machinery of government—such, for instance, as a proper budget system—was rejected by a large majority at the polls.

The state constitutions vary a good deal in the limitations which they put upon the discretion of the legislature. Some, for instance, contain the most elaborate limitations on the kind of taxation which the legislature may impose or the kind of expenses it may authorize. Thus, for instance, the constitution of the state of Georgia limits clerical expenditure in the governor's office to six thousand dollars. Other constitutions leave the legislature fairly free. But in general it may be said that the existence of strict constitutional limitations on the discretion of the legislature tends to lessen the sense of responsibility felt by the average member.

The function of the courts as the interpreters of the constitution tends to enhance this defect. In recent years, all the state legislatures have been under great pressure from public opinion to reform industrial conditions in the direction of limiting hours of labour for women in factories and so forth. In many cases, laws of this kind have been pronounced unconstitutional by the courts. This has resulted in a growing popular agitation against the judiciary as an obstacle to progress. Reformers have felt themselves unbearably cribbed, cabined, and confined within what one authority has called "our eighteenth century system of checks and balances... the legal, political and philosophical charters called bills of right by which our fathers sought to confine courts and legislatures and sovereign peoples for all time within the straight and narrow course of individualist natural law." Improvements in administration have suffered in this way no less than measures of social reform. Shortly before the outbreak of the European war an American historian[1] expressed the opinion that "so long as our courts retain their present functions, no comprehensive administrative reform is possible."

These remarks are not made with any intention of passing judgment upon American methods of government. All the questions we have touched on are matters of acute political controversy in·the United States, and they do not lack their analogies in older countries such as England and France. What we are attempting to do is not to write a treatise on American government, but to outline the recent political history of the American states, and the purpose of the foregoing sketch has been to give some slight account of the controversies which, as a matter of history, produced a strong reform movement, dating roughly from the beginning of the present century.

The state which in many respects led this movement of constitutional reform was Oregon. In a series of elections this

---

[1] Professor Brooks Adams.

state has adopted radically new constitutional methods which have come to be known as the "Oregon Plan." The first steps in this movement were taken in the year 1902, and it is interesting to note that they originated more or less in a clash between two different social strata within the state. The farmers of the interior, who, like all predominantly agricultural populations, had taken comparatively little part in politics, revolted against the conservative party leadership identified with the coast towns like Portland. This fact is of some importance, as radical movements in the western states and, to a certain extent also, in such eastern states as New Hampshire, have always tended to take this form. Not only the movements of the last twenty years, but earlier radical upheavals like the Greenback and Populist agitations and even the pre-civil-war radicalism known in American history as "Jacksonian Democracy," have originated in a revolt of the farmers against the industrial and commercial classes and the urban populations.

The Oregon Plan was an experiment in "direct legislation." Its main feature was the establishment of the initiative and referendum as a method not only of proposing or passing amendments of the constitution, but as a normal means of legislation on lesser matters. With these measures is associated another, namely, the recall—that is to say, the power of the voters to recall an elective official before the expiry of his term of office if his policy or conduct is considered unsatisfactory. The recall has been frequently used in municipalities, sometimes for good, but often for very insufficient reason. It has also been applied to state executive officials and to judges. Its use in the case of the judiciary is for obvious reasons considered more radical and has aroused more opposition among conservatives than its application to executive or legislative officers. On the other hand, the unpopularity of the courts to which we have referred made it one of the chief planks in the platform of the radicals in 1912. The recall of judges was one of the burning issues of the movement which resulted in Colonel Roosevelt's campaign for the presidency and the formation of the Progressive Party in that year, but Colonel Roosevelt, who himself disliked the proposal, converted it into a scheme for the "recall of judicial decisions" —that is to say, the right of the voters to reverse a decision of the courts in regard to the constitutionality of legislation.

The initiative, referendum and recall have been adopted in many states. They have been the centre of many political struggles and the rallying cry of many reformers in recent years. The conservatives have, however, insisted that, as a matter of fact, these proposals are at best only a shirking of the main issue. They argue that the fundamental defect in the government of the states is that the system of "checks and balances" and the excessive number of elective officers, combined with the frequency of elections and the brief terms for which officials are elected, have sapped the sense of individual responsibility on which alone democratic self-government is based, and have thrown upon the voters a mass of decisions at short intervals with which they are utterly unable to cope intelligently. They draw the obvious conclusion that the path of improvement cannot lie in the direction of measures which not only add to the burdens of the voter, already sufficiently heavy, the duty of answering "yes" or "no," in a polling booth, to a series of complicated or technical legislative proposals—ranging from the reform of the state constitution or of the system of public education to the fixing of the strength of locomotive headlights—but also, by over-riding the legislator through the initiative and referendum and by continually threatening the executive officer with the recall, cannot but tend to decrease his sense of responsibility and to make him more careful of his popularity and more astute in judging passing currents of opinion than intent upon the duties of sound legislation and administration.

It is no part of our purpose to decide between these conflicting views. But it is for this reason that not only conserva-

tive, but nearly all the wisest, reformers have long advocated
another reform in the state constitutions, commonly known
as the "short ballot"—that is to say, the reduction, so far
as possible of the number of elective offices. It is the object of
this proposal to concentrate in the hands of the governor as
chief executive the responsibility of appointing administrative officers and to relieve the voters of responsibilities which
they cannot properly discharge. While this reform has been
widely advocated, it has met with considerable opposition
from the electors who, perhaps naturally, find it difficult to
understand how reformers who fight under the rallying cry
"the remedy for the evils of democracy is more democracy"
can recommend, as the first step in that direction, a restriction
of the functions of the voters. The idea of the short ballot is,
however, steadily making headway. As an instance of the
present state of the controversy it may be of interest to quote
the platforms of the republican and democratic parties in
the state of Indiana in the pending election contest. The
republican platform contains the following clause:

We favour making the office of Attorney-General appointive
and bringing under one head, responsible to the governor, all
legal matters of the state. We favour a constitutional amendment
abolishing the office of State Superintendent of public instruction
and clerk of the Supreme Court and the re-establishment of these
offices by legislation making the same appointive, such clerk to be
appointed by the Supreme and Appellate courts.

The democratic platform on the other hand says:

We are opposed to the centralization of the government of
Indiana by taking away from the people the right to elect the
Attorney-General and other officers, and placing their appointment
in the hands of the governor.

Schemes of direct legislation, whether in the United States
or in Switzerland, may not unfairly be described as attempts
to get round the main difficulty of representative government
by making it less necessary for the people to exercise minute
care in selecting their representatives. But modern demo-

cracies are too deeply committed to representative government to make it possible to ignore the necessity of improved methods of election. We have seen above that what may be called the machinery of the suffrage has been one of the main weaknesses in American politics. It is necessary however to give a word of warning here. The general idea of the "man in the street" on this side of the Atlantic about the corruption of American party politics is perhaps largely due to the reproduction in the English press of the accusations and counter-accusations which, in the first decade of the twentieth century, were so common a feature of American political journalism. Colonel Roosevelt, in a famous phrase borrowed from Bunyan, gave to this type of political controversy the sobriquet of "muck-raking." Latterly, one or two American novels which have gained a certain popularity on this side of the Atlantic have contributed towards the same impression. Such works of fiction as Winston Churchill's *Coniston* and *Mr Crewe's Career* and Norris's *The Octopus* are, as a matter of fact, political documents of considerable importance and do represent actual conditions in New Hampshire and California in the past. But these evils are by no means peculiar to American politics. We have their counterpart in England and in France, and too much insistence upon them tends to obscure the real issues involved. The fact is that party machinery in all democratic countries tends to reflect very imperfectly the real opinions and wishes of the voters and is constantly exposed to very serious abuses. Englishmen, in studying the history of American party politics, would be well advised to remember that American politics are perhaps only more exposed to these dangers because a larger proportion of the voters in America take an active interest in public affairs than in other democratic countries where education is less widespread. This clearly makes the proper organization of politics at once more difficult and more necessary. The spread of intellectual activity and information in England is probably making such organization increasingly necessary here. Foreseeing this, even before the war, and before the present extension of the suffrage had become a burning question, Professor Graham Wallas pointed out with great force the analogies between British and American political conditions[1]. "Parliament may find itself compelled, as many of the American states have been compelled, to pass a series of acts for the prevention of fraud in the interior government of parties. The ordinary citizen would find then, much more obviously than he does at present, that an effective use of his voting power involves not only the marking of a ballot paper on the day of the election, but an active share in that work of appointing and controlling party committees from which many men whose opinions are valuable to the state shrink with an instinctive dread." The effort to reform party machinery in the United States to which Professor Wallas here refers has led to a series of measures as important as, if not more important than, the experiments in direct legislation associated chiefly with the state of Oregon.

The aim which the reformers have set out to secure cannot perhaps be more succinctly described than in the words of the Chairman of the Republican National Committee, Mr Hays, spoken only a few weeks ago: "The purpose of a political organization is to elect the candidates and not to control the party's nominations." The object of a whole series of laws passed by the various states in recent years has been to place the nomination of party candidates more directly in the hands of the voter belonging to the party, thus ensuring that a man who offers himself as republican or democratic candidate for a state or federal office shall be really representative of the members of that party instead of having been imposed upon them as their official candidate by a small clique of managers.

Legislation to this end has come to be known by the general name of "direct primaries." The "primary" is the name given to the selection of the party candidate before the

[1] *Human Nature in Politics*, pp. 233-4.

election. As we have seen above, this selection had come to be made by conventions nominally representative of the whole membership of the party, but really very largely packed by the party managers. The "direct primary" consists in the holding of an actual preliminary election at the polls, at which all the members of the party can vote for the candidate whom they desire to see contest the election. This system still leaves it open to the party managers to endorse particular candidates, and many American observers have pointed out that the "direct primary" often only throws back the wire-pulling of the party managers to an earlier stage. That is to say, a party convention tends in one form or another to precede the holding of the primary elections[1]. This danger is, however, mitigated, if not eliminated, by an additional provision, inserted in many direct primary laws, enabling any considerable group of voters, who are dissatisfied with the policy or nominations of their party, to nominate independent candidates by a signed petition.

The whole question of the direct primary system is so intricate and is giving rise today to so much controversy that it is impossible to attempt to give a full description of it

[1] This tendency cannot be better illustrated than by the following extract from a recent issue of a New York paper:

"During the past fortnight the people of New York, having by their own act done away with state conventions, held two representative political meetings which in most respects amounted to the same thing. They assembled not in convention but in conference. They did not nominate candidates, but one of them designated a state ticket and the other by means of resolutions practically indicated its choice for governor who probably will name his own associate nominees."

Quoting this extract, a Wisconsin paper comments as follows:

"So long as we have party government and large issues and sets of principles on which men differ under our form of government we are going to have these gatherings of men who are in general agreement to give their views the benefit of formal expression for organized action, and for representation in the elections and in the government.

"The direct primary elections were devised to destroy the conventions, and of course they failed because the conventions are a natural and wholesome growth and development bred of necessity and reflecting a developed political capacity."

here. The direct primary laws vary in different states, and variations which might appear to a foreign observer to be unimportant have very marked effects in actual practice. For instance, some states, such as Michigan and Iowa, require that a candidate at the primary shall receive a certain percentage of the total vote in order that his selection as a party candidate may be valid (forty per cent. of the vote in the case of Michigan; thirty-five per cent. in the case of Iowa). In other states, such as Wisconsin, Idaho, and North Dakota, a system of preferential voting is in force at the primaries under which the voter indicates both his first and his second choice for a given office, and in case no candidate receives a majority as a first choice, the candidate who receives the fewest first choice votes is dropped and his votes transferred. Again, in other states, such as Minnesota, a system of non-partizan primaries is in force for some offices; that is to say, the two parties do not hold separate primaries, but the two candidates who receive most votes at a unified primary are entitled to stand as candidates at the final election. Again, at any rate in some states, such as Wisconsin, it is possible for voters belonging to one party and intending to vote for that party's candidate at the final election, to vote at the primary of the opposite party in order there to secure the nomination of the most unpopular candidate whom their own party nominee will have the least difficulty in defeating at the final election. In such a case, the direct primary system would appear to put a premium on strong party organization because it is only a strong party, within which there is no serious competition among party candidates, which can afford to allow a considerable body of its voters to transfer themselves to the primary of the opposite party in order to defeat the latter's strongest candidate.

Another series of measures designed to improve the tone of party politics has been the corrupt practices acts which have been passed in many states. The necessity for these laws has, if anything, been increased by the direct primary system, because the latter tends greatly to "draw out the agony" of party contests, and to put a greater strain upon party funds or the private means of the candidate. Instances of such laws are those passed in Arkansas and Nevada shortly before the war, the former of which limits the campaign expenditure of candidates for congress to seven thousand five hundred dollars, while the latter limits all candidates for office to an expenditure of twenty per cent. of one year's salary. Just before the entry of the United States into the war a federal corrupt practices bill was pending in congress. In addition, one much mooted piece of legislation designed to improve party politics has been "the publicity of campaign contributions."

The purpose of direct primary legislation is to increase the responsibility and elicit the real opinions of the individual voter. No such legislation can produce its full result unless the individual actually uses his vote, and there have been various recent proposals for enabling or inducing a larger percentage of electors to come to the polls. Chief among such expedients have been the "absent voting" laws now in force in twenty-four states, beginning with Vermont in 1896, by which electors are permitted to vote at general or primary elections, or both, outside the election precinct in which they reside. The Massachusetts Constitutional Convention, which is now in session, has declared in favour of a more startling reform, in the shape of making voting compulsory. Other states have taken less drastic measures with the same object; for instance, the state of Illinois penalizes failure to vote by requiring that jurymen shall be drawn first from the non-voters' list.

No study of the development of American electoral machinery can be complete without a mention of women's suffrage. This movement has gained steadily increasing impetus in recent years. Women's suffrage has been the law in some states from very early days. In Wyoming it has been in force for nearly fifty years. In Colorado, it was approved by a majority of voters in November 1893, and became a part of the state constitution in 1901. In Utah it was incorporated in the first state constitution in 1895, after having already been in force from 1870 to 1886 before Utah had been admitted to statehood. In these cases, the measure was adopted almost as a matter of course, as inherent in the principle of democratic government; but its extension to older states has been the programme of a definite campaign carried on with increasing vigour within the last few years. The high-water mark of this campaign is represented by the adoption of women's suffrage by the state of New York in the elections last November (1917) and the movement now bids fair to capture the whole of the United States. There is still, however, a strong opposition to it in many states, and the leaders of the movement have therefore been endeavouring to secure the passage of a constitutional amendment to the federal constitution laying down women's suffrage as the law of the whole land. The President has endorsed this policy in a letter recently addressed to a member of the United States Senate which it may be worth while to quote in full:

The whole subject of woman suffrage has been very much in my mind of late and has come to seem to me part of the international situation as well as a question of capital importance to the United States. I believe that our present position as champions of democracy throughout the world would be greatly strengthened if the senate would follow the example of the house of representatives in passing the pending amendment. I therefore take the liberty of writing to call the matter to your attention in this light and to express the hope that you will deem it wise to throw your vote and influence on the side of this great and now critical reform.

To complete our survey of actual or proposed reforms in state government, we must mention the measures designed to increase the efficiency of the administrative machinery. We have already referred to the consolidation of the administrative machinery in the state of Illinois, and a similar process is being carried out in many states[1]. Many of the reforms in this sphere are so closely connected with social reform that they find their place more properly in the next lecture. Thus it would be out of place to deal here with such pieces of consolidating legislation as the Children's Code passed in Ohio in the year 1913. But two sets of measures which have been adopted in many states can more easily be mentioned here. One of these is the appointment of "economy and efficiency commissions" to survey the machinery of the state governments, and to recommend reforms. The other, connected with legislative rather than administrative efficiency, is the establishment of "legislative reference bureaux" to ensure the better drafting of bills introduced into the legislature. The pioneer in this latter class of measures was the state of Wisconsin, where a legislative reference bureau has been in operation for some years in close connexion with the state university.

This sketch of state constitutional movements would be far from complete if it omitted similar movements in muni-

[1] The following extract from the *San Francisco Chronicle* of July 27 last gives the programme of one of the candidates for governor at the pending elections in California. As a campaign document this statement should, of course, be accepted with some reserve:

"Our state affairs are honeycombed with inefficiency, duplication and waste. There are eight different commissions and officers empowered to inspect places of employment and safety conditions thereof. One could do it all. There are five different offices and commissions charged with the enforcement of laws affecting child labor, labor and welfare. One could do it all. There are eight different officers, boards, commissions, inspecting foodstuffs and drugs. One could do it all.

"There are six different boards empowered to supervise the construction of works and dams for the storage and distribution of water. One could do it all. There are five different boards and commissions authorized to investigate water resources. One could do it all. There are three different boards and commissions empowered to apportion water and permit appropriations. One could do it all!

"There are seven different boards and officers that directly and indirectly supervise the penal institutions in the state. One could do it all. There are thirteen different officers, boards and commissions that have directly and indirectly to do with the government of institutions for the insane and feeble-minded."

cipal politics. American municipalities do not stand on the
same basis as the state governments. They are not independent or sovereign entities. They have received their powers
from the state in the form of city charters and, indeed, one of
the chief movements in municipal politics during recent years
has been the movement for a fuller measure of self-government in the larger cities. The charters granted by the state
governments have tended to confine the power of the city
administration within narrow limits, and the agitation for
"municipal home rule" has been greatly strengthened by
such incidents as that which recently occurred in the state
of Indiana, where the regulation of the street railways of
Indianapolis was taken by a decision of the state supreme
court out of the jurisdiction of the city authorities and placed
within the province of the state public service commission.
Nevertheless, as has already been said, the administration of
the larger municipalities does occupy an extremely important
place in the political life of the average American citizen.
Nowhere does he feel more acutely the problems of modern
government, and nowhere has the constitutional reform
movement, which we have been considering above, as well
as the social reform movement which we shall consider in the
next lecture, been more keenly and energetically conducted.
As one prominent authority says: "The countries of Europe
have not made great changes in their machinery of municipal
government during the past half century; in this field,
America has been the world's chief laboratory for political
experimentation[1]."

---

[1] W. B. Munro, *The Government of American Cities*, 1917, p. 1.   The
following quotation from the same book provides a useful summary:
"With the adoption of commission charters, moreover, most cities
have used the opportunity to make other organic changes. The intro-
duction of provisions for direct legislation and the recall has, for example,
been a feature of charter revisions almost everywhere. The open, direct,
non-partisan primary as a means of putting candidates in nomination
for municipal offices has also found its way into many of the newer
charters. In Boston, Cleveland, Buffalo and Dayton candidates are
nominated by petition. Some other cities obviated the necessity for any

We have no space here even to begin to enter into the technical problems of municipal government. All that can be done is to give a general sketch of the most obvious tendencies.

All the experiments in constitutional government which we have noted in the case of the states have been widely put into force also in the sphere of municipal government. In many cases these experiments have been made in the municipal sphere before they were attempted in the wider sphere of the state. The recall has been perhaps more widely applied to municipal than to state administration, if only for the reason that defects and corruption in municipal administration have been more notorious and more keenly felt by the average voter than in the vaguer and more general region of state policy. Again, women's suffrage has been in the past, and is even now, in operation for municipal elections in states where women have not yet secured the suffrage in state or national elections. It would take us too long to describe here the application to municipalities of measures like the initiative and referendum and the direct primary. We must be content for this purpose with the indications already given of their operation in the sphere of state government. The same applies to reforms in the administrative sphere such as the economy and efficiency commissions and the consolidation of miscellaneous municipal authorities into sound and well-constructed departments. But there are other constitutional experiments peculiar to the municipalities which we must touch on very briefly.

serious nominating formality by the plan of preferential voting. But all these various changes in nomination methods have had the same motive behind them,—namely, to break down the power of the party leaders, and to give a fair opportunity to those candidates for municipal office who might come forward without the pledged support of any political organisation. The abolition of party designations on the municipal ballot, the simplification and shortening of the ballot itself by a reduction in the number of elective officers, the provision of new securities for fairness at elections—all these reforms have made unparalleled headway during the last ten years."

In the words of the authority already quoted, "The real renaissance in American state government has come during the last dozen years or more, and may be said to have begun with the Galveston experiment of 1901." This "Galveston Plan," as it has come to be known, consists in confiding the government of the city to a small elected commission in whose hands the whole responsibility for the administration of the city is concentrated. It is, indeed, the logical application of the principle of the short ballot to the sphere of municipal government, because its main aim is to eliminate the multiplicity of elected officials which has been a feature as much of municipal as of state constitutions. This "commission form of government" has spread rapidly in the United States. It was, indeed, preceded by an earlier movement for the concentration of power in the hands of the mayor—a movement which was at one time known as the "Tsar-Mayor" scheme. But this movement did not really produce permanent results and it is round the commission movement that the main reforms in municipal government have centred.

Much more recently, another plan of municipal government has been started which is commonly associated with the city of Dayton, Ohio. Galveston instituted its commission form of government as the result of a disaster to the city through a tidal wave. In the same way, Dayton reformed its government in order to meet the devastation caused by the Mississippi floods of 1913. The form of government which was adopted was the so-called "city manager scheme." This scheme provides for a commission as under the Galveston Plan; but the commission appoints a city manager as the general administrator of the whole municipality. The charter of Dayton provides that this manager "shall be appointed without regard to his political beliefs and may or may not be a resident of the city of Dayton when appointed." This scheme used often to be advocated as an imitation of the German system of municipal government. It has been adopted by many cities and may perhaps be regarded as the most advanced point reached by the movement now so general in the United States towards government by "experts."

This account of municipal administration is the merest outline of a series of municipal reform campaigns which has bulked almost as large in the mind of the American voter as campaigns for the reform of state and national government. These campaigns can, however, better be considered in connexion with social reform than in connexion with constitutional progress. Before we leave the question of constitutional developments in municipalities, there is, however, one point which should be made clear.

It may have occurred to the reader that, while this lecture opened with an explanation of the effect upon American politics of what often appears to be an excessive uniformity of party organisation in all spheres of government, no account has been given of any reform in the electoral machinery of the states designed to create a different alignment of parties in state affairs, from that which exists in national affairs. As a matter of fact, there have been one or two movements in the states for the creation of new parties. But even such new movements as that of the Non-Partisan League in the state of North Dakota, which is a burning question in the United States at the present moment, commonly take the form rather of an attempt to capture one or other of the old party machines than of the establishment of a new party. The Non-Partisan League, indeed, disclaims such a purpose. As we shall see at the end of this lecture, even if a new party is formed in any one of the states, its inevitable tendency is to extend its activities to national affairs. It must be remembered that, under the constitution, it lies with the state government to determine the electoral machinery by which the national government and the president are elected. Party government in the states is thus so closely bound up with the party government of the nation that, though a new party may be started in a state, there is little possibility of state politics being run for any considerable period on different party lines from those which apply in federal politics. It is in municipal politics that the need for different alignments is most keenly felt. A large and growing body of American opinion feels it anomalous that the affairs of municipalities should be dealt with by the same party machinery that deals with great national political controversies, and it is therefore in the municipalities that the system of nomination by petition has borne its fruit in the formation of parties with programmes based, not on general political considerations, but on the actual needs of the particular city government concerned. Reform movements in municipalities like those which elected Mr Mitchell as reform mayor of New York in 1913, and Mr Blankenburg as reform mayor of Philadelphia in 1912, have been "fusion" movements formed by a coalition of republicans and democrats. Even in the municipal sphere, however, it has proved difficult to prevent a relapse into the old party divisions, and all that can be said at present is that the formation of distinct parties in municipal affairs is recognised by a large body of American opinion as essential to good municipal government.

No mere enumeration of these constitutional experiments can give a proper idea of the political history of the states and municipalities during the last few years. The measures coldly set out in this lecture have been programmes about which great political campaigns have been conducted with as much fervour and with as great a sense of the issues involved as the most famous parliamentary campaigns in the United Kingdom. Reformers have staked their political lives upon them. Conservatives have opposed them, not from selfish or sordid motives, but on the highest grounds of principle. During the first decade of the twentieth century, state after state exploded as it were into radical movements of this kind. In the year 1910 two great campaigns were fought—those of Governor Johnson in California and Governor Bass in New Hampshire —which attracted the attention of the whole country.

I began this lecture by pointing out that no study of the state governments as isolated water-tight compartments could approach the full truth, and that the real key to an understanding of American politics is the concentration in the individual voter of various responsibilities as a citizen of his city, his state, and his nation. The history of these great reform movements in the various states points the moral of these reflections. They did not begin and end within the state boundaries. As soon as these movements had reached a certain point the individual voter was bound to transfer the principles and programmes for which he stood at state elections to the sphere of federal politics. These movements took place at a time when the Republican Party was in control of the federal government. Within that party there grew up, about the year 1909, what was known as an "insurgent" group, composed mainly of representatives from middle western states. This group was led by men like the late Senator Dolliver of Iowa, Senator La Follette of Wisconsin, and Mr (now Senator) Norris of Nebraska. The activities of this group culminated in 1912 when Colonel Roosevelt, having failed to capture the Republican Party itself, formed the Progressive Party and conducted a national campaign on a platform embodying the whole reform movement which had long been growing up in the various states. The history of these political developments must however be left to my next lecture.

SOCIAL LEGISLATION AND ADMINISTRATION

LORD EUSTACE PERCY, M.A.

SOCIAL LEGISLATION AND ADMINISTRATION

I T would be impossible, within the compass of an hour's lecture, to give any adequate enumeration of the social reforms which have been effected or attempted in the United States in recent years. All that I can do is to convey some idea of the origins and general direction of the reform movement.

The history which I shall try to sketch has very serious lessons for us in this country, especially at this moment. For many years past, Englishmen have too commonly regarded government in the United States as backward and defective. Yet, as a matter of fact, Americans may, with truth, point today—as the authors of the *Federalist* pointed one hundred and thirty years ago—to the "numerous innovations displayed in the American theatre in favour of private rights and public happiness." A knowledge and appreciation of American reform movements is our surest path to a better understanding between the two countries, just as it is upon the recent advances in British social policy that the increasing respect now felt in America for this country is perhaps chiefly based. Moreover, American history in this sphere has warnings for us to which it would be well for us to pay heed at the present moment, when we hope that we are nearing the end of the war.

The modern domestic history of the United States dates from the civil war, just as its history in the international sphere may be said to date from the Spanish war. The civil war roused throughout the country, north and south, an idealistic fervour of which it is difficult today to convey any adequate impression. Something of the old spirit, however, still lives today in the Memorial Day addresses of men like Justice Holmes. Both the soldiers of the north, who felt

themselves to be fighting for the highest principles of liberty,
and those of the south, who went down to defeat in defence
of their homes and of an order of society which they loved,
possessed, at the close of the war in 1865, a fund of moral
feeling and determination which seemed to open the way for
the building up of a "new world." That feeling is enshrined
for all time in the words of Lincoln's Second Inaugural—
words spoken with rare magnanimity at the close of a bitter
struggle in the name, not only of the north but of the south
as well.   .

But the material forces which converged upon the United
States in the last thirty-five years of the nineteenth century
were too strong. Rapid industrial development on an un-
precedented scale, a tremendous increase in material prosperity, and the pioneer work of settlement west of the Mississippi absorbed the energies generated by the war. The stream
of immigrants from Europe flooded the industrial sections of
the country and almost swamped the old order of American
life there. Years elapsed before Americans could find themselves again in the new problems created by these profound
changes in the very texture of their society. Finally, all
American historians are now agreed that the government's
policy towards the "rebel" states on the morning after the
war lacked both sympathy and generosity and failed to heal
divisions or, in Lincoln's words, to "bind up the nation's
wounds." That policy became the battle-ground of party
struggles and of a violent constitutional controversy between
congress and the president. The confusion and suffering of
the south in the ten years succeeding the war gave to the
word "reconstruction"—now in all men's mouths as a symbol of hope—an evil meaning in American history.

But in spite of these difficulties and failures the quarter of
a century following the civil war was marked by a sporadic
and growing radicalism. The radical movements centred
mainly in the middle western states. They represented the
discontent of the western farmers with the party machines

and with the influence of the big industrialists of the east, and their practical programmes turned largely on questions arising out of the burden of the war debt in its relation to the financial needs of the agricultural population in the more newly settled regions of the country. In the earlier years of the period indeed when, for instance, the liberal republican movement started in Missouri in 1870, this western senti- ment had leaders whose eyes were directed to broader issues —to a sounder policy of reconstruction, to civil service reform, and to a revolt against the somewhat sordid atmosphere of Washington during Grant's presidency. In the later years labour took an increasing part with the farmers in political action, and this cooperation considerably modified the charac- ter of radical programmes. But, broadly speaking, the back- bone of this western radicalism was constituted by the farmers' ideas about finance and credit. This was the actual origin of the so-called "Greenback Movement" between 1876 and 1884. The Populist Party, which made its first appearance in 1890, had a rather more complicated origin and a rather wider policy. It grew out of a combination between the Greenbackers, the Grangers and the Farmers' Alliance, representing the agriculturalists, and the Union Labour Party representing the workmen. Concurrently with the greenback and populist movements, and in varying rela- tion to those movements, a series of more or less ephemeral labour parties grew up, beginning with the National Labour Union in 1869. Without going into details as to the develop- ment of these various parties, it may be enough to say that, in so far as they did not merge again with the radical demo- crats, they took their final form in the two existing socialist parties of the present day—the Socialist Party and the Socialist Labour Party. These parties, while they play today a certain part in local politics in some states, have had little influence in the national sphere. The populists and the farmers' movement which so largely supported them merged themselves for the most part in the Democratic Party in the campaign of 1896, when the Democratic Convention at Chicago and the Populist Convention at St Louis united in selecting Mr W. J. Bryan as presidential candidate on the "free silver" platform. This campaign represented the culmination of these earlier radical movements, and its financial platform corresponded closely to the demands to which we already referred as the original motive of those movements. This financial programme proved however to be ephemeral. As a basis and starting-point for a national programme of improved industrial and general living conditions and better business methods it proved weak and mistaken, and the leadership of the social reform movement passed at the end of the century from the radical democracy of the middle west to the Republican Party under Colonel Roosevelt.

Before we consider the social reform movement as it developed under the republican *régime*—and its identification with the Republican Party was, in large measure, fortuitous—two points must be mentioned.

Towards the close of the nineteenth century, America was startled by signs of the social problems created by unrestrained industrial expansion. One or two great strikes, especially those in the Pullman Car Works at Chicago and in the Homestead Works of the Carnegie Steel Company, warned the country of the existence of labour conditions and labour unrest which threatened the peace and the good name of the United States.

The second point, to which a bare reference will be sufficient, is the beginning of government restrictions on the activities of business enterprises. The passage by congress of the original Sherman Acts and railway legislation is a subject falling more properly within the scope of Mr Kennedy's lecture on the relation between government and business, because these laws were based less upon any social reform programme than upon a desire to maintain and equalize competitive conditions in American industry. In the whole history of the American social reform movement, however, the demand for "social betterment" in the interests of the working classes and the campaign against trusts and monopolies in the real or supposed interests of the consumer are almost inextricably mingled, and it is difficult to treat them separately. The workman, apart from the submerged immigrant of the slums, is indeed recognised less in America as representing a distinct class than in the older countries of Europe, and the spectacled, insignificant, and nervous figure of the "plain citizen" is a more popular emblem of democracy in cartoons and posters than that of the manual worker. At any rate it may be said that this railway and anti-trust legislation directed the attention of public opinion towards the need for a definite programme of government action in regard to industrial conditions.

Before, however, this feeling could take shape, the Spanish war broke upon the country, and it was not until the return of peace that any social reform programme could be drawn up. Its real growth dates from the accession of Colonel Roosevelt to the presidency shortly after the close of the war, and it is with his name, more than with that of any other public man, that the new development of American internal policy is identified.

Not that Colonel Roosevelt launched any new philosophy of reform or advocated any startling innovations. It was rather his function to focus vague discontent and divergent aspirations into a rough common sense practical programme. There is, in fact, a remarkable analogy, though there are also remarkable differences, between his part in the reform movement and that played later by Mr Wilson on his accession to the presidency in 1913. In each case, reform sentiment had lost its leadership and was tending to become incoherent and violent. What Colonel Roosevelt did in taking up and developing on lines of common sense the somewhat rhetorical programmes of Mr Bryan and his predecessors, Mr Wilson did, twelve years later, in concentrating the enthusiasms of the insurgent republican and progressive movements on a thoughtful programme. The methods of the two men were, however, widely different, for while Mr Wilson seemed able, at the outset of his presidency, to cast the mantle of his eloquence over the whole range of the reformer's aspirations, addressing himself rather to the spirit behind them than to the specific causes of discontent, Colonel Roosevelt tended rather to go direct for one or two central concrete points, using simpler language and appealing to plainer moralities.

President Roosevelt's starting-point as a reform leader cannot be better marked than by the following passage from his first message[1] to congress on 3rd December, 1901:

The most vital problem with which this country, and for that matter the whole civilised world, has to deal, is the problem which has for one side the betterment of social conditions, moral and

[1] A comparison of this message with President Wilson's First Inaugural may be of interest as indicating the different genius of the two men. The following extracts from the Inaugural may be quoted:

"There has been a change of government.... It means much more than the mere success of a party.... No one can mistake the purpose for which the Nation now seeks to use the Democratic Party. It seeks to use it to interpret a change in its own plans and point of view.... We have been refreshed by a new insight into our own life.... We see that in many things that life is very great. It is incomparably great in its material aspects, in its body of wealth, in the diversity and sweep of its energy, in the industries which have been conceived and built up by the genius of individual men and the limitless enterprise of groups of men.... But the evil has come with the good, and much fine gold has been corroded. With riches has come inexcusable waste.... We have been proud of our industrial achievements, but we have not hitherto stopped thoughtfully enough to count the human cost, the cost of lives snuffed out, of energies overtaxed and broken, the fearful physical and spiritual cost to the men and women and children upon whom the dead weight and burden of it all has fallen pitilessly the years through.... At last a vision has been vouchsafed us of life as a whole. We see the bad with the good, the debased and decadent with the sound and vital. With this vision, we approach new affairs. Our duty is to cleanse, to reconsider, to restore, to correct the evil without impairing the good, to purify and humanize every process of our common life without weakening or sentimentalizing it.... The feelings with which we face this new age of right and opportunity sweep across our heartstrings like some air out of God's own presence, where justice and mercy are reconciled and the judge and the brother are one."

physical, in large cities, and for another side the effort to deal with that tangle of far-reaching questions which we group together when we speak of "labor." The chief factor in the success of each man—wage worker, farmer, and capitalist alike—must ever be the sum total of his own individual qualities and abilities. Second only to this comes the power of acting in combination or association with others. Very great good has been and will be accomplished by associations or unions of wage workers, when managed with forethought, and when they combine insistence upon their own rights with law-abiding respect for the rights of others. The display of these qualities in such bodies is a duty to the Nation no less than to the association themselves. Finally, there must also in many cases be action by the Government in order to safeguard the rights and interests of all. Under our Constitution there is much more scope for such action by the State and the municipality than by the Nation. But on points such as those touched on above the National Government can act.

When all is said and done, the rule of brotherhood remains as the indispensable pre-requisite to success in the kind of national life for which we strive. Each man must work for himself, and unless he so works no outside help can avail him; but each man must remember also that he is indeed his brother's keeper, and that each at times stumbles or halts, that each at times needs to have the helping hand outstretched to him. To be permanently effective, aid must always take the form of helping a man to help himself; and we can all best help ourselves by joining together in the work that is of common interest to all.

President Roosevelt's first steps in reform were more concerned with the control of the great corporations than specifically with labour policy. In the earlier part of the message just quoted he proposed the establishment of a new Department of Commerce and Industries, whose province it should be "to deal with commerce in its broadest sense including, among other things, what concerns labor and all matters affecting the great business corporations and our merchant marine," and in introducing this proposal he referred to the "widespread conviction in the minds of the American people that the great corporations known as trusts are in certain of their features and tendencies hurtful to the

5—2

general welfare," and "that combination and concentration should be not prohibited, but supervised and, within reasonable limits, controlled." He added: "In my judgment, this conviction is right."

As already said, it is not our province here to discuss these general economic problems. Perhaps the development of President Roosevelt's policy into the definite region of labour regulation and social reform may be said to date from another great strike which took place in the anthracite coal mines in the winter of 1902–3. This strike was settled by the appointment of the Anthracite Coal Strike Commission which presented its report to the president on the 18th March, 1903. As a result of this disturbance, a Bureau of Mines was established in Washington which has ever since that time concerned itself with a general supervision of conditions in the coal mines; but perhaps the most important work done by the commission was the embodiment in its report of the following statement which marks a definite stage in a bitter conflict between labour and capital in the whole coal industry:

It is adjudged and awarded that no person shall be refused employment or in any way discriminated against on account of membership or non-membership in any labor organisation, and that there shall be no discrimination against or interference with any employee who is not a member of any labor organisation by members of such an organisation.

It is not our purpose here to follow the development of a national labour policy, for the subject of this lecture is social legislation and administration in the states and municipalities rather than in the national sphere. This selection of a subject is justified by the narrowness of the powers of the federal government in such matters. The Bureau of Mines, for instance, is really little more than an advisory, investigatory and co-ordinating bureau with few administrative powers. The limitation on the powers of the federal government cannot better be summed up than in the following further quotation from a speech of President Roosevelt's at Sioux Falls, South Dakota, on the 6th April, 1903:

Of course the National Government has but a small field in which it can work in labor matters. Something it can do, however, and that something ought to be done. Among other things I should like to see the District of Columbia, which is completely under the control of the National Government, receive a set of model labor laws. Washington is not a city of very large industries, but still it has some. Wise labor legislation for the city of Washington would be a good thing in itself, and it would be a far better thing, because a standard would thereby be set for the country as a whole.

In the field of general legislation relating to these subjects the action of Congress is necessarily very limited. Still there are certain ways in which we can act. Thus the Secretary of the Navy has recommended, with my cordial and hearty approval, the enactment of a strong employers' liability law in the navy-yards of the nation. It should be extended to similar branches of the Government work. Again, sometimes such laws can be enacted as an incident to the nation's control over interstate commerce. In my last annual message to Congress I advocated the passage of a law in reference to car couplings—to strengthen the features of the one already on the statute books, so as to minimize the exposure to death and maiming of railway employees. Much opposition had to be overcome. In the end an admirable law was passed "to promote the safety of employees and travellers upon railroads by compelling common carriers engaged in interstate commerce to equip their cars with automatic couplers and continuous brakes, and their locomotives with driving-wheel brakes." This law received my signature a couple of days before Congress adjourned. It represents a real and substantial advance in an admirable kind of legislation.

It has been, however, necessary to give a general idea of the development of national sentiment and policy in the United States on social reform matters in order that what we have to say about state and municipal administration and legislation may fall into its proper place. Before passing on to this subject, we may conclude our consideration of the development of national sentiment by mentioning one other strike of later date which will probably be remembered in history as marking a further stage in that development. The closing years of the last and the opening years of the present century had been marked by violent labour lawlessness in the far western states, especially in the mines. That these conditions are not yet eradicated was shown last year by the activities of the I.W.W. in the lumber regions of the far west, and the strikes in the copper mines in Montana and Arizona[1]; but in its earlier and much more acute stages this anarchy was identified with an older labour body called the Western Federation of Miners, which, after terrorizing states like Colorado and Idaho for many years, was more or less broken up after the assassination of the Governor of Idaho in 1905. Some of the leaders of the Federation later transferred their activities to the organisation of the I.W.W. In February 1912, a strike broke out among the textile workers in Lawrence, Massachusetts. The workers almost all belonged to the poorer class of immigrants. They were led by two Italians —Ettor and Giovannitti. The strike was unorganised in its origin, but the I.W.W. stepped in and took over the leader-

[1] The Report of the President's Mediation Commission, which visited Arizona at the end of last year, provides a useful indication of the origins of these conditions:

"Amidst all the diversity of conditions in the four copper districts there were three basic claims urged by the men and resisted by the companies:

"(a) While not expressed in so many words, the dominant feeling of protest was that the industry was conducted upon an autocratic basis....

"(b) The men sought the power to secure industrial justice in matters of vital concern to them....

"(c) The men demanded the removal of certain existing grievances as to wages, hours, and working conditions, but the specific grievances were, on the whole, of relatively minor importance. The crux of the conflict was the insistence of the men that the right and the power to obtain just treatment were in themselves basic conditions of employment, and that they should not be compelled to depend for such treatment on the benevolence or uncontrolled will of the employers.

"Broadly speaking, American industry lacks a healthy basis of relationship between management and men....

"Too many labor disturbances are due to the absence of disinterested processes to which resort may be had for peaceful settlement."

ship. The violence of the strike, followed as it was by one or two similar labour disturbances in other cities, had a distinct effect in forcing upon the attention of the American people the magnitude of the problems connected with immigrant labour, and, coming as it did at the moment when Colonel Roosevelt was organising his campaign for the presidency on a radical reform platform, it played some part, as shown in one provision of the Progressive Party's programme quoted below, in stirring up radical feeling and pointing the moral of the possible effects of a conservative *laissez-faire* policy in regard to industrial conditions.

In the preceding lecture, we touched on the origin of Colonel Roosevelt's campaign. In order to place the reform activities of the states and municipalities in their proper light, it may be as well here to quote some of the provisions of the platform drawn up by the national convention of the Progressive Party at Chicago in the summer of 1912. That convention, which nominated Colonel Roosevelt as candidate for the presidency, and Governor Johnson of California, whom we mentioned in the preceding lecture, for the vice-presidency, was conducted amid scenes of enthusiasm difficult to describe and its platform was hailed by many leaders of social reform like Miss Jane Addams of Chicago as summing up all the programmes for which they had been struggling since the first awakening of American sentiment to a realisation of the condition of the people. The relevant passages of the platform were as follows:

DECLARATION OF PRINCIPLES

The conscience of the people, in a time of grave national problems, has called into being a new party, born of the nation's awakened sense of justice....

We hold, with Thomas Jefferson and Abraham Lincoln, that the peoples are the masters of their Constitution to fulfil its purposes and to safeguard it from those who, by perversion of its intent, would convert it into an instrument of injustice. In accordance with the needs of each generation, the people must use their sovereign powers to establish and maintain equal opportunity and industrial justice, to secure which this government was founded and without which no republic can endure....

RULE OF THE PEOPLE

The Progressive party, committed to the principle of government by a self-controlled democracy expressing its will through representatives of the people, pledges itself to secure such alterations in the fundamental law of the several states and of the United States as shall insure the representative character of the government. In particular, the party declares for direct primaries for the nomination of state and national officers, for nation-wide preferential primaries, for candidates for the Presidency, for the direct election of United States Senators by the people; and we urge on the states the policy of the "short ballot," with responsibility to the people secured by the initiative, referendum, and recall.

AMENDMENT OF CONSTITUTION

The Progressive party, believing that a free people should have the power from time to time to amend their fundamental law so as to adapt it progressively to the changing needs of the people, pledges itself to provide a more easy and expeditious method of amending the federal constitution.

NATION AND STATE

Up to the limit of the Constitution, and later by amendment of the Constitution, if found necessary, we advocate bringing under effective national jurisdiction those problems which have expanded beyond reach of the individual states....

EQUAL SUFFRAGE

The Progressive party, believing that no people can justly claim to be a true democracy which denies political rights on account of sex, pledges itself to the task of securing equal suffrage to men and women alike.

CORRUPT PRACTICES

We pledge our party to legislation that will compel strict limitation of all campaign contributions and expenditures, and detailed publicity of both before as well as after primaries and elections.

THE COURTS

The Progressive party demands such restriction of the power of the courts as shall leave to the people the ultimate authority to determine fundamental questions of social welfare and public policy.

SOCIAL AND INDUSTRIAL JUSTICE

The supreme duty of the nation is the conservation of human resources through an enlightened measure of social and industrial justice. We pledge ourselves to work unceasingly in state and nation for:

Effective legislation looking to the prevention of industrial accidents, occupational diseases, overwork, involuntary unemployment, and other injurious effects incident to modern industry. The fixing of minimum safety and health standards for the various occupations, and the exercise of the public authority of state and nation, including the federal control over interstate commerce and the taxing power, to maintain such standards. The prohibition of child labor.

Minimum wage standards for working women, to provide a " living wage " in all industrial occupations. The general prohibition of night work for women and the establishment of an eight hour day for women and young persons.

One day's rest in seven for all wage workers. The eight hour day in continuous twenty-four-hour industries.

The abolition of the convict contract labor system; substituting a system of prison production for governmental consumption only and the application of prisoners' earnings to the support of their dependent families.

Publicity as to wages, hours and conditions of labour; full reports upon industrial accidents and diseases, and the opening to public inspection of all tallies, weights, measures, and check systems on labor products.

HEALTH

We favour the union of all the existing agencies of the federal government dealing with the public health into a single national health service....

BUSINESS

...To that end we urge the establishment of a strong federal administrative commission of high standing, which shall maintain permanent active supervision over industrial corporations engaged in interstate commerce, or such of them as are of public importance, doing for them what the government now does for the national banks, and what is now done for the railroads by the interstate Commerce Commission.

THE IMMIGRANT

Through the establishment of industrial standards we propose to secure to the ablebodied immigrant and to his native fellow workers a large share of American opportunity.

We denounce the fatal policy of indifference and neglect which has left our enormous immigrant population to become the prey of chance and cupidity. We favour governmental action to encourage the distribution of immigrants away from the congested cities, to rigidly supervise all private agencies dealing with them and to promote their assimilation, education and advancement....

As indicating the other side of this struggle, the following passages of Mr Taft's speech accepting the republican nomination for the presidency in the same year may show the high ground taken by conservatives in opposition to the demands of the radicals:

In the work of rousing the people to the danger that threatened our civilisation from the abuses of concentrated wealth and the power it was likely to exercise, the public imagination was wrought upon and a reign of sensational journalism and unjust and unprincipled muckraking has followed in which much injustice has been done to honest men. Demagogues have seized the opportunity further to inflame the public mind and have sought to turn the peculiar conditions to their advantage....

In the ultimate analysis, I fear, the equal opportunity which is sought by many of those who proclaim the coming of so-called social justice involves a forced division of property, and that means socialism....

I have the fullest sympathy with every reform in governmental and election machinery which shall facilitate the expression of the popular will. But these gentlemen propose to reform the Government, whose present defects, if any, are due to the failure of the people to devote as much time as is necessary to their political duties, by requiring a political activity by the people three times that which the people thus far have been willing to assume; and thus their remedies, instead of exciting the people to further interest and activity in the Government, will tire them into such an indifference as still further to remand control of public affairs to a minority.

Instead of giving us the benefit of any specific remedies for the hardships and evils of society they point out, they follow their urgent appeals for closer association of the people in legislation by attempting to cultivate the hostility of the people to the courts and to represent that they are in some form upholding injustice and are obstructing the popular will.

The Republican party stands for none of these innovations. It refuses to make changes simply for the purpose of making a change, and cultivating popular hope that in the change something beneficial, undefined, will take place. It does not believe that human nature has changed.... We do not know any way to avoid human injustice but to perfect our laws for administering justice, to develop the morality of the individual, to give direct supervision and aid to those who are, or are likely to be, oppressed, and to give as full scope as possible to individual effort and its rewards. Wherever we can see that a statute which does not deprive any person or class of what is his is going to help many people, we are in favor of it. We favor the greatest good to the greatest number, but we do not believe that this can be accomplished by minimizing the rewards of individual effort, or by infringing or destroying the right of property which, next to the right of liberty, has been and is the greatest civilising institution in history. In other words, the Republican party believes in progress along the lines upon which we have attained progress already. We do not believe that we can reach a millennium by a sudden change in all our existing institutions. We believe that we have made progress from the beginning until now, and that the progress is to continue into the far future; that it is reasonable progress that experience has shown to be really useful and helpful, and from which there is no reaction to something worse.

The Republican party stands for the Constitution as it is, with such amendments adopted according to its provisions as new conditions thoroughly understood may require. We believe that it has stood the test of time, and that there have been disclosed really no serious defects in its operation.

Perhaps the chief feature of American internal history during the last five years, into which we have no space to enter here, is the extent to which President Wilson has been able to heal this strong division of opinion and to put the general course of social reform beyond the danger of either being swamped by revolutionary unrest or dammed by conservative principles. Unrest is indeed still at this moment a marked feature of American political life, even in the midst of all the preoccupations of war. For instance, the last two years have witnessed the rapid growth in North Dakota and the neighbouring states of a new farmers' movement, commonly known as the Non-Partisan League, and revolutionary socialism is probably, in one form or another, a common creed among considerable sections of immigrant labour; but the national policy of reform, now irrevocably launched on radical lines, is probably developing too fast and has now secured too full a measure of agreement to make such movements of permanent significance.

It is, then, in this general atmosphere of a striving after social betterment through government action that the American states and municipalities have taken up the problem of reform.

As the movement for constitutional innovation was, at the outset, particularly identified with the state of Oregon, so the new departures in social legislation and administration have been largely identified with the state of Wisconsin. For reasons which have already been partly explained in the preceding lecture, one of the first points to which the attention of the reformers has been directed, both on constitutional and on social reform grounds, has been the administration of public utilities, and especially of the railways. The method of dealing with this problem adopted in Wisconsin and many other states was the establishment of a "railroad" or "public service" commission with wide discretionary powers of regulation over railways and other public utilities, such as tramways, telegraph and telephone companies, gas and electric light companies, and even grain elevators. Many states have now established such commissions—for instance, in the year 1913, eleven states passed legislation for this purpose—and the extent of their powers may be inferred from the example of the New York Public Service Commission, which may issue orders requiring the railways to furnish safeguards and adequate services and facilities, to regulate their charges according to the rates fixed by the Commission, to provide proper switch and side-track connexions, and to keep open for public inspection the rates and fares and charges as prescribed by the Commission. But the importance of what came to be known at the time as the "Wisconsin Idea" was that it extended this principle of administrative control to other spheres of action. The leaders of opinion in the state realised very clearly the difficulty of regulating complicated industrial and social conditions by specific legislation. We have already noticed in the preceding lecture the weaknesses of state legislation and its tendency to deal piecemeal with particular problems, setting up multifarious agencies for carrying out specific enactments. Similar defects have also characterised the efforts of state legislatures to conduct investigations through committees and commissions of their own members. Americans feel, rightly or wrongly, that the proceedings of such committees have been influenced too much by party considerations and have lacked the necessary scientific impartiality. The alternative adopted in Wisconsin consisted in the establishment by statute, in the case of any given set of problems, of a great administrative commission, the task of enacting specific regulations or of conducting special investigations being left to the discretion of the commission itself. Thus, in Wisconsin, a tax commission was created in 1899, and in 1903 it was charged with the physical valuation of railways. In 1903 the banking department was reorganised and the commission was given greatly enlarged powers. In 1905 a railway commission was created with wide powers, to which in 1907 were added powers over other public utilities. Great use has been made of such expert service along the line of what is now known as the "conservation" movement, that is to say, the economical use and development of national resources. In 1899 a fishery commission and a geological and natural history survey were established; in 1901, a board of health, a board of agriculture, and a live stock sanitary board; in 1905, a board of forestry, and commissions on tuberculosis, and grain and warehouses. In 1909 a rigid "pure food" law was passed, and a commission provided to enforce it. Along the line of education, a free library commission was established in 1899. The establishment of a civil service commission is but one of a number of attempts to purify and simplify the machinery of politics. In 1909 a commission was appointed on uniform legislation, and in 1911 one on "public affairs."

In 1913, the efforts made in the state to promote cooperative agriculture culminated in a proposal to establish a market commission in the interest both of the farmers and the consumers. The bill creating this commission was, however, rejected by the legislature, but it is worth mentioning as an indication of the strong movement in the United States towards a measure of government control over marketing.

But perhaps the most interesting developments along the lines of commission government are those connected with the establishment of commissions to deal with industrial questions. Wisconsin established an industrial commission in 1911. Many states followed this example. For instance, Ohio established such a commission in 1913, consisting of three members which took over the work of eight different government departments. Its jurisdiction covers factory inspection, labour statistics, employment exchanges, boiler, mine, and building inspection, trade disputes, and compensation under the Workmen's Compensation Act. Other states have appointed commissions to deal only with a smaller range of industrial questions, such as the Californian Industrial

Accident Commission and the commissions set up in other states especially for the administration of Workmen's Compensation Acts. But great commissions like that in Wisconsin are of a far more powerful character than these. The Wisconsin commission has been called an "administrative Court of Appeal." The powers of such commissions have grown with the rapid extension of legislation regarding industrial conditions. The limitation of hours of labour, first of women and then of men, the prohibition of child labour and, finally, the establishment of minimum wages in particular industries have successively raised problems which, in the view of many reformers, can only be dealt with by administrative bodies with wide discretionary powers.

Of these laws, those relating to minimum wages are perhaps the most important. Massachusetts led the way in 1912. The Massachusetts act was interesting but comparatively moderate. It gave to a minimum wage commission power to investigate any industry and to fix a minimum wage in it, but the decisions of the commission had no mandatory force. In the event of its findings being rejected by the industry concerned, it had, however, power to publish its report, thus enabling public opinion to bring pressure to bear upon recalcitrant employers or workmen. This act also gave the courts power to set aside the findings of the commission on the ground of danger to the prosperity of the business affected. In 1913 the state of Utah passed a peculiar minimum wage law which itself fixed a classified wage rate for all female employees, thus dispensing with investigations by a commission. Other states have not followed this example. Of the minimum wage commissions set up in seven states in 1913, one was exempt from any review of its decisions by the courts, and five were liable to have their decisions reviewed on questions of law only. In the majority of cases, the decisions of these commissions had mandatory force, but their scope was confined to the fixing of wages for women and minors.

This policy of dealing with social reform by administrative commissions has been defended by its advocates on the grounds sketched above. Dr McCarthy, one of the leaders of the movement in Wisconsin, in a book written to explain the system adopted in his state, summed up the views of the most convinced defenders of the system in words which indicate the desire of American reformers to "get ahead" on practical lines without too cautious a regard for constitutional forms:

Granted that the legislature is fearless and honest, and fully able to control the most powerful commission, the question of regulation resolves itself into half a dozen concrete vital elements —the accountant, the statistician, the actuary, the chemist, red blood, and a big stick!

The system has also, however, been very strongly attacked on the ground that many such commissions have plenary powers and threaten to over-ride private rights without sufficient possibility of appeal. For instance, the average board of health established in the states has, in its own limited sphere, the most drastic authority "in condemning property, in isolating individuals and in establishing quarantines." Perhaps, however, criticism is most keenly excited by the newer methods of dealing with crime by administrative discretion rather than by fixed law. Shortly before the war, the chairman of the Massachusetts Prison Commission proposed that "all convicted persons should be turned over to a commission charged with full responsibility for their care and custody under an indeterminate sentence," and legislation of this kind has been passed in many states. Another similar measure is the extension of the jurisdiction of juvenile courts and "courts of domestic relations" with very wide powers of dealing at discretion with the lives of the poor. One great American authority, Professor Roscoe Pound, writing shortly before the war, went so far as to say that "the powers of the Court of Star Chamber extended only to misdemeanors punishable by fine or imprisonment, and, in their possibilities

of affecting the dearest interests of the ordinary man, were a
trifle compared with those of American Juvenile Courts and
Courts of Domestic Relations, and with those which many
are seeking to confer upon administrative boards after conviction and sentence."

We cannot enter here into the very large questions involved
in this controversy which is not peculiar to the United States,
but it is important to emphasise the very widespread feeling
among reformers in the United States in favour of government by "experts." As one of these reformers has said, "the
methods of applied science now inaugurated in agriculture,
engineering, and business need to be extended to sociology
and law." Along with what Americans call, and with much
justice, the " moral awakening " in their country in the
direction of social legislation, has gone a corresponding demand for "efficiency." That demand, natural in all countries
in the face of the growing complexity of modern problems,
has been given a peculiar impetus in America by reason of
previous failures in administration, defects in methods of
legislation, and the conservatism, and, in many states, the
antiquated procedure of the courts. This movement towards
"efficiency" has not been confined to the actual administration of the laws: it has also led to a multiplicity of investigatory institutions. Just before the war there were in operation
some fifty investigatory commissions appointed by state
legislatures. Examples in 1913 were the appointment in
California of commissions on immigration and housing and
on old age insurance and pensions, and the appointment in
Illinois of an " economy and efficiency commission " to
investigate the conduct of public business. In some states,
such as Wisconsin and California, state boards of public
affairs and boards of control have been created to make such
investigations as are necessary, and to introduce economy and
efficiency into the work of government departments. The
bureaux of municipal research (discussed below) have also
done considerable work for the state governments, for in-

stance, in 1913 the New York bureau conducted an investigation into the rural schools of Wisconsin. Under the same heading must be placed the "legislative reference" bureaux and libraries, to which we alluded in the last lecture, which, just before the war, existed in twenty-nine states.

It is impossible to understand the character of the American social reform movement without taking into account this cult of what has come to be known, in a cant phrase, as the "efficiocrat."

Before passing to a brief consideration of social reform in municipalities, there is one general point to be considered. The question is often raised how far the American federal system lessens the possibility of dealing in a comprehensive way with social evils. On the one hand, it is perfectly true that advanced states have frequently been deterred from passing sound but drastic legislation for fear of placing themselves at a disadvantage towards neighbouring states. Thus the backward state of legislation in regard to child labour in the southern states has been a drag on the wheels of this particular reform throughout the union, with the result that after protracted agitation the federal government recently passed a child labour law applying to the whole union. This law was, however, declared unconstitutional by the Supreme Court this spring, and the confusion thus created has had to be dealt with under the administrative war powers of the federal government. Again, limitations on hours of labour for women in Massachusetts were at one time opposed on the ground that similar legislation did not exist in the adjacent state of Rhode Island, thus giving an undue advantage to manufacturers in the latter state. These difficulties have led to a very strong movement in favour of increased control by the national government over such matters, and it is on this consideration that the demands of the Progressive Party, quoted above, for alterations in the federal constitution were based in 1912. On the other hand, there is much to be said for the view that the free play given

to various communities to experiment on a large or small
scale within their own boundaries, and the task imposed upon
these communities of encouraging their neighbours to live up
to the same level as themselves, constitute a better and more
democratic method of progress than the imposition of uniform laws by a central authority. A great deal of work is being
done towards uniform legislation. For instance, before the
war, a model vital statistics law had been drawn up and its
adoption by all states was being urged by the Federal Census
Bureau and Children's Bureau. The National Civic Federation has promulgated, among other things, a model workman's compensation law. The Committee on Uniform
State Laws of the American Bar Association has long conducted propaganda for the adoption of model laws of various
kinds, and holds, for this purpose, an annual conference of
commissioners on uniform state laws from all the states
of the union. The annual conference of state governors is
also a means of encouraging uniformity of legislation, and the
American Association for Labor Legislation has fulfilled a
similar function in regard to many matters of social reform.
At the present moment, this latter association is conducting a
widespread propaganda in favour of the adoption by all
states of health insurance legislation which is one of the
newer reforms most prominently before the American people
at the present moment. In addition, the administrative commissions of various states tend to consult together about their
work. Conferences of the Industrial Commissioners of the
various states are held every year and their deliberations have
done much gradually to lift the legislation of the various
states on to a uniformly high plane.

As a matter of fact, no one who studies American conditions
can fail to be impressed with the rapidity with which new
reform experiments are taken up and run like wildfire from
state to state. We have already seen how the Massachusetts
Minimum Wage Act was copied in various forms by eight
states within a single year. Other remarkable instances could

be quoted. For instance, in 1913 as many as thirty-one states passed legislation on the subject of child welfare. In this year was enacted the Ohio "Children's Code," one of the most comprehensive pieces of consolidating social legislation passed in America in recent years, and also the federal law creating a Children's Bureau in the Department of Labor. More remarkable still is the history of legislation establishing mother's pensions. The first instance of this rather novel reform occurred very shortly before the war. Up to the end of 1912, four states had legislation of this kind. In 1913, no fewer than thirteen states legislated on the subject. The imitative tendency is very strong and the more novel the experiment the more eagerly is it taken up.

We must close this hurried review of social reform with a few words as to reforms in municipalities. The conditions of government in great cities, especially in view of the enormous influx of immigrant labour, has naturally furnished one of the most powerful incentives to social legislation, and has provided the national movement with many of its best leaders. One of the earliest steps in the new movement was, for instance, the survey conducted by private organizations of the great steel centre of Pittsburg, which resulted in a somewhat grave indictment of the conditions of life created by that industry. For many years, too, one of the chief centres of social reform sentiment has been the settlement organized by Miss Jane Addams at Hull House, Chicago. Miss Lathrop, who was for many years closely associated with Miss Addams in this work, is now head of the Federal Children's Bureau. The part played by women like Miss Addams and Miss Florence Kelley of the National Consumers' League, as leaders of social reform in their communities, has been one of the driving forces behind the demand for woman suffrage.

We have little time to enter into any detailed discussion of municipal social reform. It exhibits many of the characteristics which we have already noticed in the states. The demand for "efficient" administration by "experts" has been made perhaps more vigorously in the case of municipalities than in any other sphere. The tendency to establish administrative commissions to deal in a scientific manner with social problems has been very marked, and the bureaux of municipal research, largely instituted by private enterprise, have played a great part in stimulating an agitation for better methods of government. These bureaux of municipal research—or "municipal besmirch," as they are pathetically called by the ward politicians—in operation in such cities as New York, Chicago, Philadelphia, Baltimore, Cincinnati, Dayton, Milwaukee, Springfield (Massachusetts) and, with perhaps a less degree of efficiency, in Memphis and St Louis, have done excellent and thorough work in showing up abuses and establishing proper standards of administration by minute surveys of city business. It may be mentioned in passing that, in 1913, the New York bureau was called in by the city of Toronto to report on and reorganise its city departments.

Municipalities are tending to adopt proper civil service systems. Professor Graham Wallas, in the work quoted in the last lecture, pointed it out as "an amazing instance of the intellectual inertia of the English people" that the application of the civil service idea to municipalities has hardly been considered in England, whereas "in America, the term 'Civil Service' is applied equally to state and municipal affairs, and Civil Service principles are understood to cover municipal as well as federal appointments." Chicago, for instance, created, during 1913, an "efficiency department" in its civil service, designed to control, not only appointments, but also promotions under an elaborate system of "efficiency ratings" for each individual official.

Perhaps the point in which foreign countries have most to learn from American municipalities is the development of park systems. The parks and amusement grounds of Chicago are models of what a poor population needs, and their equal can probably be found in few cities outside America. Boston,

Cleveland, and New York have recently done much to develop such a system, though New York is severely handicapped by the long distances which separate the different parts of the city.

These few notes are a very inadequate tribute to the sound and extensive work of reform conducted during the last few years in all the municipalities of the United States, but we have no time for more. In conclusion, however, and by way of summary, we may consider briefly one outstanding feature of municipal social reform movements which lies very near the heart of the whole problem of local government in the United States.

For reasons largely arising out of the electoral system which we tried to explain in the last lecture, municipal government had, at the beginning of the new social reform period which we are considering, fallen largely into the hands of the "bosses." The history of "boss" rule in American cities has become rather a commonplace subject of self-satisfied criticism on this side of the Atlantic. In the United States it has stirred the keenest energies of the reformers. But we should ignore one of the main problems of democratic government if we were to assume that organizations like Tammany Hall in New York—however corrupt they have been in their methods—were merely sordid excrescences in American public life. They have real strength drawn from the life of the people and fulfil real functions which cannot be dispensed with, though they should certainly be replaced and their work done in a more thorough and disinterested manner. Tammany, and societies and organizations of the same kind, have drawn their strength not merely or primarily from electoral manipulation with all its attendant corruption and "log-rolling," but from real human touch with the life of the poor. The main obstacle to reform in municipalities will, in the long run, prove to be —not the corrupt affections of politicians—but the difficulty of humanizing the processes of "efficiency" reform. Leaders like Miss Addams have recognized this, and the "social settlement" has been a real power in competition with the ward politician; but before the reform tradition can really be established in American municipalities the reformers have much to learn. However evil has been the influence of Tammany and other similar organizations in other cities, their position has been founded on a charity which may well cover a multitude of their sins. They have derived their power, not from a general benevolence like that of the reformers, which stands aloof in order that, having surveyed the whole field, it may pass well-weighed measures of social reform, but from that intimate contact and personal sympathy which find expression in coal and blankets, and, dearest of all to the poor, deal coffins and a decent funeral. The New York Polish Jew or Hungarian peasant has more affection for a city administration which illegally excludes traffic from an "East Side" street at 7 p.m. in order that children may play there and impromptu dances be held round a barrel organ, than for a mayor and council, or a commission, or a city manager, who devote their energies to efficient street cleaning, efficient accounting, and the efficient management of amusement grounds in a park three miles away. And in the heart of the slum dweller there is more joy over one policeman who conveniently turns his back when children obstruct a thoroughfare than over the other ninety-and-nine who slave fourteen hours a day to break up " gangs " or enforce the Sunday closing law. They will gather in their thousands, as they gathered on such an occasion in New York in the winter of 1913–14, to follow the coffin of their "ward leader" to the grave, when the death of a famous reformer will hardly reach their ears. Reform administrations too often get into power not, as they hope, on the general spirit of their programme, but, as in Philadelphia, on the strength of a promise to reduce the cost of gas; and they lose the next election, as the Philadelphia reformers lost it, when they find that the state of the city finances will not permit them to carry out such promises. With all their efficiency and acquaintance with the latest

German or English experiments in social reform, they have too often lacked that bond of union with the masses which in Tammany has been so largely supplied by the Roman Catholic Church; they have too often failed to provide a sufficient substitute for that common allegiance and common good fellowship which, naturally and without disparagement to the higher need, seem to find their joint expression in the priest and the saloon keeper.

If I might add one word it would be this. I have tried to convey some idea of the American reform movement. It has been hasty and sketchy, but it will not have been entirely in vain if it encourages anyone who has heard me to look to the United States as a worthy partner with the British Empire in the task of social progress. The war is in many ways revolutionizing the conditions of American life and the tendencies of American social policy. Of these developments I have had no time to speak. But Englishmen should watch them with sympathy and hold themselves ready to learn from them without pride, for it is to the British Empire and the United States that the world is about to turn for leadership in the task of reconstruction and the establishment of a secure and peaceful social order.

REFERENCE BOOKS AND STATISTICS

Government of American Cities. W. B. MUNRO. 1917. Macmillan, New York.

State Government in the United States. A. N. HOLCOMBE. 1916. Macmillan, New York.

Growth of American State Constitutions. J. G. DEALEY. 1915. Ginn & Sons.

Organised Democracy. F. A. CLEVELAND. 1913. Longmans, Green & Co., London and New York.

Cyclopedia of American Government. A. C. McLAUGHLIN (A. B. HART). 1914. Appleton & Co.

Public Opinion and Popular Government. A. LAWRENCE LOWELL. 1913. Longmans, Green & Co., London and New York.

CHARACTERISTICS OF AMERICAN INDUSTRIAL CONDITIONS

PHILIP BENJAMIN KENNEDY, A.B., A.M.

CHARACTERISTICS OF AMERICAN
INDUSTRIAL CONDITIONS

AT this time, when American industry, like the British,
French, and Italian, is mobilized for war purposes, it is
difficult to think of individual industries except in terms of
national units. It is also a time when new industrial plants are
springing up almost over night and old established plants are
often being diverted from non-essential to essential products.
Peculiar conditions also frequently necessitate the invention
of new processes. It is not my purpose, however, to attempt
to show primarily the changes in the direction of industry and
the new methods now being adopted, but to try to sketch
roughly a few of the principal features of American industrial
conditions which have characterized our economic development.

A competent European observer who visited the United
States a few years ago remarked that in America we thought
a great deal of the future and very little of the past, whereas
in Europe they thought a great deal of the past and not very
much of the future. This contrast is not pertinent at the present time because the United States is fully absorbed in the
same purposes as our European allies, and because in Great
Britain, France, and Italy the economic future is receiving a
great deal of earnest attention. It has, however, been relatively a feature of the pre-war point of view. The older European nations have been constantly influenced by traditions,
economic as well as political. In America we have become
accustomed to rapid changes in individual wealth and social
position and to the practice of tackling new economic problems in a new way. We have travelled light. American
industry has generally been characterized by speed, bustle,
and daring ambitions for the future. A visitor quickly

recognized the high tension prevailing in American business and industrial centres. Labour-saving devices, whether for the mill, the office, or the shop, have been necessary to offset the relatively high wages of American labour, and have been readily adopted. This same tendency has also been very apparent in farming and mining. The characteristic enthusiasm to get ahead has sometimes been illustrated by the mottoes one may see in offices, such as "Do it now," or "Do it better."

Whether the speed of American life has been due to the dry stimulating atmosphere or to the manifold opportunities of a new country has sometimes been a subject of discussion. An impetuous spirit is not always successful or even desirable from a standpoint of human comfort, but it gives momentum. It is the spirit of youth. This is the spirit which we bring to our gallant allies at a time when they have long been hard pressed by their great efforts and sacrifices in this war.

The traditional self-sufficiency of the United States both in industry and point of view has been due in part, at least, to the great area of the country and to its variety of national resources. Attention has been mainly focused upon local development and the home markets. Until recently American exports consisted largely of agricultural products and raw materials. Although increase in manufacture and consequent concentration of urban population have been the outstanding features of the past two decades, there is still plenty of breathing room. The area of the United States is approximately twenty-five times that of the United Kingdom, whereas the population is only a little more than twice as large.

The development of rapid means of transportation and modern methods of distributing news have done much to remove any marked differences of ideas and opinions in various parts of the country which might otherwise result from its large area. Never before in our history has the nation been so solidly unified in purpose and sentiment as it is to-day, when the great test has come.

A general understanding of American economic and social conditions, however, requires a knowledge of the background and of the special characteristics in different parts of the country. Historically, the principal sectional divergencies have been between the north and south, and between the east and west. From the time the United States became an independent nation to the civil war two quite distinct types of industrial society grew up in the north and south. The north steadily progressed in manufacture and commerce as well as in general farming. The south, after the invention of the cotton gin, devoted itself almost exclusively to cotton production. Negro slaves were found to be most profitably employed on cotton plantations and were practically all concentrated in the southern states. The capitalistic production of the northern states resulted in more rapid increase in population and wealth than in the agricultural south. At the beginning of the nation population was evenly divided between northern and southern states. In 1861, the population of the north was about double that of the south and the resources of the north were also much greater. A landed and aristocratic class had grown up in the south which had a very different point of view from the business classes in the north. Since the civil war the differences in industry and point of view have rapidly disappeared. The south is today prosperous not only on account of the cotton crop but also because of rapid industrial development along other lines. The great bulk of our numerous immigrants has, however, gone to the great industrial cities of the north Atlantic and middle western states, whereas the south has to a considerable extent grown up on the basis of its old population. The southerner still maintains a certain individuality inherited from the old régime, and has his own point of view on many local questions. He is notably high-spirited and will play a vital part in the stern programme which we have in hand.

The winning of the continent has been a march westward. It is only within the past quarter of a century that there has ceased to be a western frontier. The frontiersmen who pushed across four thousand miles of virgin country played a great part in shaping national sentiment. They were men who had to conquer nature and make homes for their families trusting to their own resources. Their spirit of independence and hardihood, of self-reliance and distrust of artificial values, has been a constant influence for a democratic spirit in national affairs, and it is an influence which is still potent.

The north-eastern states which grew rapidly in wealth found abundant opportunities for surplus investment in the development of the west, and up to the time of the present war American capital had to only a slight extent sought opportunities overseas.

The general character of different sections of the United States has been influenced by immigration. The Irish, who have come steadily in the past seventy-five years, have settled mainly in the large cities, where they have played an active part. German immigrants settled principally in the middle west, where they have been prosperous both in the cities and on the land. Scandinavians have also gone mainly to the middle west, where in some sections they are very numerous. German and Scandinavian immigrants made possible the rapid growth of agriculture in these great farming states of the middle west. Recently the bulk of immigrants who have come from southern Europe have gone to manufacturing centres in New England, the northern Atlantic states, and the middle west. They have made possible the rapid development of our manufactures which probably could not have been obtained without this plentiful supply of labour. From 1901 to 1917 the number of alien passengers and immigrants arriving at American ports was well over twelve millions. This great number of comparatively recent arrivals indicates the extent of the problem of Americanizing our new citizens. In spite, however, of the tendency of recent immigrants to congregate in foreign quarters of large cities, they rapidly absorb American ideas. Men of many races and many traditions will make up our armies, but we are confident that the test will show that they are all Americans, true to our past and loyal to the best ideals of our future.

According to the last census, that of 1910, the urban population of the United States was 42,623,383, as compared to a rural population of 49,348,883. Population of incorporated places of 2500 or more inhabitants is classed as urban. Between 1900 and 1910 urban population increased 34·8 % and rural 11·2 %. This tendency to more rapid increase in urban population has probably been maintained since the census of 1910, and it is reasonable to assume that urban and rural population in the United States are now not far from equal.

The relative importance of the different cereal crops is shown by the following statistics based upon the year 1917:

	Area	Production	Farm value, Dec. 1
	Acres	Bushels	Dollars
Corn (Maize)	119,755,000	3,159,494,000	4,053,672,000
Wheat	45,941,000	650,828,000	1,307,418,000
Oats	43,572,000	1,587,286,000	1,061,427,000
Rye	4,102,000	60,145,000	100,025,000
Barley	8,835,000	298,975,000	237,539,000

The corn (maize) belt, as it is sometimes called, consists primarily of the states of Illinois, Iowa, Missouri, Indiana, Ohio, Nebraska, Kansas, Kentucky, Minnesota, and South Dakota. These states which produced three-quarters of the entire corn (maize) crop in 1917 are in the heart of the middle west. The leading wheat-growing states are Minnesota, North Dakota, South Dakota, and Kansas, which are also in the middle west.

A prominent editor from the middle west whom I saw recently in London remarked that there seemed to be as great interest in foreign trade in Great Britain as we in the United States have in crops. The prosperity of the United States as a whole, it is true, has always been greatly influenced by the success of the harvest; in the great farming regions, however, crops are the subject of absorbing interest. The state of the weather and market prices are universal topics of conversation.

In the southern states cotton is still the basis of prosperity in spite of a considerable growth in manufactures and a very earnest effort in the direction of a sufficient production of cereal crops to make the territory self-sufficing as regards food. The American cotton crop in 1914 ran over sixteen million bales, the greatest in our history. The war made it impossible to ship normally to Europe and prices came down to a level virtually below cost of production. To assist the south a patriotic "buy a bale" movement was started and banks, business houses, and individuals bought bales of cotton to help carry the load. It was a frequent sight to see a bale of cotton displayed in shop windows in different cities. At the same time an energetic effort was made to curtail acreage, which resulted in a reduction of about one-seventh in the cotton acreage in 1915. The present war demand for cotton, however, has come to be so great that in spite of the blockade of the central powers and lessened shipments to allied countries on account of tonnage there is still a demand for a full crop at enhanced prices, and the south is sharing in the pressure for greater production.

The districts which produce food and raw materials have every incentive to increased production during the war. The feeding and equipping of our own troops adds greatly to the normal local demand. The great problem, however, is the unusual demand of our allies. In normal times the outlying parts of the world send large quantities of food and raw materials to Europe, but at present the maximum effectiveness of shipping is lessened by the long route. The nearness of American Atlantic ports to our allies makes it most economical to ship the largest possible proportion of supplies from the United States. We are trying to meet this problem by means of larger production and lessened home consumption. Wherever possible the United Kingdom is also prohibiting the importation of non-essential manufactured goods, to make the greatest possible use of available tonnage to import food and raw materials. This policy in addition to conserving tonnage provides raw material to keep British labour employed.

In 1910, the number of persons engaged in manufacturing in the United States was less than two-thirds of the number engaged in agriculture, forestry, and animal husbandry. The last census of manufactures of 1914 showed that eight and a quarter million persons were engaged in manufacturing industries, which was an increase of 7·6 % over the number so engaged in 1909. This was a marked falling off in the rate of increase of the previous five years (1904–1909) which was 23·6 %.

The greatest manufacturing district in the United States is located in the middle Atlantic states, that is New York, New Jersey, and Pennsylvania. The second district is east north central, containing the states of Ohio, Indiana, Illinois, Michigan, and Wisconsin. The third group is made up of the New England states. The great manufacturing centres are the large cities with their industrial suburbs, New York, Chicago, Philadelphia, Boston, St Louis, Cleveland, Detroit, and Pittsburg. Most of the great industries are much more scattered than is the case in the United Kingdom. There are, however, often instances of resemblance. When I visited Sheffield I was astonished at the number of tall chimneys belching smoke in a cloud over the city and could not help commenting on it to a steel manufacturer. He remarked philosophically that there was a good deal of smoke in Sheffield but that it was not as bad as Pittsburg.

In the great Lancashire district I believe there are about five hundred thousand cotton mill operatives concentrated in a relatively small area. In 1914 there were about three hundred and seventy-five thousand employees in cotton goods manufacture in the United States, which may not be strictly comparable to the industry as cited for Lancashire, since related industries are not included in the American figure. The wide distribution of the American cotton industry, however, can be illustrated in that one hundred and twelve thousand operatives are in Massachusetts, fifty-three in North Carolina, forty-six in South Carolina, and the balance scattered in twenty other states. Whereas it is possible in war time for British inspectors to pass on government cotton textile contracts with very little moving about, it is a far different problem in the United States where the mills are widely scattered.

The old cotton manufacturing district was in the New England states. Mills, however, steadily increased in the southern states, until the south caught up with the north in its output of cotton goods. This manufacturing development in the south is only partly due to nearness of raw material; a leading reason for its success is that an industrial population has grown up in the south which makes available an adequate supply of labour. The workers in the southern mills are mostly of American descent. However, in the great cotton cities of New England, Fall River, New Bedford, Lowell, Lawrence, and Manchester, the labour population is largely made up of recent immigrants. When a strike occurred in Lawrence a few years ago it was said to be difficult for the strikers to find suitable leadership because the operatives spoke forty different languages.

The development of "quantity" shoe manufacture is distinctly an American achievement. Before the invention and rapid improvement of shoe machinery, which occurred after 1880, each district had been self-sufficing. The local shoemaker turned out shoes to measure for his customers. The perfection of shoe machinery, however, has caused the almost total disappearance of the custom shoe-maker in the United States. There is a considerable localization of shoe manufacture. Brockton, Massachusetts, is the leading city in the manufacture of men's shoes as is Lynn, Massachusetts, in the manufacture

of women's shoes. Haverhill, Massachusetts, is noted as the
"slipper city." Several other cities in New England, a number
of cities in New York and New Jersey, and three or four
cities in the middle west, especially St Louis, also have extensive shoe factories. The shoe industry which originally
depended entirely upon native born American labour, still
looks to this class for all skilled workers, but in the use of
automatic machinery recent immigrants are coming to be
employed in the eastern states. In spite of the fact that new
machines have been perfected which make nearly two hundred distinct operations entirely mechanical, the shoe industry has not depended as much on new and unskilled labour
as have other industries, such as textiles.

The iron and steel industry, which in recent years has far
out-distanced that in any other country, is centred around the
Great Lakes from Buffalo to Chicago. Iron ore is shipped by
water from the head of the lakes in Michigan, Wisconsin, and
Minnesota to cities which are adjacent to a coal supply,
notably Pittsburg, Cleveland and Chicago. Improved ore-
handling machinery has been perfected which greatly cheap-
ens handling and shipment. The motto of Carnegie, "Scrap
old machinery," has been typical of the spirit of the steel industry. Constant and rapid extensions have been made along
most modern and improved lines. The large amount of unskilled and partly skilled labour needed has been supplied
in great measure by recent immigrants. Engineering and
mechanical industries have grown up in close proximity to
the steel mills.

Among recent industries none have attracted more attention than the making of automobiles and rubber goods.
Detroit easily holds the lead as the great automobile city.
Detroit, Cleveland, Toledo, and other cities on the lakes have
been near to the supply of steel and other materials used in
construction of motor cars and have been centrally located for
distribution. Seeing that the great demand for motor cars has
been in the home market, this interior location has been an

economical factor. Once an industry grows up, moreover, there are many inducements for new establishments to seek the existing centre because of the supply of skilled labour, the nearness of related industries producing accessories, and the acquired reputation of the place. In the automobile industry the American tendency to labour-saving machinery and "large-scale" production has been notable. The production of a low-priced car has extended the market to undreamed of proportions. When it is remembered that a Ford car has sold for about seventy pounds in Detroit, and that other makes have approached this low cost, it is not surprising that skilled mechanics can afford to go to work in their own motor cars. In nearly all the cities and towns men of comparatively small incomes have found that they could afford a motor car and live out far enough to have a plot of ground in the suburbs. The war has necessitated the partial conversion of automobile plants to essential war output and has accordingly diminished their production. The increase in the cost of living has, moreover, decreased the ability of people to afford motor cars.

Corresponding with the growth of the motor car industry has been the increase in rubber goods manufacture, which has been phenomenal. Akron, Ohio, the principal centre of this industry, has expanded relatively even more rapidly than Detroit because it is much smaller.

The quick expansion of manufacturing, especially in certain localities, has often constituted an acute problem in the way of housing, and manufacturers have had to devote attention to providing quarters for their employees. Where opportunities have been favourable and employers have been so inclined, a good deal of welfare work has been accomplished which has resulted in employees obtaining sanitary and wholesome surroundings and opportunities for recreation and education. The independent and self-reliant spirit of American workers usually resents any self-complacent "welfare" work on the part of employers. In so far as there has been any patronizing spirit in the way of providing better conditions of work and living, it is illogical and should be remedied. If men and women are to be most effectively employed it is fundamental that the conditions in which they do their work should be such as to make it possible for them to do their best. The employer has a genuine interest in the health and spirit of his employees, from a purely selfish standpoint. Further than this, there is every reason why the feeling of partnership in a firm should be developed among all the personnel. Pride in one's work and its achievements has too often been lost in large scale production. One of the most happy and encouraging features of American industry has been that in certain establishments, some small and some large, there has grown up a spirit of comradeship and emulation on the part of all concerned, whether managers or employees. This spirit of "pull together" is almost essential in any undertaking which would forge ahead rapidly.

The "pull together" momentum, which in certain instances normally characterized American industry, is now in war time almost universal. Great readjustments in our industries have taken place in the past year, not always as rapidly as we had hoped it is true, but the progress which has been made has been facilitated by the eagerness of both employers and labour to get ahead with the war. We have had before us the essential lesson of what has been done in this great industrial nation of Great Britain, which has been invaluable both in teaching us methods and inspiring us to put our shoulders to the wheel. Every American visitor, whether in official or private capacity, who has come to the United Kingdom has taken back home a story of the gallant work which is being done in munition factories and on the land over here. With the example of what the women, as well as the men, of Great Britain and of France are doing, it is not strange that American industry, whether agricultural or industrial, has "got on its war paint."

In the full tide of war it is not a favourable time to estimate changes which this world upheaval cannot help bringing about. It may be feasible, however, to call attention to several obvious but significant tendencies as applied to the United States. For one thing, we have discovered Europe. Whereas previously the bulk of our attention was devoted to local affairs the great interest of the American people is today focused on the war and the great problems in Europe and the rest of the world which are in process of solution. We will not relapse to our old feeling of isolation. We are committed with the allies to certain great principles in which we have a joint concern and a joint responsibility. There is no part of the country so remote that it does not realize this.

In common with our allies we are pouring our resources into the prosecution of the war, and in common with them we are experiencing high taxation and rapid increase in the cost of living. Whatever time and effort may be required to re- cover our former standard of comfort this is not a prime con- sideration today. If we have had a normal tendency to think a great deal of future ambitions, we are today living in terms of the present, which necessitates a victorious peace.

For the first time in our history we have fully recognized individual responsibility to the nation in the form of con- scription and central direction of commerce and industry. In a country where the individual has been so free to follow his own ends in his own way, this change came readily be- cause it was felt that it was necessary. It is probable that this feeling of public responsibility will be carried over into normal life and will influence our future development.

The war and the heavy burdens after the war provide every incentive for improved means of production. Progress is likely to be greatly accelerated as the result of this incentive and pre-war methods may be largely transformed. Neverthe- less, any outline of American industrial conditions, however condensed, should not fail to include a summary analysis of various factors which have facilitated our industrial progress.

A leading factor in the growth of American manufacturing has been the invention of new processes. High wages have

afforded an inducement to introduce labour-saving devices
wherever possible. Although in many instances important in-
ventions have been the work of individuals, the total momentum has been greatly accelerated by the elaborate efforts of large
firms devoted to research. Shoe machinery, textile machinery,
rubber goods, and electrical devices are a few of the lines in
which the technical work done by large establishments has
greatly advanced the whole industry. During the war the
scientific industrial work being done by the federal government through the Bureau of Standards is being much extended. The high range of prices as well as urgent necessity
should greatly stimulate the inventive output of American
technical men in the near future.

A correlated advantage which must go with the capacity to
invent new machinery is the ability of workers to operate
machinery. The general adoption of improved agricultural
machinery and implements in the United States, for instance,
which has been so important in increasing our agricultural
output, has been made possible by our farmers' ability to adapt
themselves to their use. The facility of American factory labour
to operate machinery has also been an advantage. Where skilled
mechanics were scarce and wages high, automatic machinery
has been developed which has done away with the need for
skilled labour. The increase in skilled labour could never have
kept up with our growth in manufacture. A large supply of
skilled labour, however, is constantly required and large establishments have in many instances built up special departments
for the training of apprentices. An extension of this system of
training skilled mechanics will be required by the greater
demands of the future.

Large scale production has been a special feature of American manufacture. The growth of large concerns with ample
resources has made it possible to lay out new plants on most
extensive lines. When, for instance, the great steel works at
Gary, Indiana, were built they had been planned as a whole
in advance so as to secure every possible economy. Quantity

production would in many cases have been unwise without the security of the great home market. The production of a low-priced motor car on a large scale, for example, would not be feasible unless a big market were assured.

The general use of machinery has been greatly facilitated by the standardization of parts which are carried in stock locally where users can quickly obtain them. This has reduced the cost of repairs and has obviated delay. Where the maintenance of machinery in constant operation requires technical inspection and assistance many machinery establishments have had a service department with trained men who regularly inspect their machinery in operation. If machinery is not properly operated and kept up it will not do its work and the demand for it will fall off. An American engineer told me of an experience of his own which illustrates this point. When in France he met a manufacturer who told him that he had American machinery which was no good. The engineer who had this same machinery in his own factory in America volunteered to see what was the matter. In two hours' time he had made a few adjustments which doubled the output capacity of this French establishment.

Machinery has played a great part in advancing industry, but it is not the only factor. On one occasion I asked a leading official of one of the largest and most prosperous companies in the United States what was the greatest single factor in the success of his concern. Was it, I inquired, their control of sources of supply, their technical knowledge, or their large resources? He thought for a moment and replied: "No, it is not one of the factors which you have mentioned. The greatest single factor in our success has been the personal factor." I believe that he was right. Operating organization and sound business methods depend upon the individual. A concern must be so organized as to give every employee individual responsibility and an incentive to initiative. It must be so organized as to prevent roundabout methods, and facilitate clean-cut work. A great factor in the success of leading

American firms has been the attention paid to organization, and individual incentive.

Another factor, and the last one I will mention, is the high repute which industrial and commercial callings have occupied in the United States. The expression "Captain of Industry" has so often been the subject of comment, favourable and unfavourable, that it may convey a wrong impression. If we speak of business leaders, however, it should be clear that in this period of large and complicated practical affairs, such men must have considerable technical training, a knowledge of men, and a broad understanding of general conditions. They create, organize, and carry forward to success, great undertakings. The accomplishments of men of this type have caught the admiration of the community and they occupy a position of high esteem.

There is very little place in America for the man who is not busy. The men who achieve things are the men who are prominent and who find satisfaction in the community. This public approval of practical achievement is, far more than the desire for pecuniary gain, the driving incentive of American life.

THE RELATION OF THE AMERICAN GOVERNMENT TO BUSINESS

PHILIP BENJAMIN KENNEDY, A.B., A.M.

THE RELATION OF THE AMERICAN
GOVERNMENT TO BUSINESS

AT a meeting of the American Economic Association a few years ago a well-known economist remarked that the detailed regulation of business was more difficult than the operation of business, and that the time might come when the federal government would find itself so involved in the mazes of regulation that a simpler solution would be for it to take over and operate certain major undertakings. Railway control has apparently justified this prediction. The great measure of government control which has been assumed over all lines of business during the war has, moreover, tended to bring about central management. All our traditional inclination to foster and protect individual enterprise has been put aside to meet present needs. Considering the long and vigorous efforts which have been made to prevent combinations, this new phase is especially interesting. All war expedients, however, are something in the nature of a temporary truce and the features of government regulation of business may best be considered under normal conditions.

The federal government under the terms of the constitution has the power to regulate commerce among the several states. Due to the division of industry the bulk of railway goods traffic in the United States is interstate. Moreover, since state regulation of interstate traffic has followed the main lines of federal regulation, it may be suitable to confine this discussion of government railway regulation to that which has been undertaken by the federal government.

The regulation of passenger fares is a comparatively simple matter and need not be given special attention. The regulation of freight rates, that is rates for goods traffic, however, vitally affects all lines of business and becomes very complicated.

Government regulation practically started with the so-called Interstate Commerce Act of 1887, which created the Interstate Commerce Commission and laid down certain principles as regards reasonable rates and discriminations. The Interstate Commerce Commission is an administrative body with power to see that laws and regulations passed by congress are enforced. On questions of fact the rulings of the Commission are final. Where questions of law are involved, such as the infringement of the constitution, appeal may be made to the federal courts.

One of the glaring abuses, with which federal regulation first endeavoured to cope, was discrimination among individual shippers. Competing railways had been in the habit of bidding against one another to secure the traffic of large shippers. The firms securing the lowest goods rates had a great advantage over rivals and could virtually drive them out of the field. The favourite method of giving transportation favours was in the form of rebates. Rebates worked to the advantage of so-called "trusts" which were organized in the late eighties.

It was some time before transportation favours to individual shippers were entirely eliminated. New methods of getting around the intent of the law were devised which had to be specially legislated against in acts subsequent to that of 1887. The penalty for infringement of the law was also made more severe. If a railway today reduces its rates for the benefit of a particular shipper, both the giver and receiver of the rebate are subject to a heavy fine. Although there are punishments each year for rebating, the practice has virtually disappeared.

The Interstate Commerce Commission has power in respect to classification. Various commodities are grouped in classes on which rates are based. A lower classification means a lower rate over a wide territory. In determining in what class a commodity should go two principles are involved: (1) what the traffic will bear, and (2) the cost of hauling it. High value merchandise in which the transportation cost is a small factor is usually given a high rating. Raw materials shipped in bulk are given a low rating because it is cheaper to transport them and because they will move to a wider area if goods rates are low.

One of the most vital classes of cases has related to rivalries among different localities. Rates have not as a rule been built up on a mileage basis, although this principle has been adopted to a certain extent in the region of most congested traffic. Commercial considerations have been the prime consideration. Low rates have been made to open up new markets. In certain instances reduced rates have been necessary to enable railways to compete with water transportation. A long route has had to be given as low a rate as a short route. When there has been a one way traffic, special low rates have been necessary to obtain a back haul. These few instances may illustrate the fact that goods rates have been adapted to special conditions. This flexibility has done a great deal to promote industry and commerce but it has also involved frequent litigation. The leading chambers of commerce have employed traffic experts to look after the interests of their locality before the Interstate Commerce Commission, which has been an important feature of their work.

Some of the most prominent cases in recent years have related to the general level of goods rates. Railways have had to pay increased wages to their employees, and higher prices for all their equipment and supplies, which they have felt justified increased rates. To estimate the rate of earnings the Interstate Commerce Commission has required the railways to adopt a standard form of accounting and has recently engaged in the tremendous task of making a physical valuation of the railways. Only very slight increases in general rates had been allowed, however, before the government took over the railways some months ago.

On account of the failure of the government to approve higher rates and fares and on account of the exaction of an eight hour day for employees, the feelings of railway executives towards the government have been far from cordial.

Last winter railway traffic congestion which had been serious for at least two years, as the result of the increase in export trade, became acute and the government took over the management of the railways. An endeavour is being made to eliminate competition among the different lines and to utilize the entire mileage in the most effective manner. Rates have been materially increased. Large orders have been placed for locomotives and trucks, and it is hoped that it will be possible to carry on, without delaying the war problem. The government has guaranteed railway shareholders a return equal to that of the average of three years before July 1, 1917, and that the upkeep of the properties will be maintained. It is impossible to predict whether the railways will eventually be turned back to private companies or whether the government will continue to operate them.

The expression "trust" has persisted in popular usage in spite of the fact that the type of organization to which it referred has disappeared. It was between 1880 and 1890 that trusts became prominent. A "trust" originally meant that various related firms had placed the control of certain phases of their business in the hands of a trustee. This device made possible a uniform policy as to prices and other agreed arrangements on the part of companies which would otherwise be competing. Combinations which tended to monopoly were peculiarly obnoxious to American individualistic spirit, and the famous Sherman Anti-Trust Act of 1890 was passed by congress, which was followed by acts of similar intent on the part of various states. Under these acts several of the principal trusts were dissolved by the courts and this particular form of trustee organization was abandoned. When combinations of different form were brought about, the public and especially journalistic critics kept alive the old term of trust which had already acquired a certain amount of opprobrium.

The state of New Jersey, it was found, had passed a law which permitted a company incorporated under its laws to hold the stock of other corporations. This privilege offered a favourable means for combination and gave rise to what has sometimes been called the "holding company," that is a parent company which controls other companies through stock ownership. This was the form adopted, for example, by the Standard Oil Company. The Standard Oil Company of New Jersey held the stock of the numerous subsidiary companies of which it was composed. A few years ago, it will be remembered, the Standard Oil Company of New Jersey was dissolved by order of the United States Supreme Court and the subsidiary companies were divorced from this central control and set up independently. Many of the largest corporations now own outright all the units of which they are composed, although control through partial stock ownership is still common.

The first form of combination which was adopted was horizontal, that is companies competing side by side in the production of similar commodities found it of advantage to unite to decrease production in order to maintain prices. An early example was the Whiskey Pools and later the Whiskey Trust. The production of whiskey had greatly increased during the civil war. This was because increased excise taxes were announced in advance thereby making it profitable for production to be as great as possible before the higher taxes went into effect. The whiskey producers had a hard time with their efforts to reduce production through pooling arrangements, and it was not until the trust was formed and many of the less favourably located distilleries were shut down that the industry could cope with over-production.

In the steel industry the first stage of combination was that of pooling agreement. A number of firms would agree to fix a total production and settle the percentage to which each firm should be entitled. These agreements were usually short lived because there was no effective means of enforcing them. Pooling agreements or "gentlemen's agreements" as they are now called, because they cannot be enforced at law, have never been an important characteristic of American combination. In Germany, where such agreements are enforceable at law and are encouraged by the government, they constitute the typical form.

Seeing that pools were unsatisfactory, trusts and later holding corporations were formed among companies producing similar commodities to control production and hold up prices.

A later development was vertical combination, that is a joining together of all the steps in production from raw material to the finished product. This form of integrated concern had more basis for economy of operation than the union of firms making similar articles. The most important economy effected by the horizontal combination is the concentration of production in certain plants running continuously on full time. Vertical combinations, however, may produce many economies in the close linking together of different processes and the elimination of dealers' profits on each single element in production. The vertical combination also assures a steady flow of raw, and partly finished material, and does not leave a company dependent on the temporary fluctuation of the market. There can be no doubt that in many instances integrated companies have achieved great economies and materially advanced their industry.

The Sherman Anti-Trust Act, which has been the cause of so much important litigation, aimed at monopolies and attempts to restrain trade. One of the cases which has in the past few years received considerable attention is the suit against the United States Steel Corporation. Evidence was introduced in this case to show that only about one-half of the total steel production of the United States was in the hands of this company, and that its relative ratio had actually decreased in the past fifteen years. It was also necessary to prove that no practices were indulged in which were inimical and unfair to competitors, at home or abroad. If anyone thinks that the investigation in a case of this character is not exhaustive let him some day surround himself with the testimony and findings, and he will realize the exhaustive character of the information obtained. It is obviously impossible to judge of the merits of a case by reading brief and perhaps prejudiced newspaper reports. Only a competent corporation lawyer could be trusted for advice as to what can and can not be done under the Sherman Law. Business men have sometimes protested that they ought to be told what they can do legally, but this is obviously too much to expect.

A vital question is as to whether mere bigness is a ground for the dissolution of a company. The intent of the law is to prevent monopoly; what constitutes monopoly is not, however, a question which can be readily answered because various considerations have to be given full weight.

Restraint of trade is an unfair practice designed to injure a competitor. A large company selling below cost of production in a territory where a small competitor is located, in order to drive him out of business, would be an unfair practice, and constitute restraint of trade. The question of what is, and what is not, fair practice can not be adequately answered except as the result of constant investigation and supervision. This is the reason that the Federal Trade Commission was organized to administer the Sherman Act as applied to industrial corporations in somewhat the same way that the Interstate Commerce Commission administers railway acts.

The Federal Attorney-General, who is responsible for prosecutions before the courts, is suspending activity where the government has itself during the war forced industries to form trade committees to consider the needs of a whole industry as regards priority in raw materials, coal, and shipping, and to say where the output shall go. Today, moreover, we have not only national control of many industries but also harmonious inter-allied co-operation which is becoming closer. In view of the intimate knowledge of all phases of industry now possessed by respective governments and the actual control exercised, it is futile to speak of the danger of trusts until industry has been put back on a normal competitive footing. It remains for the adjustments of peace to show us when and to what degree industry will be permitted by allied governments to resume its normal phases. The Federal Trade Commission is, moreover, fully alive to its responsibilities at the present time.

The latest and most interesting instance of American legislation as affecting combination is the Webb-Pomerene Act, which was signed by the president this spring. It permits American companies to combine for foreign trade under the supervision of the Federal Trade Commission.

Since the war a great deal has come to be known about the close combination of German concerns in dealing with foreign trade. The Webb-Pomerene Act is the direct answer to German methods and gives us the means of combating foreign combinations if directed against us. Prior to the war American copper companies sold on the market in open competition with one another. Germany, which had been a large consumer of American copper, had a single syndicate authorized to buy copper. It was customary for a number of German companies to appear to be in competition with one another whereas as a matter of fact they were actually under central control. After the war present indications are that Germany will go farther than ever before in the use of her syndicates and cartels. It would be folly to have no means of protection against this economic policy.

The extent to which American firms will elect to combine for foreign trade will depend upon circumstances. The sentiment of exporting firms generally is in favour of individual enterprise, if there is a fair field for this policy. The significance of the Webb-Pomerene Act is that it leaves the United States free to adopt foreign trade combinations, if this is necessary after the war.

The panic of 1907 clearly demonstrated that there was

something radically wrong with the American banking system. We had no central bank or any central agency which was capable of saving the situation when weakness was manifested in any quarter. In the early period of our history we had central banks. Congress refused to extend the charter of the Second Bank largely because of prejudice against the money power. The national banking system was established during the civil war to provide a stable bank-note currency and provide a market for government bonds. Both of these objects were attained. National bank-notes were secured, dollar for dollar, by government bonds and their payment in gold on demand was assured. The demand of national banks for government bonds as a basis of circulation enabled the floatation of government bonds at 2%. National banks were permitted, however, to have only a single banking office, which was the almost universal practice with state banks as well. Branch banks were so few as to be negligible. National banks in New York, Chicago, and St Louis were permitted to act as central reserve banks and carried deposits of the banks all over the country, on which they paid 2% interest. In case of a financial crisis all these depositing banks were anxious to draw out their deposits from the central reserve banks and replenish their cash account. In 1907 this system entirely broke down. Central reserve banks fearing the dangerous reduction of their cash reserves refused to pay. Each locality had to take care of itself as best it could until expedients were adopted to relieve the situation.

Congress recognizing the need for an early amendment of our banking laws appointed an able commission to make a study of the leading banking systems of the world, and recommend needed legislation. This commission recommended a central bank which would have means of providing for an elastic note issue, rediscount of commercial paper, and control of the import and export of gold. A long discussion ensued before the final adoption of the Federal Reserve Act.

Banking interests in New York preferred a single central

bank modelled after the Bank of England, the Bank of France, and the Reichsbank of Germany. This, however, met with opposition on the part of the west and south, which feared the concentration of banking power in New York. There was also the old antagonism to centralized money power which had been so effective back in 1836, when the Second Bank of the United States failed to secure an extension of its charter.

The Federal Reserve Act perfected a compromise. A central committee was set up in Washington called the Federal Reserve Board, which supervises branch federal reserve banks established in different sections of the country and determines matters of policy. The fear that the Federal Reserve Board might not be able properly to co-ordinate and direct the reserve banks has proved to be ungrounded. The federal reserve system was in working order before the heavy financial responsibilities of war came upon us and it has proved to be an agency competent and well fitted to control the financial resources of the nation. In this country so high an authority as Sir Edward Holden has recently given it his hearty commendation.

The capital stock of the reserve banks has been supplied by member national banks and state banks, which have qualified for admission. Directors are elected by member banks with certain qualifications in voting to assure geographical distribution and proper representation for smaller banks. The Federal Reserve Board is appointed by the president.

The federal reserve system has gradually taken over note issue from the national banks. Commercial paper is rediscounted for member banks on certain conditions as to character, length of time to run, and amount.

Certain features of our new banking laws have a bearing on foreign trade. Bank acceptances are now permitted in transactions arising out of trade, and banks are more and more availing themselves of this privilege. National banks of a certain capital are also permitted to establish branches in foreign countries upon making required provision for capital to be assigned to each branch. A number of the larger national banks have already established branches in South America and Europe. The law has been amended so as to allow banks to combine in establishing branches overseas and one or more important oversea banks have been founded, the stock being held by banks in different parts of the country.

In order to comprehend the importance of such a co-ordinating agency as the federal reserve system, it is essential to bear in mind that in the United States there are some twenty-seven thousand banks. The branch bank system characteristic of Great Britain and other leading countries has never developed in the United States because our national and state laws have forbidden it. In one or two states, state banks may have branches but the effects of this have been negligible. A proposed amendment is to allow national banks to have branches in the city in which their main office is located.

Amalgamation and concentration of banking strength which have been such a feature of British banking have not been permissible in American banking. A number of large banks have grown up in New York and other principal cities, but the bulk of the banks are relatively small. There is nothing on the scale of the great, amalgamated, joint stock, banks of Great Britain.

During the war the Federal Reserve Board has the heavy responsibility of maintaining the financial stability of the nation, which is now of special importance because our allies are depending upon us. A fixed rate of exchange is maintained between the sovereign and the dollar. Since American exports to Great Britain, which consist largely of food, raw materials, and war supplies, are far in excess of our imports from Great Britain, the balance is offset on the last day of each month by a loan to Great Britain. The wedding of the dollar to the sovereign also means that we must hold up Great Britain's adverse trade balance with other parts of the world as well. Every effort is being made by Great Britain to curtail non-essential imports so as to make our burden as light as possible. We also have a problem of holding up our exchange with neutral countries in Europe and South America. South America, especially, is sending us great quantities of raw materials. In order to settle as much as possible of the adverse balance against us in neutral countries, American consumers are being urged to curtail consumption so that we can send back exports. For example, before we entered the war one per cent. of our wool consumption was being utilized in foreign trade. The demands of the army programme called for a saving of wool in normal requirements, and it was suggested that export trade might be cut off. It was decided, however, to maintain the export trade in order to hold up exchange, and depend entirely on saving in civilian consumption to meet the increased requirement of wool for uniforms.

It is the Federal Reserve Board which must protect our cash reserves and hold up our credit in the face of the tremendous demands being made upon us to finance our own requirements and assist our allies. The discount rate in the United States is being kept relatively high to prevent any tendency to undue non-essential expenditure, and to protect our cash reserves.

The high American tariff is the inheritance of the civil war. At that time duties were increased to provide revenue. Since that time the industries that were protected have never ceased their persistent efforts to maintain and increase protection. The protectionists took credit to themselves for the great prosperity which the country experienced, and each new tariff act saw higher duties, until the panic of 1907 changed the sentiment of the country. The high tariff was blamed for the increase in the cost of living. President Wilson, who was elected on a tariff reduction platform, stood steadfast to his promises and procured the passage of an act providing for lower duties. There can be no doubt that the tariff had been the subject of many abuses. Special interests too often have secured protection all out of proportion to what their industry needed to maintain itself and higher prices were generally passed on to the consumers.

Tariff legislation has been particularly subject to lobbying and log-rolling. In order to obtain a scientific study of tariff problems President Taft appointed a tariff commission, which made a detailed study of several industries. President Wilson has secured a permanent tariff commission with large powers to investigate the needs of different industries and to provide congress with scientific information. The chairman of this tariff commission is Professor F. W. Taussig, of Harvard, who has been a close student of American tariff legislation for thirty years, and has written several standard books on the subject. The commission has been engaged in making a detailed survey of several industries and has held hearings on the subject of free ports, which a high protective country like Germany has found to be of great commercial value. The commission expects soon to extend its investigations to foreign countries. The information gathered by the tariff commission should be of special value when the question of tariff comes up after the war.

An interesting feature of the present American tariff law is the provision for bargaining. Preferred-nation treatment, for instance, can be withheld from any country which does not grant us this treatment. If there is to be any preferential treatment by the allies of one another the flexibility of our powers may prove useful.

The great question which American business men are asking themselves today is as to whether government regulation of business will relapse to pre-war importance when peace is secured. There is strong approval of present measures necessary to the most effective prosecution of the war, but the old spirit of individual enterprise is not dead. Whether or not government domination of industry and commerce will be greatly increased in the post-war economic system is a question which we may not try to solve in the face of urgent problems and which we can not answer until future international agreements are known. The normal attitude of American business to government regulation, however, is another matter and one which permits of a few observations.

Free play of individual initiative often brings the best result although sometimes it is fruitful of abuses. Business men have often felt that government regulation in the United States took too little consideration of business advantages of combination and that constant investigation and litigation were a severe hardship. Large American companies have had to make known every aspect of their business from time to time which they have felt gave competitors too easy access to all their affairs. The attitude of "big business" has often been that the government was doing everything possible to curtail its prosperity.

The mass of the people, however, have been constitutionally opposed to any infringements of freedom of enterprise and have eagerly pressed for the dissolution of large companies.

The plight in which large corporations have got themselves is partly their own fault. In early days powerful executives were too prone to ignore the rights of competitors and the public and very real abuses occurred. Once the tide of public opinion set against them the advantage swung to the other side. Railways long ago gave up any autocratic attitude and have endeavoured to take the public into their confidence. This same policy may have to be followed by large industrial corporations. It is only by full publicity that previous bad impressions can be removed. Large companies must bear the light of day if they wish to have public confidence. The problem of regulation is to maintain the economic advantages of large scale production and prevent abuses.

Business men who built up great railway systems and large industrial undertakings have not necessarily consciously done wrong. They have simply conceived of their business as a private matter, akin to all competitive business. When their business, however, because of its universal necessity, becomes a public utility the old practices of free competition cannot apply, and regulation in the public interest became necessary. Leaders of large affairs today are recognizing as never before the interest of the public in services of universal character and may be expected to conform more readily to the objects of government regulation.

SOME ASPECTS OF RECENT PARTY HISTORY IN THE UNITED STATES

JEROME D. GREENE, A.M.

SOME ASPECTS OF RECENT PARTY HISTORY IN THE UNITED STATES[1]

IT is now thirty years since Lord Bryce published the first edition of his *American Commonwealth*. Written for the purpose of interpreting American institutions to European readers, it has rendered even more important service in helping Americans toward a just appreciation of their own political problems. Among the most notable chapters of this epoch-making book are those devoted to the description of political parties. Much that was written then remains true today, but it must be evident to the most superficial observer of contemporary American politics that a good deal of water has flowed under the bridge since the days of Blaine and Cleveland. The practical politician of a generation ago, if suddenly brought to life today, would certainly find much to learn, and much to unlearn, before he could play a winning hand in the political game.

The two leading parties were then, as they are now, the republicans and the democrats. The republican party, formed in the fifties to resist the extension of slavery, gathered to itself in the sixties most of the thorough-going supporters of the union against secession and was responsible for the reconstruction legislation by which the north undertook to secure not only the permanence of the union and the abolition of slavery, but also an extremely radical reorganization of southern society and politics. A younger generation was coming forward which knew less of these things, but the party that saved the union, and was still led to a considerable extent by officers and soldiers of the great war, had a hold on the affections of northern voters which could not easily be

---

[1] I am indebted to my brother, Professor E. B. Greene, of the University of Illinois, for much help in the preparation of this paper.

shaken. It is worth noting in this connexion that every successful republican candidate for the presidency from 1860 to 1900 had been an officer in the union army.

Nevertheless, the republican party of 1888 was in many respects very different from that which had rallied to its colours the anti-slavery idealists of the fifties. The old traditions were steadily upheld by men like Senator Hoar of Massachusetts, but many older leaders of that type had passed away and some had left the party. During the civil war there had been a strong infusion of voters from the democratic party who, though loyal to the union, had no share in the humanitarian enthusiasm of the early days. Many of them were ardent supporters of the reconstruction programme, chiefly because it offered the best method of controlling the south in the interest of the union and the republican party.

An even more striking change in the constituency of the party had come about as a result of twenty-four years of republican administration. In 1856, and even in 1860, the financial centres of the country were suspicious of the new party whose radical ideas were considered a serious menace to business interests. After the war the attitude was almost exactly reversed. It was now the republican party which represented the established order, whose leaders were most experienced in administration, and which therefore made the strongest appeal to the conservative classes in the north. Furthermore, of the two great parties, it was the republicans who inherited more nearly the federalist and whig policy of developing the federal power, in distinction from the state governments, as the best means of promoting the business interests of the country, as, for instance, through the protective tariff.

Throughout the period under review, the republicans have nearly always had a clear majority of the voting population outside the limits of the seceding states. This preponderance was greatest in New England and Pennsylvania, whose industries looked to republican tariffs for protection, and in the rapidly growing states of the upper Mississippi valley. The extreme north-west was not yet sufficiently developed to count for much in national politics. New York, with the adjacent, and more or less tributary, areas in Connecticut and New Jersey, was less satisfactory from a republican point of view; its rural voters were preponderantly republican, as well as its leaders in business, but Tammany Hall had made of New York City, with its large working class and immigrant population, a democratic stronghold. By 1884 the republican party's effort to keep its hold on an important section of the south by means of the negro vote had clearly broken down. In that year, the republican presidential candidate did not secure the vote of a single state south of Pennsylvania and the Ohio River.

Of the chief immigrant stocks which had come in during the previous half-century, the republicans had won over only a comparatively small minority of the Irish; but they had been much more successful with the Germans and, most of all, with the Scandinavians who, until the nineties, were almost solidly republican. In this connexion it is to be noted that the German immigration to the United States contained a strong infusion of that liberty-loving element which found the Germany of 1848 intolerable.

The political calculations of the democratic party since the war have always begun with the "Solid South." In no presidential election since 1877 has the democratic party failed to win the vote of all the old seceding states, and they have usually added to this solid block most of the so-called "border states" whose sympathies during the civil war had been more or less divided. The "Solid South" resulted from the conviction that the white people must stand together and that the democratic party was their surest ally against further northern interference with the negro problem. No difference on other issues, however important, must be allowed to count in the face of this fundamental requirement. This solidarity of the southern whites enabled them, first by illegal methods and later by skilfully contrived constitutional legislation, to evade the fifteenth amendment and eliminate most of the negro vote, thus recovering control of their state governments. There was one result of this policy, however, less satisfactory to the south. In the choice of democratic candidates and the determination of party principles it became less necessary to consult southern opinions; northern democratic politicians knew that, if they could satisfy the doubtful states of the north, the southern vote could practically always be counted on, however distasteful the candidate or even the principle might be. This knowledge that southern dissent would always stop short of actual revolt often weakened its influence in party councils.

The northern democratic leaders were still largely recruited from a group of essentially conservative politicians who clung through good and evil repute to the states-rights and strict-constructionist traditions of the *ante bellum* period. During the war many of them had played the *rôle* of "conscientious objectors," over anxious about the niceties of the constitution at a time when the very life of the nation was in danger. Between this group and the positively disloyal "Copperheads" the line was not always easy to draw, and the ordinary man often failed to discriminate between them. Men of this type made their way to congress from the middle Atlantic states and from the rural areas of the middle west, the population of which had been largely drawn from the south, as, for instance, the southern counties of Illinois, Indiana, and Ohio. Though often men of integrity they did not offer an inspiring leadership.

A different type of democratic politician was coming to the front in the larger cities, notably in Boston and New York. With only a perfunctory interest in constitutional theories and the fine points of the law, he had a clear appreciation of the political game as it might be played with these crowded populations of shop and factory workers, largely of foreign birth and little acquainted with American institutions.

Through such conditions, and the negligence of the native-born population, Tammany Hall developed its great and sinister power in New York city, and there were similar groups elsewhere.

Within twenty-five years of the defeat of the confederacy, the two great parties had settled down to a rough agreement on certain fundamentals. The democrats saw the necessity of accepting once for all the supremacy of the union, the abolition of slavery, and a new conception of national citizenship. Meanwhile, the republican party, or at least its more responsible leaders, had come to see the futility of constant interference with the internal affairs of the southern states. With these fundamental issues out of the way, party contests became, as Lord Bryce pointed out, largely a matter of the "outs" trying to get "in." The republicans in the hackneyed language of political oratory "pointed with pride" to the virtues of Abraham Lincoln, and the democrat leaders recited old phrases which had little meaning for the younger voters or dwelt upon the administrative errors and crimes of the party in power.

Generally speaking the republicans believed in the vigorous exercise of national authority, while democratic statesmen proclaimed the dangers of centralization and still retained in some measure the old Jeffersonian philosophy of *laissez-faire*. Consistently with this general attitude and with the special interests of the rural south, most democrats opposed the protectionist policies of the republican party, though one of their chief leaders in the House of Representatives was a thorough-going protectionist and few of them seriously advocated a strictly free trade policy. They preferred to call themselves "revenue reformers," supporters of a "tariff for revenue only." The need of reform in the civil service was recognized by right-minded men in both parties, and was, therefore, not a party measure. The republican party had deserved well of the country by re-establishing the currency on a specie basis after the inflation of the civil war period; but in the presence of new forms of inflationist agitation, like the free silver movement, both parties often took refuge in ambiguous phrases. The prevailing forces in the republican party might roughly have been described as conservative in the European sense, but the democrats, led for the most part by southern country gentlemen and old-school lawyers, were far from being a consistently radical or even a liberal party.

The lack of clean-cut issues between the two traditional parties seemed to leave the way open for important third-party movements. One such party, the prohibitionists, has kept up a national organization for forty years, but it has rarely elected even a single member of congress, and its vote in presidential elections has been almost negligible, except in 1884, when it probably drew enough support from the republican party to insure the election of Mr Cleveland. The recent action of congress in favour of a national prohibition amendment doubtless owes something to the third-party movement, but it has been due less to the ethical and religious motives which inspired that party than to considerations of hygiene and economic efficiency and to resentment against the political activities of the liquor interests. The new disposition to accept national rather than state control in this field is fairly typical of what has happened in almost every field of legislation. In the eighties and nineties practically no politician of importance looked forward to any such outcome of the prohibitionist movement, and the republicans especially resented the formation of a national party on that issue because its voters were drawn largely from their own ranks.

The economic depression of the later seventies and the fall in prices, which came as a natural reaction from inflation and over-speculation, inevitably brought hardships to the less fortunate classes. Farmers who had mortgaged their land to make improvements found as their obligations fell due that the prices of farm products were falling. They complained also that the railways, whose construction had been made possible by federal and state subsidies, were now charging excessive rates for the transportation of grain. This feeling led to the formation of farmers' organizations which, in the north-west especially, went actually into politics, and were thus able to secure from the state legislatures the passage of the so-called "Granger Laws" for the regulation of railroads and warehouses. The old parties, however, yielded to these demands sufficiently to check, for the time being, the drift toward a distinctly agrarian party. Some of the same elements were for a time drawn into the short-lived greenback party which hoped to secure higher prices and general prosperity by lavish issues of paper money. The chief strength of northern radicalism during this period was among the farmers; the labour element was imperfectly organized and its leaders saw greater advantage in bargaining with the politicians of the older parties than in forming a new political group either alone or in alliance with the farmers.

The difficulty of securing a clean-cut alignment of parties on issues of principle was due partly to the natural inertia characteristic of all established organizations. Men who are accustomed to act together on one set of issues do not easily abandon their associations and risk their political careers on new issues which may prove to be of only temporary or local importance. The situation also resulted in part from certain aspects of party management which have since undergone radical changes.

Generally speaking, party management was then more completely than at present the business of professional politicians. They controlled party executive committees, national, state, and local; and they determined more largely the choice of candidates. These candidates were selected in party "primaries" in which any member of the party was theoretically entitled to participate, but which were as a rule poorly attended and so managed that the professional, or semi-professional, group had every advantage. Upon these local primaries were built up, through the election of delegates from the lower to the higher organizations, the county, district, state, and national conventions. In these conventions candidates were nominated of all degrees of dignity, from town collectors and county clerks to governors and presidents. In an era of enormous industrial expansion, the ordinary citizen was commonly unable, or believed himself unable, to spend the time required to get his friends out to the primaries in support of a reform candidate against the existing "machine." The natural effect of all this—of course the proposition is not exclusively applicable to the United States —was the control of state and national conventions and the drafting of party platforms by men who were much more interested in the distribution of offices and the "upkeep" of the party house in which they lived than in large questions of national policy. It was much easier for republicans to remind their fellow-voters that their party had saved the union and abolished slavery than to take sides squarely on the money question. Democrats similarly found it safer to declaim about the corrupt practices of the republican administration than to say exactly where they stood on the tariff. In this respect, at least, there has been decided progress during the past thirty years. Party nominations are now regulated by law and determined at primary elections, in which the ordinary citizen may and, generally speaking, does exercise a greater influence than under the old system.

This is an obviously rough and excessively generalized account of party politics as they were when Grover Cleveland became president in 1885. That election has little or no significance as an expression of public opinion on the issues defined in the two party platforms; the number of votes shifted from the republican to the democratic side was a comparatively small fraction of the total number cast, and in such an even balance of forces, trivial incidents may at the last have tipped the beam. Nevertheless the election of this first democratic president since the civil war remains highly significant. Thousands of republicans of the best type cast their votes for Cleveland, partly because they were attracted by the sturdy courage and honesty of his administration as governor of New York, but partly also because they desired to record their protest against that questionable bringing of business into politics which had infected the republican party in the days of its prosperity. Such men could no longer be held by appeals to sectional feeling or interested in the old party catchwords. The election, followed by four years of democratic administration, disposed effectually of the idea that the fate of the union depended exclusively on the fortunes of a particular party. It was even found possible to admit confederate brigadiers to the cabinet and the supreme court without wrecking the constitution. The way was prepared for a more rational kind of party leadership based on real political principles rather than simple desire for the spoils of office.

The Cleveland administration justified, on the whole, the expectations of the independents who had supported him. The new president took seriously his promises of economy and honesty in the public service. The cause of civil service reform made surprising progress, considering the enormous pressure naturally brought to bear upon a president whose party had been out of office for more than twenty years. What makes Cleveland's election especially notable is the fact that it gave the democrats a leader with an eye for real issues and sufficient courage to meet them squarely. Notable examples of this are his messages to congress in 1887 on the tariff.

The republicans were then generally committed to the policy of stimulating manufactures by means of protective duties, though they did not always agree on the extent to which the principle should be applied. The southern democrats had inherited a strong aversion to protective duties which, being levied on articles which they needed but did not themselves produce, seemed to them a kind of tribute paid for the benefit of northern manufacturers.. To this general proposition there were some striking exceptions, as, for instance, the sugar planters of Louisiana and later some of those who were interested in the developing iron industry of the lower south. On the whole, however, the south preserved its traditional leaning toward free trade.

Among the northern democrats, especially in Pennsylvania, the protectionist influence was stronger, sufficiently so to make the party declarations on this subject extremely cautious. Mr Cleveland, however, looked upon protectionism as objectionable, because it involved a dangerous use of governmental power for the promotion of local or private interests. This argument for the reduction of tariff duties was reinforced by other arguments among which was the condition of the treasury, then accumulating a considerable surplus which seemed to encourage extravagant appropriations.

Having reached these conclusions, Mr Cleveland embodied in his annual message of 1887 a direct attack upon the protectionist system. The challenge was at once accepted by the republican leaders, notably by Mr Blaine; and since the democratic party, though controlling the house, had only a minority in the senate, the whole question became a leading issue in the presidential campaign of 1888. With his usual dogged courage, Mr Cleveland resisted all attempts to modify his attitude, and the democratic convention sustained him. Mr Blaine was the natural leader of the republicans on this issue and would probably have been their choice for the presidential nomination, had he not refused the honour, which then went to Mr Harrison, a union general and a sound protectionist. The election was again close and Mr Cleveland actually had a much larger plurality of the popular vote than he had received on his election in 1884; but the distribution of the votes was such that General Harrison secured a decisive majority in the electoral college. It should be remembered in this connexion that the people do not vote directly for presidential candidates but for electors in the various states. It is consequently possible for a bare majority in one state to offset a much larger majority in another. The republicans also gained control of both branches of congress. Their majority in the house was exceedingly narrow, but they were ably led by the new speaker, Mr Thomas B. Reed, who exercised even more than the traditional authority of the American speaker, and in particular secured the adoption of much more stringent closure regulations. Thus it was possible for the first time in many years to carry through a definite party programme.

The republicans were not slow to take advantage of this opportunity; the McKinley tariff bill was pushed rapidly through both houses and became law in October, 1890. The new tariff was frankly based on the protective principle, existing duties on manufactured articles were generally increased and the bill even went so far as to authorize a duty for the purpose of stimulating the still unborn tin industry. On other questions party action proved to be more difficult or even impossible. When for instance an attempt was made to pass a bill for regulating national elections, it was not only attacked by the democrats as a " Force Bill "—designed to restore republican control of election machinery in the south—but it failed to receive the full party vote and was defeated. Its chief result was to give a certain plausibility to the charge that republicans were trying to revive the old sectional issues.

The republican triumph proved to be short-lived. The popular reaction to the McKinley bill was prompt and decidedly unfavourable. Notwithstanding the introduction of a few duties on agricultural products, the bill as a whole was denounced as a measure for increasing the profits of the manufacturing capitalist by raising the cost of necessaries to the consumer. There was a formidable revolt among the republican farmers of the north-west, and the democrats recovered control of the house of representatives by a majority giving them more than two-thirds of the total membership. The republicans, however, still controlled the senate.

In the election of 1890, new influences were at work which were destined to play an increasingly important part during the next six years. Among the newly elected congressmen were eight members of the Farmers' Alliance, and one of the new senators represented the same movement. Its strength was in the south and still more in the rural districts of the middle and far west. The farmers were not only dissatisfied with the tariff, but vaguely suspicious of all politicians, whom they believed to be unduly under the influence of great corporate interests. The railways were charged with fixing rates in such a way as to discriminate in favour of certain localities or companies. The combination of capital in the "trusts" was felt to be a political as well as an economic danger. The regulation of these matters was still largely in the hands of the states; federal control of inter-state commerce, provided for in the Act of 1887 and in the Sherman Anti-Trust Act of 1890, had not so far proved very effective. The farmers were especially troubled by the falling price of wheat and vaguely attributed this to an insufficient supply of money. In the seventies, the greenbackers proposed to meet the situation by lavish issues of paper money; in the nineties the cry was for the free coinage of silver, a demand naturally encouraged by the silver mine owners of the far west.

Both of the older parties recognized the strength of the free silver movement and tried to control it by concessions. The republican party put through the Silver Purchase Act of 1890, which forced the treasury to buy 4,500,000 ounces of silver a month issuing in return treasury notes to the same amount. This measure soon involved the treasury in serious embarrassments but it did not satisfy the radicals, and the free silver agitation continued with increasing force throughout the south and west until 1896.

The Farmers' Alliance tried to accomplish its objects partly by pressure upon the existing parties. By 1892, however, their leaders decided to form a new political organization to which they gave the name of the People's Party, though they were more generally known as populists. This remained on the whole a distinctly agrarian movement; efforts were made to combine with the labour element but without much success. In the next presidential election they entered the field as a national party with a presidential candidate and a fair prospect of carrying at least a few of the western states.

This situation was distinctly alarming to democrats and republicans alike, and the less courageous politicians tried to find some way of evading the troublesome issues. The republican declaration on the money question in the national platform of 1892 was distinctly evasive and the same must be said of the democratic statement. Mr Cleveland, however, who, to the great disgust of many politicians, had been recalled to party leadership, refused to go with the rising tide and was once more nominated for the presidency notwithstanding his unequivocal declaration against the free coinage of silver.

The unpopularity of the McKinley tariff bill and the revolt of the western farmers gave Mr Cleveland the election of 1892 by the largest majority given to any president since Grant's victory over Horace Greeley in 1872. For the first time since 1860, the republicans had lost not only the presidency but both houses of congress. The situation was not, however, one which the democratic politicians could regard with equanimity. The populist candidate for president had won the vote of four western states in the electoral college and scattering votes in three others. Nor did this represent the full strength of the party. Both in the south and west, it had entered into combinations with local organizations, republican or democratic, for the choice of fusion tickets by which they were able to elect congressmen who were either of their own party or in sympathy with their views. Mr Cleveland's hold on his own nominal followers in congress proved to be decidedly precarious.

On his inauguration, he found the finances in a deplorable condition. The free issue of treasury notes for silver bullion made it increasingly difficult to keep the currency on a gold basis, and the gold reserve, which was heavily drawn on for this purpose, threatened to disappear. A financial panic was already imminent and was in full swing by the summer of 1893. Mr Cleveland, as the leader of the sound money element, saw the necessity of checking this drain on the gold reserve for the redemption of the silver certificates. The treasury issued bonds for the purpose of maintaining the gold reserve and congress was asked to repeal the silver act of 1890. The president's policy was strongly resisted by the radicals in both parties who made common cause with the populists; but his own personal influence and that of the administration was sufficiently strong to carry it through, though it brought about a split in his own party reminding one in some respects of Peel's predicament after he had forced the repeal of the corn laws. The reform of the tariff on which the president now set his heart was wrecked largely as a result of this conflict within the party ranks. The so-called Wilson-Gorman tariff act was so little in accord with Cleveland's views that he refused to sign it, though allowing it to become law without his signature.

Evidently the kind of reform represented by Mr Cleveland did not satisfy the leaders of the new radical movement. Not only did he antagonize the farmers by his stand on the money question; but he also came into conflict with organized labour in the great railway strikes at Chicago, when he called out the federal troops to protect mail trains and enforce the orders of the federal courts, though the latter were charged by the labour men with an improper use of judicial injunctions to restrain the strikers. His chief opponents in this controversy were Mr Debs, head of the American Railway Union, and John P. Altgeld, the democratic governor of Illinois, who resented what he called the president's invasion of state jurisdiction. The animosities thus aroused found striking expression in the democratic convention of 1896, which refused to pass the usual party resolution commending his administration.

The republican party was ready to exploit these family quarrels. The hard times which followed the passage of the new tariff act seemed to them new evidence that prosperity was dependent upon republican administration and particularly upon protection. They found an additional argument for democratic incompetence when the income tax clauses of the act of 1894 were declared unconstitutional and the revenue expected from that source had to be given up— with the result that the surplus of 1887 was converted into a serious deficit. It was soon apparent, however, that the old alignment of parties was likely to be still further disturbed. Financial depression continued and wheat prices continued to fall. The forces of economic discontent were too strong to be met by the traditional party methods. The free silver movement grew more intense, extending to wider areas. If both of the old parties held out against these radical tendencies the populist vote would certainly assume formidable proportions.

The test came first to the republican party which unexpectedly found the tariff relegated to a subordinate place, and the money question at a point where it was difficult to avoid a definite stand. Some of the older leaders, especially in the west, were extremely reluctant to alienate the free silver elements in their own party. That was the attitude of McKinley, whose nomination for the presidency was practically assured before the convention of 1896 met. He had always been most interested in the tariff and his declarations on the money question were to say the least ambiguous. The backbone of the party was, however, in the section east of the Mississippi and north of the Potomac, and the business interests of that area were more and more insistent on strict adherence to the gold standard as the only safeguard against cheap money. As a concession to some wavering elements the convention declared in favour of bimetallism by international agreement if possible, insisting, however, that in the meantime the gold standard must be maintained. McKinley was duly nominated and in his subsequent utterances accepted the decision of his party on the money question. The protectionist policy of the party was reaffirmed but played a minor part in the campaign, especially in the earlier stages.

The democratic convention at Chicago was a remarkable assemblage. The leadership which had guided the party to victory in 1884 and 1892 was now repudiated, especially in the west and south. Revolutionary changes had been taking place in southern politics during the past few years; the representatives of the old planter class had in many cases been superseded by men of a more radical type supported by the small farmers of the up-country. They were just as insistent as their predecessors on the principle of white supremacy but they shared in many other respects the ideals of the rural west. The eastern men who pleaded for more consideration of the business interests were brushed aside and on every important test of strength the radicals carried the day. The platform declared for the free coinage of silver, attacked the supreme court for its decision on the income tax, and accepted many of the characteristic proposals of the populist party. The choice of a candidate was even more revolutionary. At the opening of the convention, the leading candidate was a second-rate politician whose chief claim to consideration was his consistent advocacy of free silver. None of the conservative candidates could rally more than a small group of voters. In this situation the convention turned to Mr William Jennings Bryan, a young man of thirty-six, whose official record was limited to a single term in congress but who knew how to express with great skill and power the ideas and emotions of his fellow-delegates and of the people who stood behind them. By its radical platform and the nomination of

Mr Bryan, the democratic party drew to itself the bulk of the populist vote, though the extreme left wing of the latter party insisted on nominating a separate ticket on which Mr Bryan's name was associated with that of a vice-presidential candidate of their own choosing. Within a few years the populists as a separate party ceased to exist.

The action of the republican and democratic conventions led to radical changes in party alignment. The free silver advocates in the republican party went over in considerable numbers to the democrats or the populists. Some conservative democrats who were opposed to free coinage of silver organized the so-called National Democratic party, though most of those who left the party voted the republican ticket.

To a greater extent than in any other election of this period the presidential contest of 1896 was a conflict between the radical and conservative forces of the country. Mr Bryan probably made a stronger appeal to the masses in town and country than any other political leader since the days of Andrew Jackson, and Jackson had no such oratorical gifts. Many of the proposals then advocated by the democrats and their populist allies have, like the "Six Points" of the English Chartists, gained respectability with the passage of time; but their failure to appreciate the importance of sound monetary standards turned against them many moderate men who might otherwise have sympathized with their protest against obvious abuses in public and private business. For many months the outcome was highly uncertain; but the republican campaign was managed with great ability by Mr Mark Hanna, who convinced the business men generally that their safety depended upon generous contributions to the republican campaign funds. Much has been said about the corrupt use of money, but the best opinion seems to be that the funds at the disposal of the republican national committee were in the main used for legitimate purposes. A more serious objection may be made to the whole practice of receiving large contributions from individuals or corporations who may become direct beneficiaries of national legislation, as for instance in the case of industries asking for protective duties. There can be no doubt in any case that the overwhelming weight of public opinion was fairly measured by the great popular majority for the republican candidate, Mr McKinley.

The election had been won mainly on the money question, but the republicans interpreted their victory also as a mandate for protection. The Dingley tariff of 1897 was framed on lines similar to those of the McKinley bill of 1890. Not until 1900 was a sufficient number of sound money votes secured to enact the gold standard in terms of a formal statute. Before the people had another opportunity to express themselves on these measures, public attention was drawn away to questions of a wholly different character.

American intervention in Cuba, brought about partly because of injury to American interests resulting from the disorders in the island, and partly through genuine sympathy with the insurgents, had far-reaching consequences which the administration had hardly foreseen. Cuba became a republic under the protection of the United States; Porto Rico and the Philippines were brought under the American flag. Public opinion on these transactions varied widely. McKinley himself probably regarded them without much enthusiasm as the only way out of a complicated situation. Some emphasized the commercial advantages to be gained from the islands. Others felt quite sincerely that the United States had in the Philippines a call to establish a new and better order, gradually preparing an untrained people for a larger measure of self-government. On these various grounds most republicans accepted the measures of the administration. The Spanish treaty was ratified, order was restored in Cuba, and American authority enforced in the Philippine Islands.

On the other hand Mr Bryan, who, in spite of his defeat, was still the acknowledged leader of his party, took his stand with the so-called anti-imperialists for an immediate, or at least an early, recognition of Philippine independence, opposing any other course as a violation of fundamental American ideals. He carried the majority of his party with him, and in the election of 1900 this question of imperialism or anti-imperialism was declared to be the "paramount issue." Some of the men who had opposed him in 1896 accepted his leadership on this question; but the country as a whole accepted the republican programme, realizing the practical difficulty of leaving the Philippines to themselves without a long preliminary training in local self-government.

The republican policies of the first McKinley administration seemed, therefore, on the whole to have received popular support. Himself a man of integrity, he gathered about him some men of great distinction like John Hay and Elihu Root. With larger experience he outgrew the narrower protectionism of his early career and began to emphasize the importance of opening foreign markets by reciprocal trade agreements. He had just made a speech setting forth his ideas on this subject when he was shot down by an assassin and the leadership passed to a man of a very different type.

McKinley was the last of the civil war veterans whom the republicans had put into the presidential chair. Theodore Roosevelt, born three years before that war began, belonged distinctly to a younger generation. In his earlier career he made his mark as a reformer but always within the party lines. He had not taken much interest in the tariff or the technique of national finance, but had proved himself an able administrative officer in various positions, including those of civil service commissioner, assistant secretary of the navy, and governor of New York, besides serving as colonel of the so-called Rough Riders in the Spanish war. His executive career in New York antagonized many old-time politicians and his radicalism did not commend him to them as a vice-presidential candidate, though it doubtless added much to the strength of the ticket. At the same time many of his opponents rejoiced at his relegation to an office commonly regarded as a *cul-de-sac* to political ambition.

Anxiety about the policy of the new president was for the time quieted by his promise to carry out the policies of his predecessor. During his first administration he retained for the most part McKinley's cabinet including Messrs Hay and Root and gave his attention to large constructive enterprises rather than to projects of legislation. He encouraged the group of able young men who were setting new standards for the conservation and development of national resources through scientific forestry and the irrigation of arid lands in the west. His vigorous personality was attractive to working men and he was able to intervene effectively in the great coal strike of 1902. The project of an interoceanic canal appealed strongly to his imagination. The Panama route was selected, the canal zone was acquired, and construction actually begun. He was keenly alive to the new influence and responsibility of the United States in world politics. Under pressure from Washington, the German Emperor consented to arbitrate the Venezuelan claims, and, in the far east, American influence continued to be exerted in favour of a just treatment of China. The new Cuban republic was set on its feet and order was restored in the Philippines, with due regard to the Filipinos and to their preparation for self-government.

Many of these things were little understood by the average voter, but he got the general impression of a vigorous, efficient administration alive to the expanding interests of the country and more concerned with real problems of contemporary life than with the traditional dogmas of either party. Especially significant was Mr Roosevelt's popularity in the far west where he had lived long enough to understand its point of view. Many republican leaders distrusted him, but his popularity with the people as a whole made any other presidential nomination by his party impossible.

Meantime Mr Roosevelt's success and the expectation of a more radical trend in his policies when he became president in his own right were depriving the radical democrats of some of their ammunition. Mr Bryan's two successive defeats, while they had by no means destroyed his hold on the party, had somewhat weakened it and correspondingly encouraged the conservative wing. In consequence, the democrats now nominated for the presidency a New York judge of more cautious temper, who definitely rejected free silver and hoped to profit by the suspicion current in conservative eastern circles that Roosevelt was an unsafe man. These tactics failed completely. Roosevelt held the McKinley areas in the east and recovered several of the western states where the Bryan following had been particularly strong.

In his second administration Mr Roosevelt felt himself free to develop his own independent policies, and the trend toward radicalism was more marked. Public attention had been sharply directed toward serious abuses in corporate management to the detriment of investors as well as of the general public. It was known that large contributions had been made to the campaign funds of political parties, with the expectation, in some cases at least, of political favours in return. All these things seemed to justify more drastic measures of government control. The Inter-State Commerce Act was strengthened and suits were instituted under the Sherman Anti-Trust Act to dissolve certain great combinations of capital. Measures of this kind, with some picturesque phrases like "malefactors of great wealth," increased the hostility to the president not only in Wall Street but among conservative politicians of his own party. Toward the close of his administration these elements in congress succeeded in blocking certain measures in which he was interested; but his hold on the people at large was unshaken and when on his retirement he recommended his friend and associate, Mr Taft, as his successor, the party followed his advice. The democratic party now returned to Mr Bryan, but the momentum of Roosevelt's popularity and a republican promise to reform the tariff, supposedly downward, carried Mr Taft into the White House.

When Mr Roosevelt left the United States on his famous African journey, the position of the republican party seemed fairly secure. Recent administrations had apparently justified the republican claims of superior efficiency, and the progressive elements in the organization seemed to have the upper hand sufficiently to deprive the democrats of much valuable capital. Within a little more than a year the situation was decidedly changed. Mr Taft's cabinet did not add much to his political prestige. In certain disputes between conservative and progressive elements in the administration he sustained the former, alienating in this way some of Mr Roosevelt's closest supporters. Though he carried out the party pledges by calling a special session of congress to revise the tariff, and exercised a certain moderating influence, the extreme protectionists were on the whole victorious. The result was general popular resentment against a measure believed to have been dictated by the protected interests, and a strong insurgent movement within the party set in. Mr Cannon's use of the speakership in the interest of the conservative group also caused dissatisfaction and a demand for the revision of the house rules. These things outweighed in the public mind many excellent features of Mr Taft's policy —his effort to secure commercial reciprocity with Canada, his advocacy of a scientific budget system, and his promotion of international arbitration. Under the combined fire of democrats and insurgent republicans, led by Senator La Follette of Wisconsin, the administration suffered a severe defeat in the congressional elections of 1910 and the democrats secured control of the house for the first time since 1896. Neither party was able to control legislation, but the democrats took advantage of their majority in the house to carry through a revision of the rules which materially reduced the speaker's power.

When Mr Roosevelt came back from his tour of Africa and Europe, he found the situation quite different from that which he had left behind him. Many of those with whom he had been most closely associated were now in opposition and his old enemies, the "standpatters," seemed to be most in favour at court. Gradually his attitude toward the Taft administration became more critical, until in 1912 he announced his own candidature for the presidency, taking more radical ground than in any earlier utterances.

The significance of the Roosevelt programme can hardly be understood without recalling certain aspects of American radicalism during the previous decade. With the passing of the frontier and the increasingly rapid exploitation of natural resources public attention was more and more devoted to the importance of a well-considered policy of conservation in such matters as mineral resources, forests, and water power. It seemed important also that such resources should be so controlled as to serve the interest of the whole people rather than of a small group of owners. In short, there was a growing demand which may fairly be called socialist, in the broad sense of that word, for government control or even government ownership of such national interests. This tendency may be measured partly by the growth of the socialist party vote which was considerable during this period; but much more adequately by the expression of such ideas in the platforms of both the older parties and in legislation, both state and national. In short, political democracy was beginning to be thought of not merely as an end in itself but as a means of securing a more democratic economic order. In order to realize such a programme effectively and speedily, the radical elements urged the necessity of democratizing still further the machinery of government. Elective officials should be subject to recall or removal by special popular vote, even before the expiration of their terms, if they failed to respond to the popular will; legislative action should be controlled more directly by the people through the initiative and referendum. The action of ultra-conservative judges in declaring unconstitutional some of the new social legislation led to extreme demands for the recall of judges, or, as even

Mr Roosevelt proposed, for the reversal of constitutional decisions by direct popular vote.

The importance of parties as a means of democratic control was realized also. In the old days, parties, whether local or national, were voluntary organizations without legal status. It was evident, however, that in the choice of elective officers the party caucus or primary was often more important than the formal election, and that the choice of a party chairman might have more serious consequences than the election of a congressman. The result was the enactment of legislation in one state after another by which the whole party machinery was subjected to legal regulations. There are now virtually two elections for every office, both equally under the control of the state. The first determines who shall be the candidates of their respective parties; the second which of these candidates shall actually hold the office. Similarly the choice of party committees and the instruction of delegates to national nominating conventions has been determined in several states by the direct action of the voters in their primary elections.

Naturally enough changes of this kind were regarded with serious misgiving by many men of moderate views as well as those of more conservative temper. Measures like the initiative, the referendum, and the recall, seemed to them at bottom an attack on the whole conception of representative government. From this point of view the people, having chosen their representatives, should leave them free to exercise their best judgment, subject to a strict accounting when their term of service was over, without attempting to intervene directly in the processes of legislation and administration. Some of those who sympathized with the radical programme in other respects were repelled by the attacks on the independence of the judiciary and believed that the judicial review of legislation was, in spite of occasional abuses, a valuable part of the American system.

In the election of 1912, the conservative forces gathered about the candidature of Mr Taft, who, with the resources of the administration behind him and the support of the older party managers, secured the republican nomination after a hard fight in the convention. The Roosevelt forces complained that they had been unfairly treated by the refusal of the men in power to seat delegates who were believed to have been duly elected. However this may be, the final decision of the convention undoubtedly did not represent the real wishes of the republican voters in the country at large. When, therefore, Mr Roosevelt and his followers refused to accept Mr Taft's nomination and formed the new progressive party, the old organization was split in two and party success in the election became practically impossible.

For the first time since the civil war the democrats entered a presidential contest with a reasonable certainty that a strong nomination would bring a victory at the polls. Once more there was a conflict within the party between those who under the leadership of Bryan fought for a straight-out radical programme and their opponents who favoured the compromise tactics of 1908. Two of the leading candidates represented the latter element. The third, Speaker Clark, had drawn his original support largely from the old Bryan following, but was now suspected of too good an understanding with the opposite faction, especially with Tammany Hall. The result was that Mr Bryan transferred his support to Governor Wilson of New Jersey who seemed to him a safer representative of the progressive element. Mr Wilson's nomination was thus assured.

Though Mr Wilson's opponents were accustomed to refer to him as Professor Wilson, by way of suggesting his unfitness for the rough-and-tumble of practical politics, nevertheless he had not only been a serious student of government but as a university president had dealt with administrative problems of a very practical kind. As governor of New Jersey he was able, in the face of strenuous opposition from some of the "bosses" of his own party, to carry out a fairly radical and yet not unreasonable programme for the control of industrial corporations. As a younger man, he held some views which would now be regarded as conservative, but as president of Princeton university his desire for a more democratic organization of student life brought him into conflict with some of his associates in the administration. This tendency toward the left became still more marked during his governorship, though his presidential candidature was supported by some elements of a different sort.

In the campaign which followed, the republicans and progressives devoted themselves largely to attacking each other, though Mr Roosevelt sought with some success to draw radical voters from all the parties. Mr Wilson's campaign was dignified and on the whole held his party together. In all the northern states except two, the republicans lost the electoral vote, sometimes to the progressives but more often to the democrats. Mr Wilson received much less than half of the popular vote, but it was so distributed that he had an overwhelming majority over both of his opponents in the electoral college. Roosevelt's vote came largely from former republicans, but there was also some loss on the democratic side as shown by the fact that Wilson's popular vote was less than that cast for Mr Bryan in 1908. This loss was partially offset by the action of a few conservative republicans who regarded the defeat of Mr Roosevelt as the first consideration. With the presidency the democrats gained control of both houses of congress.

It seemed not impossible for a time that the progressive party might take its place as the chief antagonist of the democratic organization. There were, however, obvious difficulties. Not all progressives were really hostile to the republican party; they were rather opponents of the existing management. Many were not even progressive in the ordinary sense of that term, but had been drawn away by enthusiasm for Roosevelt's personality, or sometimes by purely factional motives. There was another difficulty in the fact that, while the progressives had been surprisingly successful in winning

votes for their presidential candidate, they had not developed
their organization sufficiently to secure much representation
in congress, the state legislatures, or the state executives.
Consequently, so far as the actual machinery of government
was concerned, the republicans held their place as the main
party of opposition. Lastly, it became evident that the democratic party had not only elected a new president but had
found a real leader whose knowledge of political strategy was
far from academic. Mr Wilson's policy throughout his first
term was that of winning the genuinely progressive voters by
a legislative programme at once radical and constructive. In
the alignment which was likely to follow, the comparatively
conservative elements were likely to gravitate toward the
republican party, and the progressive party as such would
probably disappear.

Precisely that result did come about. The force of old
associations gradually carried back to the republicans not
only those who had no keen interest in the principles of the
new party but others, more truly progressive in spirit, who
distrusted the traditions of the democratic party and especially its capacity for efficient administration. On the other
hand, Mr Wilson, having the support of his party in congress
more completely even than Mr Roosevelt himself, actually
carried through an extraordinarily extensive programme of
legislation including many measures advocated by the progressives. The tariff was reduced, a new federal banking
system was organized, and some important labour legislation
enacted. Many of these measures received support in all of
the parties, but final success was largely due to the driving
power in the White House.

Before this programme was completed, however, the
country was forced to take account of international issues
quite unforeseen by the leaders on either side. The selection
of Mr Bryan as secretary of state was due partly to his claims
as a party leader, but it also seemed to indicate sympathy with
his well-known interest in the cause of international peace.

The pacific temper of the administration was illustrated by the so-called Bryan arbitration treaties and by the extreme forbearance shown toward Mexico. The president also proved his determination to maintain the national honour by scrupulous good faith in the performance of international engagements. One of the first measures adopted by congress at his request was the repeal of the law exempting American ships from the payment of tolls in the Panama Canal—an exemption properly held to be incompatible with national good faith.

When the European war broke out the problem of defining America's attitude was extremely difficult. All American tradition was strongly against intervention in European affairs. The sympathies of the population were divided. Of those who had any clear convictions on the subject, the over-whelming majority undoubtedly sympathized with the allies; but to a great body of Americans the contest was so remote that it was difficult for them to realize it. The group which favoured the central powers was more consciously organized for influencing public opinion and was supported in sub-terranean ways by German agents. Only gradually was the whole scope and character of German policy brought home to the consciousness of the American people. The adoption of a neutral policy was at first accepted as a matter of course by nearly all the leaders of both parties. The democratic party probably had the larger proportion of pacifist advo-cates; the republican, on the other hand, had the larger constituency of German voters, especially in the middle west.

As the president's first term drew to a close the policy of neutrality was still maintained, though with increasing diffi-culty. The president's speeches had begun to recognize the necessity not only of military preparedness but also of in-tellectual preparation for a larger responsibility in inter-national affairs. A presidential election carried on under these circumstances was a severe test of the political steadi-ness of the American people.

The republicans nominated a man of high character and ability in the person of Mr Justice Hughes, and the great majority of the progressives followed Mr Roosevelt back into the republican party, whose platform was carefully drawn with a view to attracting this group of voters. Notwithstanding the comparative radicalism of Mr Wilson's attitude, the platforms of the two main parties were strikingly similar. The chief question was whether Mr Wilson or Mr Hughes was to be accepted as a safer guide in these trying times. It is almost impossible to determine the motives which controlled a large proportion of the voters. In the same community, ardent pro-ally voters denounced Wilson for his neutrality when he ought to have taken sides, while pro-Germans insisted that he had consistently violated neutrality to the prejudice of the German cause. Mr Hughes originally received a considerable amount of German support, because it was thought essential to "punish" Mr Wilson; and much of this vote was held to the end, though, in the east especially, many of Hughes's supporters declared that he would take a firmer stand against German aggression than Wilson had done. Many former supporters of Mr Wilson voted against him because of this belief.

When the vote was finally counted, it appeared that, while the republicans won the majority of the progressive voters, Wilson's legislative programme had won for him a sufficient number of Roosevelt's former followers to secure his re-election by a round majority in the electoral college. Sectionally speaking it looked like a victory of the south and west over the north-east; but such a generalization is far from being exact. It should not be forgotten that the popular vote went to Wilson in a somewhat larger proportion. Some indication of radical support for Wilson may be seen in a considerable reduction of the socialist vote since 1912.

Limits of space and the difficulty of seeing recent events in just perspective prevent much consideration of party divisions as affected by the great war. It is perhaps sufficient to say

here that the chief aim of responsible leaders, whether republican or democratic, is to prove that their own party is
the more competent to solve the difficult problems involved
in the successful prosecution of the war, on whose main issues
as defined by President Wilson they are substantially agreed.
Meanwhile the rank and file of both parties, as well as many
of their leaders, are, as individuals, actually enlisted in the
great work of carrying on the war, recognizing that Mr Wilson
has defined with accuracy, as well as eloquence, the cause
to which the American people are now committed with a
unanimity unapproached in the one hundred and forty-two
years of their national history.

The opposition of the socialist party organization has
attracted attention in some localities, but does not seem formidable in the country at large. There is but one socialist
representative in either house of congress.

One other point may be noted in conclusion. When the
American Commonwealth was first published, it seemed to
some observers that the conditions of American politics
tended to keep men of first-rate capacity for leadership out
of the presidential office. Such an observation seems less
appropriate after a survey of the period between 1885 and
1918, more than two-thirds of which is covered by the administrations of Grover Cleveland, Theodore Roosevelt, and
Woodrow Wilson.

AMERICAN UNIVERSITIES: THEIR BEGINNINGS AND DEVELOPMENT

JOHN W. CUNLIFFE, D.Lit. (Lond.)

AMERICAN UNIVERSITIES: THEIR BEGINNINGS AND DEVELOPMENT

THE beginnings of American university life go back without a shadow of doubt to this university of Cambridge, which counted some forty or fifty graduates among the little band of settlers who, nearly three hundred years ago, took possession of the fringe of coast about Massachusetts Bay. Probably no community not professedly academic has ever counted so large a proportion of university graduates among its inhabitants, and their first thought after building a few log huts was to provide a college for their children. To quote a contemporary account:

> After God had carried us safe to New England and we had builded our houses, provided necessaries for our livelihood, reared convenient places for God's worship, and settled the civil government, one of the next things we longed for and looked after was to advance learning and perpetuate it to posterity; dreading to leave an illiterate ministry to the churches, when our present ministers shall lie in the dust. And as we were thinking and consulting how to effect this great work, it pleased God to stir up the heart of one Mr Harvard (a godly gentleman and a lover of learning, there living amongst us) to give one half of his estate (it being in all about £1700) towards the erecting of a college, and all his library. After him another gave £300, others after him cast in more, and the public hand of the state added the rest.

As early as 1638 the name of the little settlement of Newtown, which was chosen by common consent to be the site of the college, was changed by order of the general court, the local governing body of the colony, and it was called Cambridge. The magistrates and teaching elders (or congregational ministers) of the six nearest churches were appointed to be for ever governors or overseers of the college, and every family in each colony gave a peck of corn or twelve pence for its support—an early example of the esteem in which education has been held by the American people and of the generosity with which they have contributed to its maintenance. Of course, for these devoted souls, who had barely occupied a small tract, twenty miles by thirty, of a vast continent, and who were still struggling with wild beasts and hostile Indians, the way of the new college could not be free from financial and personal embarrassment. The astonishing thing was that the effort was made at all; the astounding thing was that it was successful.

This was largely due to the courage and devotion of the first president, Henry Dunster, who took his B.A. at Magdalene College, Cambridge, in 1630 and his M.A. in 1634. He was the real founder of American higher education, and I should like to linger a moment by a figure I find singularly sympathetic. He organized the curriculum on the Cambridge model and obtained in 1650 the charter by which Harvard is still governed. On a salary sometimes paid in kind instead of in cash, and sometimes not paid at all, he built himself a house, and, practically unaided, taught the first students, who soon increased in number from the first class of nine (all duly graduated at the commencement of 1642) to nearly a score. They were required, as a preliminary to admission, to read and write "true Latin" (prose and verse) and to read ordinary Greek, and they were not allowed to use their mother tongue except in public oratory. Their training consisted mainly in "declamations in Latin and Greek and disputations, logical and philosophical," which upon set days, once a month, were conducted "in the audience of the magistrates, ministers and other scholars"; degrees were granted "according to the custom of the English universities," and the regulations drawn up for undergraduate conduct and education would have served with very little change for a Cambridge college in contemporary England. The provision of "commons" preceded that of "lectures and exercises," and Harvard still retains the Cambridge fashion of providing rooms and meals for its students as well as class-rooms and laboratories. Nothing could be more in the spirit of the old world than this extract from the "Body of Laws for Harvard College made by the President and Fellows thereof and consented to by the Overseers of the said College anno domini 1734":

Fellow Commoners shall have the privilege of dining and supping with the fellows at their table in the hall, and shall be excused from going on errands, shall have the title of Masters, and shall have the privilege of wearing their hats as masters do, but shall attend all duties and exercises with the rest of the Class, and be alike subject to the Laws and Government of the College; and shall sit with their own Class, and in their place in the Class at the worship of God in the hall and meeting-house.

The indebtedness to the old country is not surprising, but it is notable, for it means that the English tradition was handed on not only to American colleges, but to American life. There is, however, one striking omission from the statutes—no theological tests were imposed on either students or teachers, and theology was omitted from the curriculum. Dunster, the first president, was known to be a disbeliever in infant baptism, but so long as he made no open profession of this heresy, he was not disturbed. When, however, he advocated his views in church meeting, he was indicted by the grand jury, convicted, and obliged to resign the presidency, on account of the influence his learning and personality were known to exercise. Accepting the loss of his office without protest, he addressed to the general court a manly and temperate plea to be allowed to stay in the house he had built till the winter was over, and from this I will quote a sentence or two, for the letter gives us a glimpse of a soul in which high-mindedness mingled with gentleness:

1. The time of the year is unseasonable, being now very near the shortest day, and the depth of winter.

2. The place unto which I go, is unknown to me and my family, and the ways and means of subsistence to one of my talents and

parts, or for the containing or conserving my goods, or disposing of my cattle, accustomed to my place of residence.

3. The place from which I go, hath fire, fuel, and all provisions for man and beast, laid in for the winter. To remove some things will be to destroy them; to remove others, as books and household goods, to hazard them greatly....

4. The persons, all besides myself, are women and children, on whom little help, now their minds lie under the actual stroke of affliction and grief. My wife is sick, and my youngest child extremely so, and hath been for months, so that we dare not carry him out of doors,...The whole transaction of this business is such, which in process of time, when all things come to mature consideration, may very probably create grief on all sides; yours subsequent, as mine antecedent. I am not the man you take me to be....But our times are in God's hands, with whom all sides hope, by grace in Christ, to find favour, which shall be my prayer for you, as for myself, Who am, honoured Gentlemen, yours to serve.

The court allowed him to stay, but it did not pay the arrears of his salary, and at his death he left his affairs to be arranged by his successor in the presidency and a ministerial colleague, who had described his gifts as "the venom and poison of the Evil One." He was a puritan saint without a touch of bigotry or bitterness, and one wishes that the New England leaders had better appreciated the nobility of his spirit.

His successor, Charles Chauncey, had taught Greek and Hebrew at Trinity College, Cambridge, before coming to the new world. He also was unorthodox on the subject of baptism, but only as to the manner in which the rite should be administered. He believed in the immersion of infants—that they should be "washed all over"; but as this custom was unsuited to the climate, he did not press his view, and was allowed to hold it and the presidency unmolested.

Harvard and its sons have played a part in every great crisis in the history of the colony and the nation, and a review of its contributions to American life would be a fitting subject for many lectures. All that I have time to say here is that its influence and the influence of its graduates has been on the side of learning and of liberty, and it has continued to hold the position of leadership in American higher education for which its early foundation gave it the first opportunity. Under the guidance of Charles W. Eliot (President 1869–1909), still its revered President Emeritus and one of the most honourable and honoured figures in American life, Harvard liberalized its curriculum so as to include modern subjects. This gave the undergraduate a freedom of choice which was sometimes bewildering, but on the whole salutary, and by the end of the nineteenth century the elective system, as it was called, was gradually extended to every American university of importance. About the same time (1870) Harvard revolutionized the study of law by the establishment of what is known as the case system, and won for its school of medicine and graduate school a well-deserved reputation. No other American university can boast of having had so many men of distinction on its professorial staff.

Harvard also took the lead in the athletic contests which have since become as notable a feature of college life in the United States as they are, or were before the war, in the English colleges. Harvard won the first college boat race rowed in American waters in 1852. In contrast to the elaborate training undergone by modern crews it may be noted that these mid-nineteenth century oarsmen had rowed only a few times before the race "for fear of blistering their hands," and had continued their ordinary diet except that on the day of the race they abstained from eating candy. But this is a digression.

Political and national vicissitudes are better illustrated by the fortunes of William and Mary College, established at Williamsburg, Virginia, in 1693. It is perhaps significant that while the New England settlers relied on their own resources and exertions, and were thus left for more than half a century in sole possession of the field of American higher education, the Virginian colony turned for help to the mother country.

There was an attempt in 1622 to found an "Academia Virginiensis et Oxoniensis," but this came to nothing, and the founder and first president was a graduate of Edinburgh. He succeeded in obtaining a charter under William and Mary, whose names the new college accordingly bore. The college, however, needed funds as well as royal patronage and appealed to the lord treasurer. "What do you want the money for?" he abruptly asked the president of the infant college, and the president murmured in confusion, "To save souls." "Souls," he replied, "damn your souls; grow tobacco." It was as a matter of fact largely in a tax of one penny a pound on all tobacco exported from the colony that the college revenue consisted, in addition to a grant of land. Unlike the other early foundations, it has remained an old-fashioned college of classical learning in a delightful southern town, and has never sought to develop into a modern university. But it was within its walls that the first Greek letter society "Phi Beta Kappa" was organized in 1776; membership of this society with its old-fashioned motto, "Philosophy—the Guide of Life," remains the cachet of academic distinction throughout the United States, and the later fraternities, which developed into social rather than learned organizations, have become a characteristic feature of American college life.

A word of explanation is perhaps necessary as to the difference between Phi Beta Kappa and its successors. They are alike in extending to the principal colleges and universities of the United States, the parent organization having established practically autonomous chapters in all the great academic centres. A Phi Beta Kappa chapter consists of members elected year by year, the number being limited, from the graduates of a particular university, mainly, though not exclusively, on their academic record, some regard being paid to personal qualities; its social functions are slight, the chapter being called together almost exclusively for the transaction of business, chiefly the election of new members, or to hear an address or poem from some person of distinction, not necessarily connected with the society. The fraternities (or sororities as other Greek letter societies are called when they consist of women students) are mainly social; few of them make any pretence of seeking academic distinction. They are self-administering residential halls, in the case of the sororities with the assistance (in the French sense) of an elder woman as chaperon or matron. I say "in the French sense," for it is a common saying that the ideal chaperon is blind, deaf and largely dumb. As a matter of fact, these young people manage their affairs with astonishing capacity, but, as is natural when a considerable number of undergraduates are gathered together under one roof, their common efforts are directed rather to entertaining than educating each other. The "rushing" of possible candidates—that is, strenuously cultivating their society with a view of ascertaining their suitability for membership—and the ceremony of their initiation are conducted with much solemnity, but my impression is (I am, of course, not a member of any) that the secrecy in which these proceedings are involved is merely the air of ingenuous mystery that delights the heart of romantic youth. There is no doubt, however, that in some colleges the annual elections provoke as much excitement, heartburning, and tears (these, of course, in women's colleges) as a hotly-contested bye-election in an English constituency. They have become exceedingly wealthy by the gifts of prosperous graduates, and form a kind of college aristocracy which is undoubtedly very helpful to its members, but is often regarded with suspicion and dislike by the outsiders, whom the fraternity members are in the habit of describing as "barbarians."

I hope I shall be pardoned this digression, for the fraternities to some extent supply the place, in a characteristically American democratic fashion, of the English college system.

About the same time that Phi Beta Kappa was founded at William and Mary, the famous Virginia orator Patrick Henry made its halls resound with the historic "Liberty or Death" speech, which heralded the revolution, and many of the

William and Mary graduates, who were original members of Phi Beta Kappa, were also among those who signed the Declaration of Independence. When Washington was occupied by British troops, William and Mary College was taken by British soldiers, and it is pleasant to record that they treated it with respect. The college was less fortunate in the civil war, when the federal troops burnt it to the ground, and it has never entirely recovered from the loss suffered at that time. Williamsburg, the ancient capital of the colony of Virginia, has remained rather apart from modern commercial developments, and is still a charming country town with wide streets and embowering trees, a home of ancient learning and of generous southern hospitality to the few visitors attracted by its distinguished history.

The first year of the eighteenth century saw the foundation of a college in Connecticut "wherein youth may be instructed in the arts and sciences, who through the blessing of Almighty God may be fitted for public employment, both in church and state." Its later name it derives from the timely generosity of a Connecticut merchant adventurer Elihu Yale, who became Governor of Madras, and some years of unsettlement preceded its permanent establishment at New Haven. It was founded by ten congregational ministers, all but one of them Harvard graduates, who were partly dissatisfied with the tendency of their alma mater to tolerate heresy, partly eager to give the growing colony of Connecticut a college more accessible than that at Cambridge, Massachusetts. Bishop Berkeley in 1733 endowed scholarships for graduate work, and graduate courses in philosophy and the arts were begun in 1846. Yale made great progress in the middle of the nineteenth century under the vigorous administration of President Dwight. Besides the college, scientific school, and graduate school, the university now includes schools of fine art, forestry, law, medicine, music and religion. Its reputation for strict congregational orthodoxy has been transferred in more recent times to social and commercial influence and athletic prowess;

but it has never ceased to be a home of learning and the sons of Eli have been for generations prominent in every department of the national life. Without despising or neglecting intellectual distinction, it has put the emphasis more on life than on letters, and has been justified by the important public services its alumni have been able to render. The words of President Clap a century and a half ago are still largely true: "Most of our superior gentlemen who have shined brightest at the council board, on the bench, at the bar, or in the army, have had their education in this society."

The presbyterians of New Jersey in 1746 established a college which later took the name of Princeton, and has come to be joined with Harvard and Yale in friendly rivalry not only in football, but in more strictly academic pursuits and in public service. It attracted considerable attention some years ago under the energetic administration of President Woodrow Wilson, who introduced a modification of the English tutorial system in the face of considerable opposition. The establishment of a graduate college led to an equally violent controversy, and Mr Wilson left the academic arena to become Governor of New Jersey and President of the United States.

All these early colleges were in comparatively small places, for although Harvard is only a few minutes from Boston by the modern subway, it was sufficiently far away in the seventeenth and eighteenth centuries to be obliged to lead its own life. The middle of the eighteenth century saw, however, the foundation of colleges in two growing cities, King's College (afterwards called Columbia) in the city of New York (1754) and Pennsylvania (1755) in the city of Philadelphia. The great Philadelphian Benjamin Franklin is credited with the foundation of the University of Pennsylvania, and its first provost, William Smith of Aberdeen, brought to America the reformed Scottish curriculum which soon after its introduction at Philadelphia was adopted, with some modifications, by the other American colleges. This was the first substantial

reform of the scholastic curriculum introduced since the
establishment of the Cambridge course of study at Harvard
by Henry Dunster more than a century before, and no
further step in advance was taken for almost another century.
William Smith emphasized the division into years, which has
remained a characteristic feature of American college life
(though the names of the classes—Freshmen, Sophomore,
Junior, and Senior—point back to a Cambridge origin), and
he gave American college education a Scottish tinge it has not
entirely lost. The separation of the colonies from the mother
country was a disadvantage rather than a gain from the
educational point of view, for the French influence which
came in for a time had no permanent effect, though traces of
it may be found in the plans of Thomas Jefferson for the
University of Virginia and in the appointment in 1784 of a
president of the University of the State of New York after
the example of the University of Paris. The development of
Columbia, as King's College was called after the revolution,
followed the development of New York city and came into
real significance and power in the latter half of the nineteenth
century and the early years of the twentieth. The same is to
be said of the University of Pennsylvania. Both universities
draw their support from the wealth of the communities in
which they are placed and give their students and professors the opportunities for cultivation in a wide sense
offered by the resources of a great American city outside as
well as inside the walls of the university.

The connection of Roger Williams, a Pembroke man, the
American apostle of religious liberty, with Providence, Rhode
Island, gives an especial interest to the foundation in that
city in 1764 of Rhode Island College, now called Brown
University. Its charter provided that of the thirty-six trustees,
twenty-two should be baptists, five quakers, four congre-
gationalists and five episcopalians; of the twelve fellows,
eight should be baptists and the rest of any denomination;
that the president should be a baptist, but that the other

members of the faculty might be of any protestant faith. It was further provided that "into this liberal and catholic institution shall never be admitted any religious tests, but on the contrary all the members hereof shall for ever enjoy full, free, absolute and uninterrupted liberty of conscience and the sectarian differences of opinion shall not make any part of the public and classical instruction." This was an extension of the honourable tradition of liberty established at Harvard (as already noted) and continued at Yale, both of them congregationalist, and at Princeton, which was founded by the presbyterians. President Clap of Yale said in 1766: "persons of all denominations of protestants are allowed the advantage of an education here, and no inquiry has been made, at their admission or afterwards, about their particular sentiments in religion." The second charter of Princeton, granted in 1748, stipulated that the laws of the college should not exclude "any person of any religious denomination whatsoever from free and equal liberty and advantage of education, or from any of the liberties, privileges, or immunities of the said college on account of his or their being of a religious profession different from the said trustees of the said college." At King's College (Columbia), which was episcopalian, the aim of the institution at its foundation was said to be to train the students "in all virtuous habits and all such useful knowledge as may render them creditable to their families and friends, ornaments to their country and useful to the public weal in their generation. As to religion there is no intention to impose on the scholars the peculiar tenets of any particular sect." The charter forbade the authorities to "exclude any person of any religious denomination whatever, from equal liberty and advantage of education, or from any of the degrees, liberties, privileges, benefits or immunities of the said college, on account of his particular tenets in the matters of religion." In the University of Pennsylvania, another episcopalian foundation, no religious tests were allowed. At William and Mary, which was also episcopalian, the professorship of divinity was abolished at the revolution with the remark: "It was formerly instituted for the purposes of the church of England which is here established, but it is now thought that establishments in favour of any particular sect are incompatible with the freedom of a republic, and therefore the professorship is entirely dropped. The doors of the university are open to all." This spirit of liberality, characteristic of the beginnings of the older American colleges, became thoroughly interwoven with the national life as a fundamental principle of education in all grades, and the great American republic has thus been saved from the complications and friction which religious controversies in connection with education so often arouse in less favoured lands. Undenominationalism is a central principle of public education in the United States, and any attempt to encroach upon the liberty thus gained is keenly resented by public opinion.

The opening up of the West in the nineteenth century gave the early settlers the opportunity of carrying thither the enthusiasm for education and for the principles of religious liberty which they had inherited from their colonial forefathers. In the very first year of the century, when the population of Northern Ohio could not have exceeded 1500, petition was made to the territorial legislature for the grant of a charter to what later became Western Reserve University:

We consider our present national character abroad and our civil and religious liberties at home to have their foundation laid (under God) by the early institution of public schools and colleges for the education of youth. We apprehend that the continuation of the rights and liberties of our country does depend under Divine Providence on the continued exertion of our political fathers and the people of information in general to devise and promote ways and means for education.

It was with these aims in view that Western Reserve College was established in 1828 at Hudson, Ohio, to be later reorganized as a university at Cleveland, and that

Washington University was founded at St Louis, Missouri, in 1853.

The legislatures of the middle west and of the Pacific slope provided generously by taxation for university education, and I am relieved, as well as pleased, to know that the story of the state universities is to be told in this hall to-morrow evening by my honoured colleague, Dr G. E. Mac-Lean, who, as former Chancellor of the University of Ne-braska and ex-President of Iowa University, is pre-eminently qualified to deal with the subject. Mention must, however, be made of two conspicuous private benefactions—the foundation of the University of Chicago by Mr John D. Rockefeller and that of Leland Stanford Junior University by Mr and Mrs Leland Stanford in memory of their son. The history of these two universities goes back little more than a quarter of a century, but their large endowments have enabled them to make very remarkable progress.

The state universities are co-educational, and in them men and women students meet on a footing of absolute equality. On the eastern seaboard, separate colleges for women sprang up and placed themselves at once on a level with the men's colleges as educational and social institutions. I should have more to say about them if the whole subject of the position of women in the United States were not at this meeting in the competent hands of Mrs Bowlker, who is to speak to you to-morrow afternoon. I turn, therefore, to a brief survey of general developments in university instruction in the United States during the modern period.

In the days of the colonial colleges all the instruction was given by the president, with the aid of a few tutors. William and Mary, which was supposed at the time of the revolution to be working on the Oxford curriculum, had five professors: the first (president), of mathematics and natural philosophy; the second, of law and police; the third, of chemistry and medicine; the fourth, of ethics and belles-lettres; the fifth, of modern languages. The professorship of humanity was abolished with that of divinity after the Declaration of Independence. The course was one of extraordinary liberality. To quote the words of the president in 1780:

> The doors of the university are open to all, nor is even a knowledge of the ancient languages a previous requisite for entrance. The students have the liberty of attending when they please and in what order they please or all the different lectures in a term if they think proper. The time for taking degrees was formerly the same as Cambridge but now depends upon the qualifications of the candidate. He has a certain course pointed out for his first degree and also for the rest. When master of either, the degree is conferred.

This seems to combine laxity of class attendance with a go-as-you-please examination system, and if it is rightly described in 1780 as the Oxford system, it was Oxford at its worst. It is not unlikely that it was at its worst towards the end of the eighteenth century and the beginning of the nineteenth. Edward Everett wrote from Oxford in 1818:

> I have been over two months in England, and am now visiting Oxford, having passed a week in Cambridge. There is more teaching and more learning in our American Cambridge than there is in both the English universities together, though between them they have four times our number of students.

The fact is that about a century ago university education on both sides of the Atlantic was at a low ebb. At Yale, as late as 1825, every class at entrance was broken up into divisions of about forty students each, and each division of forty was assigned to a tutor who remained their sole instructor in all branches of study, to the end of the junior year, when they passed as seniors under the direct care of the president. After that date the practice grew up at Yale and elsewhere of assigning professors to subjects rather than to students, and the Yale curriculum of 1828 was a distinct step in advance. The foundation of the Lawrence Scientific School at Harvard in 1847 and of the Sheffield Scientific School at Yale in 1859 marks the arrival of a new and powerful competitor among the subjects of academic study. A further step forward was taken at both Harvard and Yale by the organization of graduate schools in 1872 and by the foundation at Baltimore in 1876 of Johns Hopkins as a centre for graduate study with D. C. Gilman as president. The organization of graduate work at all three universities was carried out under German influence, for reasons which need not here be dwelt upon. It is enough to say that in 1835 there were four American students in German universities, in 1860 there were seventy-seven, in 1880 there were one hundred and seventy-three, and in 1891 there were. four hundred and forty-six. The effect upon American higher education of an increasing tide of American professors trained in Germany was by no means all for good; it strengthened American education at the point where it least needed it—in systematic organization—but as the tide is now over, and will, we hope, flow in other directions henceforth, we need not stay to lament the past. It is enough to quote the latest historian of university education in the United States, Dr Louis F. Snow:

Our colonial colleges were English in their traditions and curriculum. These modern modifications of methods and material must have been German in their origin. But the essential character of the structure has never been altered, the assimilation of the foreign strain has but strengthened and more deeply rooted the native stock.

The history of the American universities during the last thirty years has been one of continuous and exceedingly rapid development, especially in the directions of scientific and professional education, which now includes schools not merely of law, medicine and engineering, but of agriculture, horticulture, forestry, domestic science, journalism, diplomacy, pharmacy, dentistry, and commerce. At any of the larger universities a student may prepare himself (or herself) for almost any calling in our highly complex American civilization.

Usually such professional training is necessarily preceded

by a college course, and for those who wish to pursue advanced studies in literature or pure science, graduate courses are provided of sometimes bewildering variety. If I may be pardoned for using my own university and my own subject as an illustration, it is sometimes a subject of academic chaff that I hold the thirteenth chair of English at Columbia, and all thirteen of us, together with my younger colleagues, are giving graduate courses in English literature. Other subjects and other graduate schools have proportionately large staffs of specialists. Though it is difficult to obtain precise figures, there is no doubt that in consequence of the development of opportunities for graduate study at home, even before the war the number of American professors trained in Germany had greatly fallen off. In medicine and in technical science a considerable number of American students still sought instruction abroad; but in the literary subjects the American universities had become largely self-supporting.

It will be seen that we have reached a stage of highly organized specialization—perhaps too highly organized—and it may be asked why American students, with these opportunities at their own doors, should wish to come to English universities where the organization of graduate teaching is less advanced. Well, there are reasons, and very good reasons, which I must not stay to elaborate. My chief desire is, and my chief occupation during the last few months as Director of the London Branch of the American University Union has been, to facilitate the interflow of students and professors between the two great Anglo-Saxon nations. I am sure American students will find much to their profit in your ancient halls of learning, and still more outside of them in the knowledge of English life and the English countryside; and I think English students might learn something by a visit to our institutions for advanced study and research. In any case, the travelling student will do his share to increase the mutual understanding, liking, and respect between the two nations upon which depends the future, not only of the United Kingdom and the United States, but of modern civilization.

UNIVERSITIES

A FEW BOOKS AND FACTS

A History of Higher Education in America. By CHAS. F. THWING. 1906.
The College Curriculum in the United States. By LOUIS F. SNOW. 1907.
American College and University Series (Oxford University Press).
"Columbia." By F. P. KEPPEL.
"Harvard." By JOHN H. GARDINER.
"Princeton." By V. L. COLLINS.
"Vassar." By JAS. MONROE TAYLOR and ELIZABETH HAZELTON HAIGHT.

Name	Place	Founded	Students	Staff
Harvard	Cambridge, Mass.	1636	6306	892
William and Mary	Williamsburg, Va.	1693	242	19
Yale	New Haven, Conn.	1701	3254	478
Princeton	Princeton, N.J.	1746	1535	215
Columbia	New York	1754	15,494	1215
Pennsylvania	Philadelphia	1755	9000	630
Brown	Providence, R.I.	1764	1100	100
Western Reserve	Cleveland, Ohio	1826	3168	340
Washington	St Louis, Mo.	1853	1304	226
Johns Hopkins	Baltimore, Md.	1876	2666	340
Leland Stanford Jr.	Palo Alto, Cal.	1891	1500	225
Chicago	Chicago, Illinois	1891	10,448	600

STATE UNIVERSITIES, SCHOOL SYSTEMS, AND COLLEGES, IN THE UNITED STATES OF AMERICA

GEORGE EDWIN MACLEAN, Ph.D., LL.D.

STATE UNIVERSITIES, SCHOOL SYSTEMS, AND COLLEGES, IN THE UNITED STATES OF AMERICA

THE lecture by Professor Cunliffe, my esteemed colleague, has shown that the British universities, and pre-eminently Cambridge, were mothers of American universities planted in colonial times along the Atlantic seaboard.

As the state and not the federal government is the educational unit; my subject includes the institutions planted since the American Revolution, owned and controlled, in whole or in part, by the forty-eight present states in the union. These institutions, founded and manned by those who came from the colonial colleges, are the grandchildren of the British universities, but possessed particularly by the spirit of the Cromwellian commonwealth and of the "glorious revolution" of 1688.

As a part of their zeal for religion, the Puritan Fathers cherished scholarship. The saying of the New England mother is famous, "Child, if God make thee a christian and a scholar thou hast all I ever asked for thee."

My colleague's lecture has shown that that mother's spirit still possesses the commonly called "endowed universities," but better named, non-state universities, since state institutions also have endowments. The state institutions are a supreme proof of the spread of the spirit which President Angell of Michigan named "the American passion for education." An eminent American-born scholar confirms, but disparages, this "passion for education." In the *Cambridge Modern History*, he says, "in America a faith in the saving grace of education seems more deeply rooted than even religion itself. In short, the nation that we are trying to understand is

12—2

a nation whose most prominent characteristic at this moment is its superstitious devotion to education." This passage from an American justifies a recent British writer in saying "the Americans have become educationally mad." He approvingly adds, "however, that is a very healthy form of national insanity."

It is fair to you that I, as a New Englander, whose life work has been done in three state universities in the middle west, should avow that I have this "superstitious devotion to education." Before I finish perhaps you will have just occasion to use the expression of an Oxford don after he had received a lengthy and tedious *questionnaire* seeking information as to Oxford from a university in the States named "Western Reserve." The don exclaimed "If this is Western Reserve, what would be Western exuberance?"

Our topic is threefold, treated in order of time, state universities, state school systems, and state colleges, each worthy of a series of lectures. They are a supreme manifestation of Americanism. Their remote origins may be traced to Europe, but they take their definite form from the time of the founding of the republic. The fathers of the republic, in the wilderness of the new world, smote the rock of freedom whence gushed forth the waters of learning with a miraculously increasing stream.

First speaking of the state universities, no less an authority than President Pritchett of the Carnegie Foundation writes: "The rise of these great universities is the most epoch-making feature of our American civilization, and they are to become more and more the leaders and makers of our civilization. They are of the people."

The immediate origin of these universities may be traced to the ordinance for the government of the North-Western Territory, adopted in 1787, by the Congress of the Confederation, and precedent to the adoption of the constitution of the United States. You will recall that the thirteen colonies on the Atlantic seaboard, when they had secured their independence, had to provide government for the vast tract of land west of the Alleghanies and north-west of the Ohio river extending to the Mississippi and the British possessions on the Great Lakes. This country was uninhabited except by Indians and a few white men in British trading posts and French settlements. The ordinance provided that not more than five states should be organized out of the territory and a state might be set up when it had a population of sixty thousand. Each state was to have equal standing with the thirteen original states, instead of being a subject colony. This was a magnificent concession by the original thirteen states.

This first experiment in far flung federation was the first-fruits of the American revolution, ultimately resulting in the present federal union of forty-eight states. Two other pregnant ideas of the ordinance were that slavery should not be extended into the states of the territory and the mandate for state education. The ordinance may be called the Magna Carta of state educational institutions. A famous sentence of the ordinance is emblazoned in golden letters in the great assembly halls of the universities of Michigan and of Iowa: "Religion, morality, and knowledge, being necessary to good government and human happiness, schools and the means of education shall forever be encouraged."

Please observe the educational trinity in which "religion, morality, and knowledge" are one and inseparable. And also note the twofold basis for state education. First, it is a necessity to good government in a republic; since the acts extending the suffrage in Britain you have expressed it in the phrase, "We must educate our governors." Second, the recognition of the necessity of education to human happiness implies the right of every human being in a democracy to have equal opportunity for the highest education of which he is capable.

In the course of time five states, Ohio, Indiana, Illinois, Michigan and Wisconsin, three of which have each an area about equal to that of England and Wales, were carved out of

the North-Western Territory. By congressional acts townships
of thirty-six square miles were surveyed in each state, with
every sixteenth section (one square mile) in each township
reserved for the support of schools and two entire townships
for the support of a state university. This became a precedent, in the admission of new states to the union, for land
grants and educational systems with a state university as a
crown. Indeed four of the original thirteen states, and it is
noteworthy they were in the south, North Carolina, South
Carolina, Georgia and Virginia, also established state universities. In recent times the influence of the state university
idea has effected the establishment of a state university in
Maine and a semi-state university—Cornell—in New York.
At present there is a total of forty-two state universities, only
nine states having none. These nine states are of the original
thirteen which are well supplied with institutions on private
foundations.

Our time will only permit us to outline a typical western
state university. Upon the admission of the state into the
union provision was made for the sale of the lands of the two
university townships reserved by congress in order to create
a building and endowment fund. In most cases these lands
were disposed of at ridiculously low prices and the universities were opened as petty institutions in a poverty-stricken
condition among scattered settlements of impecunious but
ambitious pioneers. This waste of the proceeds of the federal
grants, intended to create an ample endowment, has resulted
in a claim upon the conscience of the states to make the
original endowment more than good, so that within the last
forty years the states have made liberal appropriations and
have laid "millage" taxes which have sustained the prodigious
growth of these institutions.

The governing board of the university, now ordinarily a small
body of nine to fifteen men, known as a board of regents, or
of trustees, or of education, was at first commonly appointed
by the governor of the state and confirmed by the senate.

As early as 1851 in Michigan and later in Nebraska the board was elected directly by the people. The board elects a resident chancellor or president as the head of all the faculties. Ordinarily the board appoints the professors upon the recommendation of the president, and deans of the colleges, and heads of the departments concerned. The president is either a member of the governing board, or sits with them and presents the agenda. He has a responsible leadership. He is, with scarcely an exception, a person of the teaching profession, supposed to have executive ability, a prolonged tenure of office, and to be a representative of the various elements in the university. He has the five-fold task of retaining the confidence of the governing board, of the faculties, of the student-body, of the graduates, and of the people of the state, especially as represented in their legislature. Is it a wonder that he has been challenged as the "American Boss President," and even depicted by an eccentric professor as "a black beast in the academic jungle"? An answer is found in the progress of the universities that have retained the leadership, in a business age, of efficient presidents as compared with that of universities frequently changing their presidents; or having only a rotating chairman of the faculty, as was formerly the case in the University of Virginia. If further proof be required, a famous case may be cited. A democracy realized the dream of Plato in making a "philosopher, ruler," by elevating the President of the University of Princeton to the Presidency of the United States in the person of Woodrow Wilson.

The qualifications for appointment to the staff of instruction are in practice not unlike those set out for the appointment of university professors or readers in the University of London, namely: a consideration of the candidate's "(1) contributions by research to the advancement of science or learning; (2) his powers as a teacher; (3) generally his eminence in his subject or his profession."

In the States weight is laid upon the possession of a Ph.D.

degree or its equivalent as an indication of not less than three years of successful research work beyond the first degree. The educational management and discipline of the university are committed to the teaching body subject only to approval by the governing board which is supposed to devote itself to the financial administration.

The curriculum of the university at first was inherited from the New England college and was compulsory through a course of four years devoted chiefly to Greek, Latin, mathematics including some elements of natural science, mental and moral science, rhetoric, logic and even Paley's *Natural Theology* and *Evidences of Christianity*. So strong were the traditions of the classics that university towns were named Athens. The extreme strength of the classical tradition is illustrated in the grotesque coining of words from Greek in the legislative act of 1817 establishing the University of Michigan.

"Be it enacted by the Governor and Judge of the Territory of Michigan that there shall be in the Territory a Catholepistemiad, or University denominated the Catholepistemiad, or University of Michigania. It shall be composed of thirteen didaxum or professorships: First a didaxia, or professorship of Catholepistemia, or universal science."

The happy outcome of the New England college tradition is that the core of all these universities is what is now generally known as the faculty and college of liberal arts giving the B.A. degree. The cast iron four years compulsory course has given place to what is known as an elective system with groups of cognate studies into which the newer subjects of study have been introduced. A group of studies corresponds roughly to a tripos at Cambridge, or an honour school or one of its subdivisions at Oxford.

Not infrequently the college of liberal arts in the state university has by law been made the measure by which the many independent or non-state colleges should be standardized. The multitude of institutions ambitiously professing and calling themselves colleges but with low terms of admission led, in the opening of the twentieth century, the state and non-state universities in co-operation with the best preparatory and secondary schools to attempt to secure a standard of college entrance requirements. In 1906 the National Conference Committee on Standards of Colleges and Secondary Schools was formed. The result has been the almost universal adoption of sixteen so-called "units" for admission to a "standard college," which would ordinarily require four years of study in a secondary school, after from six to eight years of elementary and intermediate study. "A unit represents a year's study in any subject in a secondary school, constituting approximately a quarter of a full year's work." It may seem meticulous thus to safeguard the admission to a standard college, but it has become necessary amidst the competition of many colleges and in the interest of innocent parents and youth. No regular student can matriculate in a standard college with less than fourteen units, whereas a generation ago, about one half of that amount would have been accepted. No less important than the raising of the standards and securing a degree of uniformity in measuring them has been the increase in the flexibility of entrance requirements. The formerly compulsory subjects covering the entire preparatory course have been reduced to a minimum of seven or eight units, leaving seven or eight units for elective studies. English language and literature, one foreign language, and mathematics at the most remain compulsory. The electives, with limitations as to the amount in any single subject, may include even manual training, or domestic science, agriculture, drawing, fine arts and music.

The articulation of the secondary school with the college is made closer. It is not forgotten that the spirit and ideals of the college defy objective standards. As your public schools and provincial universities have been largely manned by graduates from Cambridge and Oxford, so the traditions of the old American colleges have been handed on from professor to professor, so that every true college has an atmosphere. The proof of this is in the consecration of the professors to their life work—a consecration so great that they live upon low salaries, sometimes lower than the wages of bricklayers. The much abused word "culture," when understood in the broad sense in which Principal Shairp defined it as "sympathy with intelligence," is a note of the true college.

Time has been given to the liberal arts college, not only because it has held its own as the centre for the professional and technical schools in the few highly developed state universities, but because the majority of state universities are still only in the collegiate stage of development. Only eleven state universities[1], as indeed only eleven universities on private foundations, have as yet attained the standards requisite for membership in the Association of American Universities. Though universities in name they remained only colleges until the revival of patriotism and the prosperity of the country which followed the civil war after 1865. Then professional and technical schools were grouped about the college of arts and science. In the last half century the following schools or colleges have been incorporated in the university, viz. of law, of medicine (including the training of nurses), in a few cases of homoeopathic medicine, of dentistry, of pharmacy, of applied science and engineering, of agriculture, of commerce, of library training, of music and fine arts, of education and—as the touchstone of a true university—a graduate college.

Summer sessions, real university terms, have been universally added, and a university extension division. The university extension movement, which originated in the University of Cambridge with the late lamented Professor James Stuart as its father, was so congenial to the American spirit that it was soon taken up.

[1] The state universities of Illinois, Indiana, Iowa, Kansas, Michigan, Minnesota, Missouri, Nebraska, Ohio, Virginia, and Wisconsin.

Naturally the state universities, close to the people and recognized servants of the state, have developed mȯdern forms of university extension by which centres for practical instruction for adults are organized in every part of the state. The University of Wisconsin is mentioned the world over as an example of this work, but the other states are now catching Wisconsin up.

The University of Virginia, the Mother of Universities of the south, with the exception of those of North and South Carolina and Georgia which antedate its foundation, is a variation from the type of the state universities of New England lineage in the north-west. Its story is filled with the personality of one of the greatest founders of the republic and the third President of the United States, Thomas Jefferson. It has been pointed out that the story is a remarkable illustration of Emerson's epigram that "an institution is the lengthened shadow of one man." The last seven years of his life were given to the erection of the university buildings according to an original and classical plan. The university he ranked among his highest accomplishments. In the epitaph he himself composed which is inscribed upon his monument we read, "Here was buried Thomas Jefferson, author of the Declaration of American Independence, of the Statute of Virginia for Religious Freedom, and Father of the University of Virginia." By his omission of "twice President of the United States" he seems to make the Father of the University greater than a President of the United States.

Jefferson once said he "had sworn upon the altar of God eternal hostility to every form of tyranny over the mind of man." He carried out this oath not only politically but in his plans for the university in which he gave to the students the opportunity of free choice or of election of studies. This resulted in the abolition of a prescribed curriculum and of the four-year class system. It introduced specialization. Jefferson even reduced discipline to a minimum so that the University of Virginia has become known the world over for its "honour system" of student government. In examinations there is no invigilator. The students over their signature upon their examination papers pledge their honour that they have neither received nor given assistance. The public sentiment of the students makes it impossible for a student to violate his pledge and longer remain at the university.

Jefferson's plan for university organization broke away from the dogma that a university must have its foundation in arts or consist of the four faculties of theology, law, medicine and philosophy. He substituted distinct schools or cognate groups of studies, e.g. ancient languages, modern languages, etc., an idea which may be traced to the University of Paris. Jefferson acknowledged that there were some "novelties" in his university, like those of a professorship of principles of government, of instruction in the Anglo-Saxon tongue, and of agriculture. With his radical views of government he stipulated that there should not be a principal or president, but that the professors should in turn be chairman of the faculty for a year. In 1904 the University of Virginia felt so strongly the need of the leadership of a president that the statute was changed—and the university now flourishes under its first president.

A totally different type of state university which we can only mention is the University of the State of New York. Alexander Hamilton the great political antagonist of Jefferson is credited with inspiring its plan. It was an adaptation of a French centralized, standardizing, and examining body, but it never became a teaching university. It exists to this day as an influential educational agency.

The latest type of state university is that which has been evolved since 1862 out of colleges of agriculture and mechanic arts, of which I shall speak under the heading of state colleges.

The second subject assigned to me is the school systems. The state university has officially been declared "an integral part of the school system." The system began from the university. It is an illustration of the saying that in the kingdom of education, as in the kingdom of heaven, the movement is from above downward. Where there are state universities—normally they are the head or perhaps better the heart of the school system.

There are several types of systems. As we have seen in New York state there is a highly centralized plan. The commissioner of education, in conjunction with the university, has control of elementary and secondary schools, of examinations for promotion and admission to the professions, and authority in chartering institutions of higher learning.

Iowa, Indiana and the middle western states generally represent school systems less centralized, in which the state through a state superintendent or board of education divides the authority and the responsibility in differing degrees with the localities through their county and city superintendents and town or district committees.

In Oregon the county is the real educational unit, while the state oversight and control is weak.

In states like Ohio, Missouri and Arkansas the state school systems are only nominal. In effect there are a series of small, local, school systems. Townships in Ohio and districts in Missouri and Arkansas are the real educational units.

In recent years there has been an increasing tendency toward centralization. Petty school districts with the one-room rural school-house have been consolidated and pupils transported at public expense to central schools. High schools have been established at least one in every county and the state pays the tuition of non-resident pupils. State commissioners of education with permanent tenure of office have been appointed in place of state superintendents elected periodically by the people. There are state school inspectors and in many cases the inspection of the high schools is conducted by the state university.

In a number of states there is a complete system even with kindergartens. Commonly, there are eight grades or years in the elementary and intermediate schools and four in the high schools. In addition to these twelve grades, in some places the four years in the undergraduate course of the state university, and the three or four years in the graduate college or professional school are reckoned as rounding out nineteen or twenty grades of the free (except for nominal fees in the university) public school system. The pupils are promoted from grade to grade oftentimes semi-annually. A leaving certificate given to a graduate of a high school and containing a record of his standing in the subjects accepted for admission by a university, together with a testimonial of the high school principal that, in his judgment, the pupil in character and ability is fitted to undertake collegiate education, is accepted from inspected high schools in lieu of an entrance examination.

These school systems, in some states more and in others less developed, represent the fulfilment of the prophecies of many generations. John Knox in 1560 had the vision of schools in each parish, and academies preparing for the universities. The example of Scotland and the academies set up by dissenters in England doubtless impressed the colonial forefathers. The earliest instance of colonial school systems is found in the quaintly worded law of the Massachusetts Bay Colony in 1647. It runs "It being one chief project of that old deluder Satan, to keep men from the knowledge of the Scriptures,... It is therefore ordered by the court that every township within this jurisdiction, after the Lord hath increased them to the number of fifty householders, shall then forthwith appoint one within their own town to teach all such children as shall resort to him, to write and read." "And it is further ordered that where any town shall increase to the number of one hundred families or householders, they shall set up a grammar-school, the master thereof being able to instruct youths so far as they may be fitted for the university."

In the legislature of Virginia in 1779, Jefferson's proposal was another anticipatory dream, to connect primary, secondary and higher education and to send "the boy of best genius" on to the nearest grammar school to be educated gratis, and finally, after six years of public training, to William and Mary College. Huxley's "educational ladder from the gutter to the university," and the Worker's Educational Association's "highway" were old in the states, before the day of these modern leaders.

In these days of war it may not be superfluous to remark that these dreams of school systems were not "made in Germany" and antedate the far-famed Prussian school system. From the middle of the nineteenth century, the German and particularly the Prussian influence became considerable, especially in the universities, but was declining before the war with the rise of American graduate colleges.

The administration of the school system is more or less effective in the hands of the forty-eight state superintendents or commissioners of education, aided in 1915 by 2768 county superintendents and 2263 city superintendents.

Generally a state or county graded certification of teachers prevails. The ideal, which as yet is far from realized, is that common school teachers shall be graduates of high schools, high school teachers graduates of colleges, and college teachers and superintendents graduates of universities.

If one gains the impression that the school systems are mere caudal appendages of the universities, it may be said that they have almost become strong enough to wag the dog. It must also be remarked that there is an increasing feeling that the systems must be reconstructed from bottom to top. There are proposals to telescope the grades, to reduce the eight pre-high school grades to six, to telescope the last two years of the high school and the first two years of the college, not only to save time but to afford more opportunity for adaptation of courses to the abilities and life work of the pupils. The idea is to make the systems vital-organisms instead of organizations.

The third significant educational step for which the way

had been prepared by the state university and common school movement, and which was precipitated by the on-coming of the industrial age and the crisis of the greatest war in history next to the present war, was the movement which established the land grant or state colleges of agriculture and the mechanic arts. In July 1862 President Lincoln approved an act of congress known, from the name of the author of the bill, as the Morrill Act. The act donated to each state in the union public land scrip to the amount of thirty thousand acres for each senator and representative then in congress. The income from the sale of the scrip "should be for the endowment, support, and maintenance of at least one college whose leading objects were to be, without excluding other scientific and classical studies, and including military tactics, to teach such branches of learning as are related to agriculture and mechanic arts." The act did not use the name "university" common to the earlier land grant acts, but "college." The act did not contemplate industrial *universities*, but colleges which might become a part of existing univer-sities. In some twenty of the states the legislatures when accepting the land grant added the colleges to the others in the state university. In the other states they were set up as separate colleges, which in two or three of the states have developed into universities. As the United States is primarily an agricultural country, despite the recent diversification of its industries, the word agriculture is one to conjure with in congress and in legislatures. Successive land grants and finally direct appropriations by congress have been made, which in turn have stimulated the states to make appropria-tions.

Agricultural experiment stations, now numbering sixty-one, of which every state and territory has one or more, followed the passage of the Hatch Act in 1887 granting fifty thousand dollars per annum federal aid to each state and territory. In 1906 by the Adams Act an additional grant of fifteen thousand dollars was made to these stations. With a few exceptions the stations were established as departments of the colleges of agriculture and mechanic arts. The revenues of these stations in 1916 aggregated more than five million dollars, two millions of which were derived from direct appropriations by the states. The personnel of their staffs, men given to research, included nearly nineteen hundred persons.

The university or college extension movement has culminated in cooperative extension work in agriculture and home economics as provided for in the Smith-Lever Congressional Act of 1914 making hugely increased federal grants to every state. The main features of this cooperative extension system are the county agricultural agents (men), the home demonstration agents (women), the establishment of boys' and girls' clubs, the maintenance of moveable schools of agriculture and home economics, reinforced by the work of the college and experimental station specialists. The statistics of this work in 1916 are astonishing. Special efforts were made in fifteen southern states where demonstrations under the supervision of county agents were carried on by upwards of one hundred and ten thousand farmers, involving the growing of crops on a million and a half acres from which records were obtained, showing on the average an increase of production and profit of one hundred per cent. over ordinary yields and profits. In the northern and western states one hundred and eight thousand field demonstrations were conducted and more than one million seven hundred thousand people were reached through meetings, about eighty-one thousand farmers were enrolled in the farm bureaux, and nearly eighty thousand cows were tested for milk production. The women home demonstration agents were until recently employed exclusively in the southern states. These agents gave instruction to over eighty thousand women and girls. The work began as a rule with an effort to increase the earnings of the women through the home garden, canning and preserving, marketing of eggs, butter, fruits, and vegetables, poultry raising, etc., and the improving of the farm diet. Home sanitation, the use of labour saving devices, combating of insect pests, serving, the care of children, and the beautification of the home also received attention.

In 1916 analyses were made of the business of over fifteen thousand farmers, with the result that over six thousand began keeping farm accounts and many made changes in their methods of farming, putting it on a better economic basis.

For the fiscal year beginning July 1st, 1916, the total fund available for extension work from federal, state, and local sources was over six million dollars. These dull figures are, I submit, rather dazzling in their promise of the attainment of well-nigh universal education and increased production. They will be particularly refreshing in these times of food rationing, and help to explain how our food administrator, Mr Hoover, can warrant sufficient supplies for the allies.

There is only time to mention that there are state normal schools or colleges, several schools of mines, and various affiliated research organizations. The last are ordinarily affiliated with or under the control of the university. Illustrations of these are the state geological survey, the state library commission, the state conservation commission, the bureau of plant diseases and destructive insects, the state bacteriological, chemical and other laboratories, the state museum of natural history, the state water survey and state historical societies.

Thus the university, in addition to its functions of teaching youth and of research, has become almost an arm of the government, or certainly, as President Van Hise expressed it, "the expert adviser of the state."

I hope that you will not think that in the enumeration of so many state educational activities I have strained a point as did the Kansas farmer who wished to make a good report for the government census. He claimed that he had twenty-six head of stock—the return showed two cows, two horses and twenty-two hens!

The sketch I have so inadequately outlined of American state education illustrates the intense idealism of the people which the allies have so generously recognized since we came into the war. Our survey discloses educational ideals only the beginnings of which have been realized. Universal and practically free education, without distinction of race, creed or sex, predominantly by the state, is supplemented by church colleges and institutions on private foundations. This makes the three-fold cord of education, which is not soon broken, on which our civilization largely depends. It may not be a violation of our not too well-known American modesty to cite the opinion of a non-American authority. Lord Bryce has written in his book *The American Commonwealth*: "It is the glory of the American universities, as of those of Scotland and Germany, to be freely accessible to all classes of the people." "In every civilised country the march of scientific discovery has led to an enormous increase of the applications of science to productive industry.... Nowhere, perhaps not even in Germany, has this movement gone so fast or so far as in the United States.... One who surveys the progress of the United States during the last fifteen or twenty years finds nothing more significant than the growth of the universities in number, in wealth, and in the increased attendance of students from all ranks of life. They have become national and popular in a sense never attained before in any country.... They have turned a university course from being the luxury which it has been in the old world into being almost a necessary of life." A text-book on *Government and Politics in the United States* summarizes it: "From the first century A.D. down to the very beginning of the nineteenth century, education was almost universally controlled by the church, and was confined to the wealthier classes; while to-day education is generally recognized as a function of the state, and its benefits are freely offered to all children, the expense being borne by the community. Nowhere has this modern conception of free public education been more fully realized than in the United States."

These tributes, if written today in view of the stirrings in your universities and of the education act just put on your statute-book under the leadership of Mr Fisher, would constrain the authors to place Great Britain beside the United States. Henceforth they will be side by side. To this end there must be a study of each people by the other. This venerable university, "the mother of us all," has portended, by the selection of the subject of the United States for this summer session, the creation of an intellectual understanding and sympathy to ensure the leadership of the English speaking peoples in peace as well as in war.

This day the prophecy of Jefferson, of more than one hundred years ago, in seeking to have English teachers in Virginia is being fulfilled in our ears. He said: "For these two nations holding cordially together have nothing to fear from the united world. They will be the models for regenerating the condition of man, the sources from which representative government is to flow over the whole earth."

REFERENCE BOOKS AND STATISTICS

A Cyclopedia of Education. Ed. by PAUL MONROE. 1913. Macmillan & Co.

The New International Year Book. 1907. Dodd, Mead & Co.

Education in the United States. Its History. RICHARD G. BOONE. 1889. Appleton.

American State Universities. Their Origin and Progress. ANDREW TEN BROOK. 1875. Cincinnati.

History of the Higher Education of Michigan. A. C. McLAUGHLIN. 1891. U.S. Bureau of Education.

Cambridge Modern History, vol. 7. United States. 1903. Cambridge University Press.

Thomas Jefferson and the University of Virginia. HERBERT R. ADAMS. 1888. U.S. Bureau of Education.

UNIVERSITIES, SCHOOLS, AND COLLEGES 197

Jefferson's University. JOHN S. PATTON, *et al.* 1915.

Indiana University. Ed. by SAMUEL B. HARDING. 1904. Bloomington, Indiana.

Illinois. By ALLAN NEVINS. American University Series. 1917. Oxford University Press.

A Decade of Development in American State Universities. GEORGE E. MACLEAN. 1896. University of Nebraska.

Present Standards of Higher Education in the United States. GEORGE E. MACLEAN. 1913. U.S. Bureau of Education.

Education and Economic Success, Some Lessons from America. The Fortnightly Review, August, 1918.

State Universities	First opened
†Alabama, University of ...	1831
*Arizona, ,, ,, ...	1891
*Arkansas, ,, ,, ...	1892
*California, ,, ,, ...	1869
†Colorado, ,, ,, ...	1877
*Florida, ,, ,, ...	1884
*Georgia, ,, ,, ...	1801
*Idaho, ,, ,, ...	1892
*Illinois, ,, ,, ...	1868
‡Indiana University	1824
*Purdue University (Indiana)	1874
†Iowa, State University of	1855
†Kansas, University of	1866
*Kentucky, State University of ...	1865
*Louisiana State University	1860
*Maine, University of	1868
‡Maryland, Johns Hopkins University (semi-state)	1876
†Michigan, University of	1841
*Minnesota, ,, ,, ...	1869
†Mississippi, ,, ,, ...	1848
*Missouri, ,, ,, ...	1847
†Montana, ,, ,, ...	1895
*Nebraska, ,, ,, ...	1871
*Nevada, ,, ,, ...	1886
†New Mexico, ,, ,, ...	1891

* Indicates that the College of Agriculture and Mechanic Arts is in the University.

† Indicates that the College of Agriculture and Mechanic Arts is separate but engineering is taught in the University.

‡ Indicates that the College of Agriculture and Mechanic Arts is separate and engineering is *not* taught in the University.

State Universities					*First opened*
*New York, Cornell University (semi-state)				...	1868
†North Carolina, University of	...	...	...		1795
†North Dakota, University of	...	...	...		1884
*Ohio State University	...	...	...	...	1872
‡Ohio, Ohio University	...	...	...	...	1808
‡Ohio, Miami University (semi-state)	...		...		1824
†Oklahoma, University of		...	...	...	1892
†Oregon, University of	...	...	...	...	1876
†Pennsylvania, University of (semi-state)			...		1755
†South Carolina, University of	...	...	...		1805
†South Dakota,	,,	,,	...	...	1882
*Tennessee,	,,	,,	...	...	1794
±Texas,	,,	,,	...	...	1883
†Utah,	,,	,,	...	...	1850
*Vermont,	,,	,,	...	...	1800
†Virginia,	,,	,,	...	...	1823
†Washington,	,,	,,	...	...	1861
*West Virginia University		...	...	...	1868
*Wisconsin, University of		...	...	...	1848
*Wyoming,	,,	,,	...	...	1887

   * Indicates that the College of Agriculture and Mechanic Arts is in the University.

   † Indicates that the College of Agriculture and Mechanic Arts is separate but engineering is taught in the University.

   ‡ Indicates that the College of Agriculture and Mechanic Arts is separate and engineering is *not* taught in the University.

     State Colleges—separate from Universities   *First opened*

Michigan College of Agriculture and Mechanic Arts ...   1857
26 other Colleges   ,,   ,,   ,,   *between* 1865 *and* 1895

    246 State Normal Schools or Teachers' Colleges

In 1916—1917	Total staff of instruction	Total students
State Universities	8,111	128,956
State Colleges of Agriculture and Mechanic Arts	3,340	42,855
State Normals and Teachers' Colleges	532	9,350
Totals in State Institutions	12,983	181,161
Total 574 Universities and Colleges reported in U.S.		259,511

LITERATURE IN CONTEMPORARY AMERICA

HENRY SEIDEL CANBY, Ph.D.

LITERATURE IN CONTEMPORARY AMERICA

THE analysis of conditions and tendencies in contemporary American literature which I wish to present in this lecture, requires historical background, detailed criticism, and a study of development. I have time for none of these, and can only summarize the end of the process. If, therefore, in trying to gather ideas and fling them into one lecture, I seem to generalize unduly, I hope that my deficiencies may be charged against the exigencies of the occasion. But I generalize the more boldly because I am speaking, after all, of an English literature; not in a Roman-Greek relationship of unnaturalized borrowings (for we Americans imitate less and less), but English by common cultural inheritance, by identical language, and by deeply resembling character. Nevertheless, the more American literature diverges from British (and that divergence is already wide) the more truly English, the less colonial does it become. A Briton should not take unkindly assertions of independence, even such ruffled independence as Lowell expressed in *The Biglow Papers*:

> I guess the Lord druv down Creation's spiles
> 'Thout no *gret* helpin' from the British Isles,
> An' could contrive to keep things pooty stiff
> Ef they withdrawed from business in a miff;
> I han't no patience with such swellin' fellers ez
> Think God can't forge 'thout them to blow the bellerses.

Vigorous independence is essential for the ambitious son of a famous father.

I desire neither to apologize for American literature, nor to boast of it. No apology is necessary now, whatever Sydney Smith may have thought in earlier days: and it is decidedly not the time to boast, for so far literature has usually been a by-product in the development of American aptitudes. But it may be useful to state broadly at the beginning some of the difficulties and the closely related advantages that condition the making of literature in the United States.

The critic of American literature usually begins in this fashion: America, in somewhat over a century, has built up a political and social organization admittedly great. She has not produced, however, a great literature: great writers she has produced, but not a great literature. The reason is, that so much energy has been employed in developing the resources of a great country, that little has been left to expend in creative imagination. The currents of genius have flowed toward trade, and not aesthetics.

This explanation is easy to understand, and is therefore plausible, but I do not believe that it is accurate. It is not true that American energy has been absorbed by business. Politics, and politics of a creative character, have never lacked good blood in the United States. Organization, and organization of a kind requiring the creative intellect, has drawn enormously upon our energies, especially since the civil war, and by no means all of it has been business organization. Consider our systems of education and philanthropy, erected for vast needs. And I venture to guess that more varieties of religious experience have been given a local habitation and a name in America than elsewhere in the world in the same period. After all, why expect a century and a half of semi-independent intellectual existence to result in a great national literature? Can other countries, other times, show such a phenomenon?

No, if we have been slow in finding ourselves in literature, in creating a school of expression like the Elizabethan or the Augustan, the difficulties are to be sought elsewhere than in a lack of energy.

Seek them first of all in a weakening of literary tradition. The sky changes, not the mind, said Horace, but this is true only of the essentials of being. The great writers of our common English tradition—Chaucer, Shakespeare, Milton, and many others—are as good for us as they are good for you. It is even whispered that our language is more faithful to their diction than is yours. But the conditions of life in a new environment bring a multitude of minor changes with them. Our climate, our birds, our trees, our daily contact with nature, are all different, to begin with little things. Your mellow fluting blackbird, your wise thrush that sings each song twice over, your high-fluttering larks we do not know. Our blackbird creaks discordantly, our plaintive lark sings from the meadow tussock, our thrush chimes his heavenly bell from forest dimness. And this accounts, may I suggest in passing, for the insistence upon nature in American writing, from Thoreau down. Our social and economic experience has been widely different also; and all this, plus the results of a break in space and time with the home country, weakened that traditional influence which is so essential for the production of a national literature. It had to be; good will come of it; but for a time we vacillated, and we still vacillate, like a new satellite finding its course.

Again, the constant shift of location within America has been a strong delaying factor. Moving-day has come at least once a generation for most American families since the days of William Penn or " The Mayflower." The president of a western university, who himself, as a baby, had been carried across the Alleghanies in a sling, once told me the history of his family. It settled in Virginia in the seventeenth century, and moved westward regularly each generation, until his father, the sixth or seventh in line, had reached California. On the return journey he had got as far as Illinois, and his son was moving to New York! The disturbing effect upon literature of this constant change of soils and environment is best proved by negatives. Wherever there has been a settled community in the United States—in New England of the 'forties, in the south of the 'forties and again in the 'nineties, in the middle west and California today—one is sure to find a literature with some depth and solidity to it. The New England civilization of the early nineteenth century, now

materially altered, was a definable culture, with five generations behind it, and strong roots in the old world. From it
came the most mature school of American literature that so
far we have possessed.

Still another difficulty must be added, the social. Pessi-
mists, who see in our eastern states a mere congress of all
the white races, and some not white, bewail the impossibility
of a real nation in America. But the racial problem has always
been with us, nor has it by any means always been unsolved.
Before the revolution, we were English, Scottish, Welsh, Low
German, Huguenot, Dutch, and Swedish. Before the civil war,
we were the same plus the Irish and the Germans of '48.
And now we add Slavs, Jews, Greeks, and Italians. I do not
minimize the danger. But let it be understood that while our
civilization has always been British (if that term is used in its
broadest sense) our blood has always been mixed, even in
Virginia and New England. This has made it hard for us to
feel entirely at home in the only literary tradition we possessed
and cared to possess—yours. We have been like the man with
a ready-made suit. The cloth is right, but the cut must be
altered before the clothes will fit him.

And finally, America has always been decentralized intel-
lectually. It is true that most of the books and magazines are
published in New York, and have always been published
there, or in Boston or Philadelphia. But they have been written
all over a vast country by men and women who frequently
never see each other in the flesh. There has been no centre
like London, where writers can rub elbows half-a-dozen times
a year. Boston was such a capital once; only, however, for
New England. New York is a clearing-house of literature
now; but the writing is, most of it, done elsewhere. It is
curious to speculate what might have happened if the capital
of the United States had been fixed at New York instead of
Washington!

From this decentralization there results a lack of literary
self-confidence that is one of the most important factors in

the intellectual life of America. The writer in Tucson or Minneapolis or Bangor is dependent upon his neighbours to a degree impossible in Manchester or Glasgow or York. He is marooned there, separated in space and time, if not in mind, from men and women who believe, as he may believe, in the worth of literary standards, in the necessity of making not the most easily readable book, but the best. Here is one cause of provincialism in America.

Nevertheless, this very decentralization may have, when we reach literary maturity, its great advantages. It is difficult to over-estimate the colour, the variety, the *verve* of American life. And much of this comes not from the push and "hustle" and energy of America—for energy is just energy all the world over—but is rather to be found in the new adjustments of race and environment which are multiplying infinitely all over the United States. It is true that American civilization seems to be monotonous—that one sees the same magazines and books, the same moving-picture shows, the same drug-stores, trolly cars, and hotels on a New York model, hears the same slang and much the same general conversation from New Haven to Los Angeles. But this monotony is super-ficial. Beneath the surface there are infinite strainings and divergences—the peasant immigrant working toward, the well-established provincial holding to, the wide-ranging mind of the intellectual working away from, this dead level of conventional standards. Where we are going, it is not yet possible to say. Certainly not toward an un-British culture. Certainly not toward a culture merely neo-English. But in any case, it is because San Francisco and Indianapolis and Chicago and Philadelphia have literary republics of their own, sovereign like our states, yet highly federalized also in a common bond of American taste and ideals which the war is making stronger—it is this fact that makes it possible to re-cord, as American writers are already recording, the multi-farious, confused development of racial instincts working into a national consciousness. Localization is our difficulty;

it is also the only means by which literature can keep touch
with life in so huge a congeries as America. If we can escape
provincialism and yet remain local, all will be well.

So far I have been merely defining the terms upon which
literature has been written in America. Let me add to these
terms a classification. If one stretches the meaning of literature to cover all writing in prose or verse that is not simply
informative, then four categories will include all literary
writing in America that is in any way significant. We have an
aristocratic and a democratic literature; we have a dilettante
and a vast bourgeois literature.

In using the term aristocratic literature I have in mind an
intellectual rather than a social category. I mean all writing
addressed to specially trained intelligence, essays that imply
a rich background of knowledge and taste, stories dependent
upon psychological analysis, poetry which is austere in content or complex in form. I mean Henry James and Mrs
Wharton, Agnes Repplier and George Edward Woodberry.

By democratic literature I mean all honest writing, whether
crude or carefully wrought, that endeavours to interpret the
American scene in typical aspects for all who care to read.
I mean Walt Whitman and Edgar Lee Masters; I mean a
hundred writers of short stories who, lacking perhaps the
final touch of art, have nevertheless put a new world and a
new people momentarily upon the stage. I mean the addresses
of Lincoln and of President Wilson.

With dilettante literature I come to a very different and less
important classification: the vast company—how vast few even
among natives suspect—of would-be writers, who in every
town and county of the United States are writing, writing,
writing what they hope to be literature, what is usually but a
pallid imitation of worn-out literary forms. More people seem
to be engaged in occasional production of poetry and fiction
—and especially of poetry—in America, than in any single
money-making enterprise characteristic of a great industrial
nation. The flood pours through every editorial office in the

land, trickles into the corners of country newspapers, makes short-lived dilettante magazines, and runs back, most of it, to its makers. It is not literature, for the bulk is bloodless, sentimental, or cheap; but it is significant of the now passionate American desire to express our nascent soul.

My chief difficulty is to explain what I mean by bourgeois literature. The flood of dilettante writing is subterranean; it is bourgeois literature that makes the visible rivers and oceans of American writing. And these fluid areas are like the lakes on maps of Central Asia—bounds cannot be set to them. One finds magazines (and pray remember that the magazine is as great a literary force as the book in America), one finds magazines whose entire function is to be admirably bourgeois for their two million odd of readers. And in the more truly literary and "aristocratic" periodicals, in the books published for the discriminating, the bourgeois creeps in and often is dominant. The bourgeois in American literature is a special variety that must not be too quickly identified with the literary product that bears the same name in more static civilizations. It is nearly always clever. Witness our short stories, which even when calculated not to puzzle the least intelligence nor to transcend the most modest limitations of taste, must be carefully constructed and told with facility or they will never see the light. And this literature is nearly always true of the superficies of life, to which, indeed, it confines itself. Wild melodrama is more and more being relegated to the "movies," soft sentimentality still has its place in the novel, but is losing ground in the people's library, the magazines. Life as the American believes he is living it, is the subject of bourgeois literature. But the sad limitation upon this vast output is that, whether poetry, criticism, or fiction, it does not interpret, it merely pictures; and this is the inevitable failure of pages that must be written always for a million or more of readers. It is standardized literature, and good literature like the best air-planes, cannot be standardized.

Now the error made by most English critics in endeavouring to estimate the potentialities or the actualities of American literature, is to judge under the influence of this crushing weight of clever, mediocre writing. They feel, quite justly, its enormous energy and its terrible cramping power. They see that the best of our democratic writers belong on its fringe; see also that our makers of aristocratic literature and our dilettantes escape its weight only when they cut themselves off from the life beat of the nation. And therefore, as a distinguished English poet recently said, America is doomed to a hopeless and ever-spreading mediocrity.

With this view I wish to take immediate issue upon grounds that are both actual and theoretical. There is a fallacy here to begin with, a fallacious analogy. It is true, I believe, in Great Britain, and also in France, that there are two separate publics; that the readers who purchase from the news stands are often as completely unaware of literary books for literary people as if these bore the imprint of the moon. But even in England the distinction is by no means sharp; and in America it is not a question of distinctions at all, but of gradations. In our better magazines are to be found all the categories of which I have written—even the dilettante; and it is a bold critic who will assert that pages one to twenty are read only by one group, and pages twenty to forty only by another. We are the most careless readers in the world; but also the most voracious and the most catholic.

And next, let us make up our minds once for all that a bourgeois literature—by which, let me repeat, I mean a literature that is good without being very good, true without being utterly true, clever without being fine—is a necessity for a vast population moving upward from generation to generation in the intellectual scale, toward a norm that must be relatively low in order to be attainable. Let us say that such a literature cannot be real literature. I am content with that statement. But it must exist, and good may come of it.

This is the critical point toward which I have been moving

in this lecture, and it is here that the hopeful influence of the American spirit, as I interpret it today, assumes its importance. That spirit is both idealistic and democratic. Idealistic in the sense that there is a profound and often foolishly optimistic belief in America that every son can be better than his father, better in education, better in taste, better in the power to accomplish and understand. Democratic in this sense, that with less political democracy than one finds in Great Britain, there is again a fundamental belief that every tendency, every taste, every capacity, like every man, should have its chance somehow, somewhere, to get a hearing, to secure its deservings, to make, to have, to learn what seems the best.

A vague desire you say, resulting in confusion and mediocrity. This is true and will be true for some time longer; but instead of arguing in generalities let me illustrate these results by the literature I have been discussing.

When brought to bear upon the category of the dilettante, it is precisely this desire for "general improvement" that has encouraged such a curious outpouring from mediocre though sensitive hearts. The absence of strong literary tradition, the lack of deep literary soil, has been responsible for the insipidity of the product. The habit of reference to the taste of the majority has prevented us from taking this product too seriously. Without that instinctive distrust of the merely literary common to all bourgeois communities, we might well be presenting to you as American literature a gentle weakling whose manners, when he has them, have been formed abroad.

Aristocratic literature has suffered in one respect from the restraints of democracy and the compulsions of democratic idealism. It has lacked the self-confidence and therefore the vigour of its parallels in the old world. Emerson and Thoreau rose above these restrictions, for reasons I have given elsewhere; and so did Hawthorne and Poe. But in later generations especially, our intellectual poetry and intellectual prose is too frequently less excellent than yours. Nevertheless, thanks to the influence of this bourgeois spirit upon the intellects that in American towns must live with, if not share it; thanks, also, to the magazines through which our finer minds must appeal to the public rather than to a circle or a clique, the nerves of transfer between the community at large and the intellectuals are active, the tendons that unite them strong. I argue much from this.

Now theoretically, where you find an instinctive and therefore an honest passion for the ideals of democracy, you should find a great literature expressing and interpreting the democracy. I have given already some reasons why in practice this has not yet become an actuality in America. Let me add, in discussing the bearing of this argument upon the third category of American literature, the democratic, a final one.

I doubt whether we yet know precisely what is meant by a great democratic literature. Democracy has been in transition at least since the French Revolution; it is in rapid transition now. The works which we call democratic are many of them expressive of phases merely of the popular life, just as so much American literature is expressive of localities and groups in America. And usually the works of genius that we do possess have been written by converted aristocrats, like Tolstoi, and have a little of the fanaticism and over-emphasis of the convert. Or they represent and share the turgidity of the minds they interpret, like the less excellent work of Walt Whitman. All this is true, and yet a careful reader of American literature must be more impressed by such prose as Lincoln's, by such poems as Whitman's, such fiction as Mark Twain's at his best, or Howell's, than by many more elegant works of polite literature. For these—and I could add to them dozens of later stories and poems, ephemeral perhaps but showing what may be done when we burst the bourgeois chain—for these are discoveries in the vigour, the poignancy, the colour of our democratic national life.

I have already hinted at what seems to me the way out and

up for American literature. It will not be by fine writing that
borrows or adapts foreign models, even English models which
are not foreign to us. It will not come through geniuses of the
backwoods, adopted by some coterie, and succeeding, when
they do succeed, by their strangeness rather than the value of
the life they depict. That might have happened in the romantic decades of the early nineteenth century, if our English
literary tradition had not been a saving influence which kept
us from *gaucherie*, even if it set limits upon our strength. Our
expectation, so I guess, is in the slowly mounting level of the
vast bourgeois literature that fills not excellently, but certainly not discreditably, our books and magazines. There,
and not in coteries, is our school of writing. When originality
wearies of stereotypes and conventions, when energy and
ability force the editorial hand, and appeal to the desire of
Americans to know themselves, we shall begin a new era in
American literature. Our problem is not chiefly to expose and
attack and discredit the flat conventionality of popular writing.
It is rather to crack the smooth and monotonous surface and
stir the fire beneath it, until the lava of new and true imagin-
ings can pour through. And this is, historically, the probable
course of evolution. It was the Elizabethan fashion. The
popular forms took life and fire then. The advice of the
classicists, who wished to ignore the crude drama beloved of
the public, was not heeded; it will not be heeded now. Our
task is to make a bourgeois democracy fruitful. We must
work with what we have.

Much has been said in the last few months of the advantage
for us, and perhaps for the world, which has come from the
separation of the American colonies from Great Britain.
Two systems of closely related political thinking, two national
characters, have developed and been successful instead of one.
Your ancestors opened the door of departure for mine, somewhat brusquely it is true, but with the same result, if not the
same reason, as with the boys they sent away to school—they
made men of us. And now, when we Americans are returning

with serious intent, it is with a deep sense of affection that we find the door open again, and a welcome within. And we come, as we went, not empty handed.

So it is with literature. American literature will never, as some critics would persuade us, be a child without a parent. In its fundamental character it is, and will remain, British, because at bottom the American character, whatever its blood mixture, is formed upon customs and ideals that have the same origin and a parallel development with yours. But this literature, like our political institutions, will not duplicate; like the seedling, it will make another tree and not another branch. We are still pioneers. I think that it may be reserved for us to discover and send back to you a literature for the new democracy of English-speaking peoples that is coming after the war—a literature for the common people who do not wish to stay common. Like Lincoln's, it will not be vulgar; like Whitman's, never tawdry; like Mark Twain's, not empty of penetrating thought; like Shakespeare's, it will be popular. If this should happen, as I believe it may, it would be a just return long owing upon our share of a great inheritance, and upon a debt to you for thought and ideas and culture that has run between us now for well nigh three hundred years.

TWO AMERICAN PHILOSOPHERS, WILLIAM JAMES AND JOSIAH ROYCE

GEORGE SANTAYANA, Ph.D., Litt.D.

TWO AMERICAN PHILOSOPHERS, WILLIAM JAMES AND JOSIAH ROYCE

FOR some twenty-five years—from 1885 to 1910—there was at Harvard College an interesting conjunction of philosophers. Why at Harvard in particular? We must remember that ever since the establishment of Christianity philosophy in the west has become an authoritative tradition —an orthodoxy (though not always the same orthodoxy) with its heresies. Under these circumstances the chief prerequisite to a relative originality in thinkers is a relative freedom. Now liberalism and orthodoxy are matters of degree, and at that time in Boston and at Harvard both were in the unitarian stage. The old college was becoming a university; granted diligence, sobriety, and theism, no professor was expected to agree with any other. Philosophers could be almost happy there, and came together from opposite ends of the United States—and even from beyond—because that was then the American community in which opinion was most ripe and most free.

William James enjoyed in his youth what are called advantages: he lived among cultivated people, travelled, had teachers of various nationalities. His father was one of those somewhat obscure sages whom early America produced; mystics of independent mind, hermits in the desert of business, and heretics in the churches. They were intense individualists, full of veneration for the free souls of their children, and convinced that everyone should paddle his own canoe, especially on the high seas. William James accordingly enjoyed a stimulating if slightly irregular education: he never acquired that reposeful mastery of particular authors and those safe ways of feeling and judging which are fostered in great schools and universities. In consequence he showed an almost physical horror of club sentiment and of the stifling atmosphere of all officialdom. He had a knack for drawing, and rather the temperament of the artist; but the unlovely secrets of nature and the troubles of man preoccupied him, and he chose medicine for his profession. Instead of practising, however, he turned to teaching physiology, and from that passed gradually to psychology and philosophy.

In his earlier days he retained some traces of polyglot student days at Paris, Vienna or Geneva; he slipped sometimes into foreign phrases, uttered in their full vernacular; and there was an occasional afterglow of Bohemia about him, in the bright stripe of a shirt or the exuberance of a tie. On points of art or medicine he retained a professional touch and an unconscious ease which he hardly acquired in metaphysics. I suspect he had heartily admired some of his masters in those other subjects, but had never seen a philosopher whom he would have cared to resemble. Of course there was nothing of the artist in William James, as the artist is sometimes conceived in England, nothing of the aesthete, nothing affected or limp. In person he was short rather than tall, erect, brisk, bearded, intensely masculine. While he shone in expression and would have wished his style to be noble if it could also be strong, he preferred in the end to be spontaneous, and to leave it at that; he tolerated slang in himself rather than primness. The rough, homely, picturesque phrase, whatever was graphic and racy, recommended itself to him; and his conversation outdid his writing in this respect. He believed in improvisation, even in thought; his lectures were not minutely prepared. Know your subject thoroughly, he used to say, and trust to luck for the rest. There was a deep sense of insecurity in him, a mixture of humility with romanticism: we were likely to be more or less wrong anyhow, but we might be wholly sincere. One moment should respect the insight of another, without trying to establish too regimental a uniformity. If you corrected yourself tartly, how could you know that the correction was not the worse mistake? All our opinions were born free and equal, all children of the Lord, and if they were not consistent that was the Lord's business, not ours. In reality, James was consistent enough, as even Emerson (more extreme in this sort of irresponsibility) was too. Inspiration has its limits, sometimes very narrow ones. But James was not consecutive, not insistent; he turned to a subject afresh, without egotism or pedantry; he dropped his old points, sometimes very good ones; and he modestly looked for light from others, who had less light than himself.

His excursions into philosophy were accordingly in the nature of raids, and it is easy for those who are attracted by one part of his work to ignore other parts, in themselves perhaps more valuable. I think that in fact his popularity does not rest on his best achievements. His popularity rests on three somewhat incidental books, *The Will to Believe*, *Pragmatism*, and *The Varieties of Religious Experience*, whereas, as it seems to me, his best achievement is his *Principles of Psychology*. In this book he surveys, in a way which for him is very systematic, a subject made to his hand. In its ostensible outlook it is a treatise like any other, but what distinguishes it is the author's gift for evoking vividly the very life of the mind. This is a work of imagination; and the subject as he conceived it, which is the flux of immediate experience in men in general, requires imagination to read it at all. It is a literary subject, like autobiography or psychological fiction, and can be treated only poetically; and in this sense Shakespeare is a better psychologist than Locke or Kant. Yet this gift of imagination is not merely literary; it is not useless in divining the truths of science, and it is invaluable in throwing off prejudice and scientific shams. The fresh imagination and vitality of William James led him to break through many a false convention. He saw that experience, as we endure it, is not a mosaic of distinct sensations, not the expression of separate hostile faculties, such as reason and the passions, or sense and the categories; it is rather a stream of mental discourse, like a dream in which all divisions and units are

vague and shifting, and the whole is continually merging together and drifting apart. It fades gradually in the rear, like
the wake of a ship, and bites into the future, like the bow
cutting the water. For the candid psychologist, carried bodily
on this voyage of discovery, the past is but a questionable
report, and the future wholly indeterminate; everything is
simply what it is "experienced as being."

At the same time, psychology is supposed to be a science,
a claim which would tend to confine it to the natural history
of man, or the study of behaviour, as is actually proposed by
Auguste Comte and by some of James's own disciples, more
jejune if more clear-headed than he. As matters now stand,
however, psychology as a whole is not a science, but a branch
of philosophy; it brings in the literary description of mental
discourse and the scientific description of material life, in
order to consider the relation between them. What was
James's position on this crucial question? It is impossible to
reply unequivocally. He approached philosophy as mankind
originally approached it, without having a philosophy, and he
lent himself to various hypotheses in various directions. He
professed to begin his study on the assumptions of common
sense, that there is a material world which the animals that
live in it are able to perceive and to think about. He gave a
congruous extension to this view in his theory that emotion
is purely bodily sensation, and also in his habit of conceiving
the mind as a total shifting sensibility. To pursue this path,
however, would have led him to admit that nature was automatic and mind simply cognitive; conclusions from which
every instinct in him recoiled. He preferred to believe that
mind and matter had independent energies and could lend
one another a hand, matter operating by motion and mind
by intention. This dramatic way of picturing causation is
natural to common sense, and might be defended if it were
clearly defined; but James was insensibly carried away from
it by a subtle implication of his method. This implication
was that experience or mental discourse not only constituted

a set of substantive facts, but the *only* substantive facts; all else, even that material world which his psychology had postulated, could be nothing but a verbal or fantastic symbol for sensations in their experienced order. So that while nominally the door was kept open to any hypothesis regarding the conditions of the psychological flux, in truth the question was prejudged. The hypotheses, which were parts of this psychological flux, could have no object save other parts of it. That flux itself therefore, which he could picture so vividly, was the fundamental existence. Where one's gift is, there will one's faith be also; and to this poet appearance was the only reality.

William James shared the passions of liberalism. He belonged to the left, which, as they say in Spain, is the side of the heart, as the right is that of the liver; at any rate there was much blood and no gall in his philosophy. He was one of those elder Americans still disquieted by the ghost of tyranny, social and ecclesiastical. Even the beauties of the past troubled him; he had a puritan feeling that they were tainted. They had been cruel and frivolous, and must have suppressed far better things. But what, we may ask, might these better things be? It may do for a revolutionary politician to say: "I may not know what I want—except office—but I know what I don't want"; it will never do for a philosopher. Aversions and fears imply principles of preference, goods acknowledged; and it is the philosopher's business to make these goods explicit. Liberty is not an art, liberty must be used to bring some natural art to fruition. Shall it be simply eating and drinking and wondering what will happen next? If there is some deep and settled need in the heart of man, to give direction to his efforts, what else should a philosopher do but discover and announce what that need is?

There is a sense in which James was not a philosopher at all. He once said to me: "What a curse philosophy would be, if we could'nt forget all about it!" In other words, philosophy was not to him what it has been to so many, a consolation and sanctuary in a life which would have been unsatisfying without it. It would be incongruous, therefore, to expect of him that he should build a philosophy like an edifice to go and live in for good. Philosophy to him was rather like a maze in which he happened to find himself wandering, and what he was looking for was the way out. In the presence of theories of any sort he was attentive, puzzled, suspicious, with a certain inner prompting to disregard them. He lived all his life among them, as a child lives among grown up people; what a relief to turn from those stolid giants, with their prohibitions and exactions and tiresome talk, to another real child or a nice animal! Of course grown up people are useful, and so James considered that theories might be; but in themselves, to live with, they were rather in the way, and at bottom our natural enemies. It was well to challenge one or another of them when you got a chance; perhaps that challenge might break some spell, transform the strange landscape, and simplify life. A theory while you were creating or using it was like a story you were telling yourself or a game you were playing; it was a warm, self-justifying thing then; but when the glow of creation or expectation was over, a theory was a phantom, like a ghost, or like the minds of other people. To all other people, even to ghosts, William James was the soul of courtesy; and he was civil to those theories as well, as to more or less interesting strangers that invaded him. Nobody ever recognised more heartily the chance that others had of being right, and the right they had to be different. Yet when it came to understanding what they meant, whether they were theories or persons, his intuition outran his patience; he made some brilliant impressionistic sketch in his fancy and called it by their name. This sketch was as often flattered as distorted, and he was at times the dupe of his desire to be appreciative and give the devil his due; he was too impulsive for exact sympathy; too subjective, too romantic, to be just. Love is very penetrating, but it penetrates to possibilities rather than to facts. The logic of opinions, as well as the exact opinions themselves, were not things James saw easily, or traced with pleasure. He liked to take things one by one, rather than to put two and two together. He was a mystic, a mystic in love with life. He was comparable to Rousseau and to Walt Whitman; he expressed a generous and tender sensibility, rebelling against sophistication, and preferring daily sights and sounds, and a vague but indomitable faith in fortune, to any settled intellectual tradition calling itself science or philosophy.

A prophet is not without honour save in his own country; and until the return wave of James's reputation reached America from Europe his pupils and friends were hardly aware that he was such a distinguished man. Everybody liked him, and delighted in him for his generous, gullible nature and brilliant sallies. He was a sort of Irishman among the Brahmins, and seemed hardly imposing enough for a great man. They laughed at his erratic views and his undisguised limitations. Of course a conscientious professor ought to know everything he professes to know, but then, they thought, a dignified professor ought to seem to know everything. The precise theologians and panoplied idealists, who exist even in America, shook their heads. What sound philosophy, said they to themselves, can be expected from an irresponsible doctor, who was not even a college graduate, a crude empiricist, and vivisector of frogs? On the other hand the solid men of business were not entirely reassured concerning a teacher of youth who seemed to have no system in particular —the ignorant rather demand that the learned should have a system in store, to be applied at a pinch—and they could not quite swallow a private gentleman who dabbled in hypnotism, frequented mediums, didn't talk like a book, and didn't write like a book, except like one of his own. Even his pupils, attached as they invariably were to his person, felt some doubts about the profundity of one who was so very natural, and who after some interruption during a lecture—and he said life was a series of interruptions—would slap his forehead and ask the man in the front row "What *was* I talking about?" Perhaps in the first years of his teaching he felt a little in the professor's chair as a military man might feel when obliged to read the prayers at a funeral. He probably conceived what he said more deeply than a more scholastic mind might have conceived it; yet he would have been more comfortable if some scholastic had said it for him. He liked to open the window, and look out for a moment. I think he was glad when the bell rang, and he could be himself again until the next day. But in the midst of this routine of the class-room the spirit would sometimes come upon him, and leaning his head on his hand, he would let fall golden words, picturesque, fresh from the heart, full of the knowledge of good and evil. Incidentally there would crop up some humorous character-isation, some candid confession of doubt or of instinctive preference, some pungent scrap of learning; radicalisms plunging sometimes into the sub-soil of all human philo-sophies; and on occasion thoughts of simple wisdom and wistful piety, the most unfeigned and manly that anybody ever had.

Meantime the mantle of philosophical authority had fallen at Harvard upon other shoulders. A young Californian, Josiah Royce, had come back from Germany with a reputa-tion for wisdom; and even without knowing that he had already produced a new proof of the existence of God, merely to look at him you would have felt that he was a philosopher; his great head seemed too heavy for his small body, and his portentous brow, crowned with thick red hair, seemed to crush the lower part of his face. "Royce," said William James of him, "has an indecent exposure of fore-head." There was a suggestion about him of the benevolent ogre or the old child, in whom a preternatural sharpness of insight lurked beneath a grotesque mask. If you gave him any cue, or even without one, he could discourse broadly on any subject; you never caught him napping. Whatever the textbooks and encyclopaedias could tell him, he knew; and if the impression he left on your mind was vague, that was partly because, in spite of his comprehensiveness, he seemed to view everything in relation to something else that remained untold. His approach to anything was oblique; he began a long way off, perhaps with the American preface of a funny story; and when the point came in sight, it was at once enveloped again in a cloud of qualifications, in the parliamentary jargon of philosophy. The tap once turned on, out flowed the stream of systematic disquisition, one hour, two hours, three hours of it, according to demand or opportunity. The voice, too, was merciless and harsh. You felt the overworked, standardised, academic engine, creaking and thumping on at the call of duty or of habit, with no thought of sparing itself or any one else. Yet a sprightlier soul behind this performing soul seemed to watch and laugh at the process. Sometimes a merry light would twinkle in the little eyes, and a bashful smile would creep over the uncompromising mouth. A sense of the paradox, the irony, the inconclusiveness of the whole argument would pierce to the surface, like a white-cap bursting here and there on the heavy swell of the sea. His procedure was first to gather and digest whatever the sciences or the devil might have to say. He had an evident sly pleasure in the degustation and savour of difficulties; biblical criticism, the struggle for life, the latest German theory of sexual insanity, had no terrors for him; it was all grist for the mill, and woe to any tender thing, any beauty or any illusion, that should get between that upper and that nether millstone! He seemed to say: If I were not Alexander how gladly would I be Diogenes, and if I had not a system to defend, how easily I might tell you the truth.

But after the sceptic had ambled quizzically over the ground, the prophet would mount the pulpit, to survey it. He would then prove that in spite of all those horrors and contradictions, or rather because of them, the universe was absolutely perfect. For behind that mocking soul in him there

was yet another, a devout and heroic soul. Royce was heir to
the calvinistic tradition; piety, to his mind, consisted in
trusting divine providence and justice, while emphasising
the most terrifying truths about one's own depravity and the
sinister holiness of God. He accordingly addressed himself,
in his chief writings, to showing that all lives were parts of
a single divine life in which all problems were solved and all
evils justified.

It is characteristic of Royce that in his proof of something
sublime, like the existence of God, his premiss should be
something sad and troublesome, the existence of error. Error
exists, he tells us, and common sense will readily agree,
although the fact is not unquestionable, and pure mystics and
pure sensualists deny it. But if error exists, Royce continues,
there must be a truth from which it differs; and the existence
of truth (according to the principle of idealism, that nothing
can exist except for a mind that knows it) implies that some-
one knows the truth; but as to know the truth thoroughly,
and supply the corrective to every possible error, involves
omniscience, we have proved the existence of an omniscient
mind or universal thought; and this is almost, if not quite,
equivalent to the existence of God.

What carried Royce over the evident chasms and assumptions in this argument was his earnestness and passionate
eloquence. It was not the fact of error that supplied these
ingenious transitions, but the fervent aspiration to escape
from it. Error was no natural, and in itself harmless, incident
of finitude; it was a sort of sin, as finitude was too. It was a
part of the problem of evil; a terrible and urgent problem
when your first dogma or postulate is that moral distinctions
and moral experience are the substance of the world, and
not merely an incident in it.

To this old problem Royce could only give an old answer,
although he rediscovered and repeated it for himself in many
ways, since it was the core of his whole system. Good, he said,
is essentially the struggle with evil and the victory over it; so

that if evil did not exist, good would be impossible. I do not think this answer set him at rest; he could hardly help feeling that all goods are not of that bellicose description, and that not all evils produce a healthy reaction or are swallowed up in victory; yet the fact that the most specious solution to this problem of evil left it unsolved was in its way appropriate; for if the problem had been really solved the struggle to find a solution and the faith that there was one would come to an end; yet perhaps this faith and this struggle are themselves the supreme good. Accordingly the true solution of this problem, which we may all accept, is that no solution can ever be found.

Royce passed for an eminent logician, because he was dialectical and fearless in argument, and delighted in the play of formal relations; he was devoted to chess, music, and mathematics; but all this show of logic was but a screen for his heart, and in his heart there was no clearness. His reasoning was not pure logic or pure observation, but always secretly malicious or enthusiastic; and the result it came to had been presupposed. I remember a saying of his that seems to sum up the man. There was no conflict, he observed, between science and religion, but the real conflict was between religion and morality. There could indeed be no conflict in his mind between faith and science, because his faith began by accepting all facts and all scientific probabilities in order to face them religiously. But there was an invincible conflict between religion as he conceived it and morality, because morality takes sides and regards one sort of motive and one kind of result as better than another, whereas religion according to him gloried in everything, even in the evil, as fulfilling the will of God. Of course the practice of virtue was not excluded; it was just as needful as evil was in the scheme of the whole; but while the effort of morality was requisite, the judgments of morality were absurd. Now, without entering upon this question on its merits, I think we may say that a man who finds himself in such a position has a divided mind, and that while he has wrestled with the deepest questions like a young giant, he has not won the fight. I mean, he has not seen his way to any one of the various possibilities about the nature of things, but has remained entangled, sincerely, nobly, and pathetically, in contrary traditions stronger than himself. In the goodly company of philosophy he is an intrepid martyr.

These two thinkers are certainly the most original, in technical philosophy, that America has yet produced. The little I have been able to say of them will have shown you that in things intellectual America is an integral part of the European world; its philosophy differs from that of Britain only in that the men who philosophize are Americans; they merely say perhaps more crudely, and perhaps more frankly, what professors of the same schools might have said in England or in Germany. But in the personalities of these two men I think we may feel something of the open vistas, the directness and the generosity which are characteristic of the new world.

THE POSITION OF WOMEN IN AMERICA

MRS BOWLKER

THE POSITION OF WOMEN IN AMERICA

I AM very grateful for the opportunity to come here today, to tell you something of the position of women in America, and to explain to you more clearly the ideals which are represented in our democracy by the women. I believe that every increase in our knowledge of each other leads to closer intimacy and truer friendship, and that it will be only through the enduring friendship between our two nations of English speech that the great ideals of justice and freedom, of ordered liberty and permanent peace, for which both our peoples stand, will become lasting realities upon earth.

We all know that it is the democracy of the allied nations which has won the victory in this great war, and that this democracy will henceforth govern the world; so that the issue of most vital significance to each one of us is to ensure that the public opinion of our own country shall become intelligently educated and organized, not a mere chaos of anarchy which spells disaster.

Today, democracy stands at the crisis of its fate, on trial in the allied nations before the judgment seat of history. Will it triumph and assure to mankind a form of government, a way of living, that shall bring prosperity and happiness to all, or will it go down, broken, crushed, destroyed, beneath the weight of an ideal too great for frail humanity to bear?

The answer to this question must be given by us who live today, and the responsibility for what that answer shall be rests in as great a measure upon the women as upon the men of our two great English-speaking democracies, Great Britain and the United States of America; for as in all things else, so with democracy, the conception which man forms and embodies in his life differs from the conception of woman, though each is needed to complement and fulfil the other, if we would find the truth.

Men and women are alike in essentials, yet we all realize that the emphasis each lays upon life is different from that of the other, even though the things that they do may be quite identical. Man's emphasis, as far back as we can trace him in history, has been placed primarily upon acquisition; to him happiness is secondary. The mighty compelling instinct of his nature which urges him forward continually is his need to acquire possessions for himself and for others, his desire to gain gifts for mankind; first, food for the tribe, then property, knowledge, art, science, everything that can beautify and enrich our common life. No gift can be greater, and none is more wide in its uses, than the power to acquire, the force which enables men to master all things.

Woman's emphasis is different. From the dim early beginnings of human life her chief labour has ever been to take the gifts man brings to the common life, and out of these to weave a magical new substance—it is the garment of human happiness that woman weaves to cover with its beauty the nakedness of all mankind! For woman's deepest instinct, the compelling hunger of her nature, has been always the need to create happiness for all those she loves, to maintain for those dependent upon her the environment which each one needs for perfect development. Such an environment is happiness.

Woman is born endowed with an instinct unique, all her own, which man does not possess, a power whose teaching shows her how to make of every place where she happens to live, be it large or small, a home for all those who come there—a home where those who dwell with her may develop in safety and bring to maturity all the best possibilities that lie dormant within them. Every woman possesses this power, if she be given the chance and be taught to develop it; therefore the leaders of thought among women know that woman will have failed to fulfil the possibilities of her life in the great life of the race, if she fail to create the environment which humanity needs for perfect development, if she fail to enlarge her dream of home until it includes within its scope the city, the whole community, the very earth itself, wherever mankind may find a place to dwell.

Democracy, as man has made it, is a political institution, a form of government, the granting to everyone of an equal right to make the laws; but all those other things that man has dreamed of in democracy, even the happiness he has hoped to conquer with his gift of acquisition, remain still an unrealized ideal; for happiness comes to human beings not as the result of some great gift to mankind, but as the uncounted sum of myriads of little daily deeds of quiet ministration, deeds that only woman's patience is glad to do again and yet again and always again, till human joy is made complete.

Democracy, as woman sees it, is not a mere form of government, but a uniting force of unmeasured power. It is a way of living, which shall give concrete embodiment in the community to those things for which *all* women care; for the deep underlying interests of all of us are the same, they centre in the very core of life out of which the vital things grow, the things which concern the heart of humanity. Each added gift of knowledge only draws this bond more close; for science is daily teaching us that no one is safe while foul disease, physical, mental, and moral, breeds in the slum close by, while feeble-mindedness and drunkenness and crime, while war and selfish lust of universal domination, lurk in the dark corners of the earth.

We cannot ensure individual happiness for ourselves or others, it is too frail and too elusive, but of one fact we can be absolutely certain, that our only possibility of permanently securing it is by basing it upon the universal well-being of the whole community.

The treasure for which women care in their hearts is the health and happiness of those they love. We know today that this treasure can only become with any hope of certainty our own, when every other person enjoys and shares it with us, and helps us to gain and keep it.

Man's emphasis upon acquisition, notwithstanding the marvellous gifts it has brought to human life, the civilization it has given us, has proved as yet to be, not necessarily but in actual fact, a centrifugal, separating force in human life, driving men apart, keeping them asunder, class and race and creed, far from one another. But woman's instinct to create happiness, rightly understood, wisely developed and utilized, will become a centripetal, convergent force of subtle power, drawing all human beings close to one another; for the treasure which women labour to acquire is not lessened, even seemingly, but grows greater with every individual's gain.

Men and women as human beings are alike in essentials, it is in emphasis only that they differ, supplementing each the other. In the hands of both *together*, acquiring, uniting, democracy can never fail.

This is our belief in America, this is the faith for which our people stand, and the object of all the public activities of women in the United States is that they may do their share in the practical ways of daily life, to make of this ideal of democracy a living reality.

The two salient points in the position of women in America are these: first, the men and the women are *friends*; second, both men and women think of the women *collectively* as mothers. This statement may sound trite, a mere platitude, yet in no other country are these two characteristics combined in the thought and the life of the people as they are in America where they give to the women a quite unique position.

To begin with the first point, the friendship between the sexes, let us consider the legislation of the United States as it illustrates this relation of mutual confidence. The men have always legislated for the women as their friends. Before there was any thought of woman's suffrage, the laws were invariably framed by the men to give equal rights and equal protection to both sexes, except that in certain respects the law grants more favoured treatment to women. For instance, the laws which regulate the possession of property give to the woman, whether married or single, the absolute right of control and disposal over all her own property; the husband has no right over his wife's possessions. The wife has a right of dower in all her husband's real estate, and he may not alienate any piece of it unless his wife signs a release of her dower right; but the husband has no corresponding right of dower in his wife's real estate. The wife has a legal right to maintenance from her husband, and therefore a first lien on his wages, but the husband has no right of support from his wife. The husband is legally responsible for all his wife's debts unless he makes a public announcement disclaiming such responsibility for the future, but no wife can be held responsible at law for the debts of her husband. The law of divorce is the same for both sexes, and a divorce is granted for precisely the same causes to both men and women. The laws which concern social welfare and the conditions of labour illustrate clearly the same friendly relation between the sexes; for such legislation has not been framed by the men with a feeling of antagonism to the women, in fear of their competition. The labour laws on the contrary have been drafted by men and women, consulting together in order to secure for both sexes better conditions of work. These laws require shorter hours and more hygienic surroundings for women, and forbid to them night work and all very heavy manual labour. But these safeguards have been provided on account of the weaker physique of the women and not because of a desire on the part of the men to secure for themselves a monopoly of labour.

In public life, in the United States, the same feeling of comradeship exists between men and women. In many states, women now have the vote, but the significant fact to be emphasized is that, wherever women have been given the vote, it has been granted to them by the men upon the basis of an equal franchise for both sexes, namely, universal adult suffrage for all municipal, state, and federal elections, and equal eligibility with the men to all public office. At the present time, in many states, women have been elected to positions of trust and responsibility, and the men invariably treat the women in office as their comrades and friends.

A striking illustration of this friendly consideration was given by the men in congress when the first woman elected to the house of representatives took her seat. The men might have been discourteous to her, they might have shown distrust of her judgment, ridicule of her actions, but instead they showed to her the same sympathy, the same kindly, helpful courtesy that they would have given to a young man in a similar position.

The friendships between men and women in America are not more numerous or more intimate than in other countries, yet it is a fact that the close comradeship between the sexes which exists in the United States gives to the women a more direct influence upon public affairs than they exert elsewhere. If we attempt to analyse the causes which have led to this friendship and co-operation between men and women, we shall find the most obvious one in the educational system of the country; for everywhere except in the east the method of co-education prevails. Boys and girls attend the same schools in childhood, the same colleges in youth, sharing together their work and their recreation, learning to judge each other according to the merits of each individual, not losing their perspective through the influence of sex. True comrades from baby-hood, "pals" in American slang, what wonder that each sex learns to rely on the other, what wonder that a feeling of mutual confidence and respect, of esteem and under-standing, exists between men and women, and endures throughout life. The close friendship between boys and girls is especially noticeable in the social class from which the soldiers are drawn, the great middle class of the country.

Question one of these boys, ask him what he misses most here, what he longs for to give him the feeling of home that he needs, and the answer invariably given by every type of man will be this: " I want to know nice girls, the kind of girls that I know at home, girls who will be my *friends*."

The second salient characteristic in the position of women in America, namely that both men and women think of the women collectively as mothers, may seem a more commonplace statement, equally true of the women of every country. Yet it is just this mental attitude which causes the women to consider themselves and to be regarded by the men as responsible to the nation for the social welfare and the happiness of the whole people, it is precisely for this reason that women have gained such direct far-reaching influence in public affairs.

Family affection in America is no deeper, no warmer than in other countries: on the contrary it is in Italy and France that the individual mothers have perhaps the greatest influence and power over their sons, even in mature life. Yet in neither Italy nor France are the mothers organized together "as mothers" to do public work as they are in the United States. In a letter from America written last winter Ian Hay said, "one of the most noticeable characteristics of the American soldier is that he is a 'mother's boy' to an extent unknown elsewhere." This statement, though true, requires an explanation to be understood here. To give an illustration. In the autumn of 1917, a nation-wide campaign to save food in America became necessary in order that, through voluntary rationing by the people in the States, the allies in Europe might be kept from starvation. Five hundred thousand women organized themselves as "crusaders," visited literally every household in every town and village, and went to each isolated farm-house throughout the country asking the "house mothers" (as the women are called) to sign the Food Pledge Card, promising in the name of their families to follow the rules for food-saving suggested by the food administrator, Mr Hoover. In one week eighteen million of the twenty-two million families in the United States signed the pledge, and the huge total of food exported to Europe proves that this voluntary pledge has been loyally kept. Few people in England realize that there was *no* exportable surplus of food in the United States in 1917-18, and therefore all the wheat and the meat exported to Europe was literally given off their own plates by our people[1]. The following anecdote connected with this campaign emphasizes the attitude of the men towards the women everywhere in America, and illustrates one aspect of what Ian Hay meant when he said that the soldiers were "mothers' boys." In Iowa 25,000 boys in training at a soldiers' camp sent a petition to the state food administrator, asking that they might be allowed to sign a special Man's Food Card, because as they said "we want to help the 'war mothers,' who are canvassing the state." Such a phrase and such an action would be impossible in Europe!

Another illustration of the prominent position of the women as mothers is the proclamation recently issued by President Wilson, appointing the date for the annual celebration of "Mothers' day." This is a yearly observance in the United States, when there are services in all the churches, and many other meetings are held: it is not a war-time measure for a peculiar emergency but an habitual custom.

----

[1] *Pre-war* average export of all food from the United States to the allies for two months, March and April = 196,000,000 lb.; in March and April 1918 = 754,000,000 lb. In the autumn of 1917, the exportable surplus of wheat over the normal consumption of the people was about 10,000,000 bushels. By July 1st, 1918, the United States had exported to the allies 144,000,000 bushels of wheat, the difference being saved from their own ration by the people.

The cattle had not increased, and the hogs had decreased since 1914, yet in the four months from November to March, 1917–1918, the United States exported to the allies 165,000,000 lb. of beef, and 200,000,000 lb. of pork. In the corresponding period *pre-war*, the export of beef was 25,000,000 lb., of pork 4,000,000 lb.

The common speech of the people shows the feeling that lies at the heart of the nation, for throughout the middle class in all parts of the country the women are always addressed by their husbands as "mother," the soldiers are called "our boys," and no one ever speaks of the place where they live as their "house," it is always their "home."

In America the domestic life of the family is planned upon a more patriarchal system than in England, the opportunities for employment are much greater, and therefore no boy or girl grows up with the feeling that in order to earn a living or make a career it will be necessary to leave the country. On the contrary every boy expects to enter his father's business, or, if that is impossible, he intends at least to follow some employment in his native town. Moreover when the children marry it is a widespread custom for parents, whose means enable them to own a country estate, to build upon their own property a house for each child, and this patriarchal way of living gives added emphasis to the influence of the mothers.

It is very difficult to generalize on the position of women in America because the country is so vast and the population is composed of many different races. Nor is it easy for English people to realize conditions so different from their own life, in a small island, with an almost homogeneous population and the ancient traditions of a feudal past.

In the United States today the people of British descent form a very small minority of the population of one hundred and ten millions, although they constitute the dominant power. The language is English, the system of law and government was brought from Great Britain, the customs and habits of life are largely English. Yet the people are not British, for as Americans they belong to a nation which draws its life and inspiration from the national thought and traditions of every race upon earth. During the fifteen or twenty years immediately preceding the war, one million immigrants landed each year in the United States, and almost every individual of that vast horde of people came from the backward, the oppressed races of south-eastern Europe: the Balkans, Armenia, Syria, with great numbers of Polish and Russian Jews.

The ignorant, illiterate, immigrant women have affected to a certain extent the position of all women in America, and therefore it is impossible to comprehend fully the national position of women unless we first understand the problem of the immigrant. The foreign women constitute a very grave menace to our democracy, for they almost invariably represent one of two extreme mental types, both equally dangerous to the stability of our institutions. One type consists of individuals who have sought refuge in America from oppression in their own country, people who have had no previous experience of self-government, and have no conception of the true meaning of democracy—ordered liberty. They come to America brimming over with theories which they hope to practise in the United States; they misunderstand the meaning of the laws and institutions and customs of the country, they misinterpret these things to each newcomer; and, knowing that Liberty begins with a capital "L," they immediately proceed to spell it Licence! It is from their ranks that the labour agitators and anarchists come. The other type of immigrant comprises the opposite mental extreme, clinging ignorantly and passionately to all the ancient traditions and customs, and even to the language of the land of their birth. Their religious belief is almost invariably Roman Catholic or Jewish of the most bigoted and ignorant type, and the women if Roman Catholics are entirely under the influence of the priests. In the state of Massachusetts, more than half the population is Roman Catholic, and three-quarters of the people are of foreign birth or parentage.

Throughout the United States large groups of aliens live in great colonies where the people work at the same occupations, unable to speak or understand any language but their native tongue, each race entirely isolated from every other. In the new draft army, according to the statistics of the Federal Bureau of Americanization, almost one man in ten has been unable to speak English, and it has therefore been necessary to establish in every training camp classes to teach these men the language of the country, in order to enable them to understand the words of command, and even to communicate with the men standing next them in the ranks.

Unfortunately the tests required by law for naturalization are not difficult for the immigrant to pass, and as the vote is easily gained by the foreigner, so it is easily gained from him for political purposes either by money or in more subtle ways, through the help and sympathy given to him in his need by unscrupulous native politicians or by ambitious self-seekers of his own nationality. In America nearly three-quarters of the unskilled manual workers cannot speak or understand English, and these people become an easy prey to every form of industrial exploitation and unrest.

There is no sex antagonism in the United States, yet there is a very strong feeling of class antagonism and an intense hostility between the different races, so that it is almost impossible for the native American, especially if well educated and of good social position, to gain influence over the immigrant. The urgent problem of America today which demands immediate solution is the "Americanizing of the immigrant." The war is giving to the country momentarily a breathing space which every social agency, every board of education, even the federal bureaux, are utilizing in the endeavour to discover the best method to make of the foreigner a loyal American citizen. The education of the adult immigrant woman is one of the most pressing needs of today, and everywhere women are seeking to learn the best way to make of her an intelligent American.

The feudal past of England affects the present conditions here to a degree that perhaps only Americans fully realize when they contrast this country with their own. In England, except in the ranks of labour, the poor women are grateful for sympathy and guidance given to them by ladies of inherited education and position if that help be offered with kindness and tact. But in America the poor women, the native as well as the foreign born, resent every effort to help them no matter how kindly given, regarding it as an impertinent intrusion into the privacy of their domestic lives.

These are the conditions which make the question of suffrage for women so complex a problem in America. The men are ready and willing to vote the suffrage to women as soon as they desire it, it is the women not the men who are making the delay. In the states of the middle west, where the population is smaller and more homogeneous than in the east and the immigrants are fewer in numbers and better educated, the problem is comparatively simple. But on the eastern seaboard with the present unrestricted immigration and the easy naturalization laws, the work of assimilating the immigrants and fitting them for intelligent citizenship is so vast that the extension of the franchise by granting the vote to women has become a matter of doubtful expediency. The wisest course for the national welfare seems to lie in delay. The state of New York has recently adopted woman's suffrage, and the result of the first election in that state at which women will cast their vote is awaited with eager interest throughout the whole country.

There is no political Woman's Party in the United States, the only political organizations of women in states where women have no vote are organizations for and against the granting of the suffrage to women. In the states where women already vote they are organized like the men politically into parties, and the vote of the women is divided at elections on almost the same lines as the vote of the men, not because the women follow the guidance of the men, but simply because the mind of the woman is not very unlike the mind of the man and she decides the same issues in the very same way. The women show a greater tendency to emphasize the need of better legislation for social welfare, while the emphasis of the men is placed more upon financial legislation to regulate business conditions. But this diversity of interest has not yet produced any very marked effect, although it is becoming of increasing importance with the wider education of women as experts in social knowledge.

In America the opportunities of advancement for everyone are so unlimited that the different classes shade into one another as is not the case here. The types accordingly are more various, and in order to gain a clear idea of the position of women as a whole it will be necessary to consider the different types in detail.

First, the university women. Many years ago women in the United States obtained the right to an equal education with men, to an equal opportunity to enter any occupation or employment. The learned professions—the bar, medicine, science—were opened to them upon an equal footing with men, and today women have the right to fill any position in any employment to which their capacity entitles them, and are taking their place in every occupation side by side with the men, as their comrades and friends. A college education is usual for both boys and girls if the parents have sufficient means to defray the expense, but in cases where a choice must be made between the children it is the custom, at least in the west, to send the girl to college while the boy earns his living. The result is that in the middle classes the education of the women differs greatly from that of the men. The intellectual vigour of the men in America is centred in their business, they study it as a profession or a science is studied, they make of it a mental pursuit. But they study nothing beyond business, and are quite content to leave to the women the knowledge of literature and history and art, not because the men undervalue this knowledge, for they are extremely proud that their wives and daughters should possess it, but simply because they have no leisure for such study.

In every western state there is a state university, and this is also the case in some of the eastern states. All state universities are supported by taxation and are co-educational, free to both sexes as students on equal conditions, and both men and women if duly qualified may become members of the teaching staff—the faculty. In the east the colleges for women are entirely separate from the men's colleges, the faculty of the women's colleges being composed of both men and women, or, as at Radcliffe College and at one or two other women's colleges, selected, from the teaching staff of a men's university. The president of a women's college is always elected by a mixed board of trustees, and the office may be held either by a man or a woman. The standard of education in the colleges for women is as high as in men's colleges, but the post-graduate courses and the original research work are not as highly developed. The number of women qualified to fill the highest professorships is still very limited, and it is for this cause, and not from a desire on the part of the men to exclude them, that so few of the highest positions in the teaching staff of the state universities are as yet filled by women.

Women professors and women graduates of colleges take a very prominent and influential position in many directions in the national life, not only through their influence upon the development of academic education, but by the emphasis they are placing upon the necessity of scientific research and of scientific training for women in the various branches of domestic economy and kindred subjects. At Mount Holyoke College, in Massachusetts, there has been started this year a summer school for health officers where college graduates are trained for work in the ordnance department of the federal government. These health officers will be given the entire responsibility for the physical health and the social welfare of all girls working in government or private factories engaged in war industries. This new branch of study is merely typical of the many specialized activities, in addition to the usual academic curriculum, which are carried on in women's colleges to fit the students for their special share of the work of the nation.

The conference called by Mr Hoover last winter in

Washington is an interesting illustration of the prominent position held by college women in America. Every woman president and every professor of domestic economy in all the women's colleges were invited to attend this conference. They were asked by Mr Hoover to take the entire responsibility of organizing a great campaign of education throughout the country, to teach the women the necessity to save food for the allies, and the need to use substitute foods. Expert college women planned and carried to successful accomplishment this very large work.

Second, the club women. In America the club woman is a very influential person, not by herself but because she belongs to a club! A woman's club does not mean a place of residence, it means a society organized to do useful work. Every town in the United States has many clubs. Even the little villages have each a woman's club whose members do active work for the community, and almost every woman whether rich or poor, educated or ignorant, belongs to a club. These thousands of clubs are associated together to form the National Federation of Women's Clubs, which has a membership of more than two million women. The members of the federation belong to every class and every type of woman in the country, college graduates and trades women. Each club sends delegates to the biennial sessions of the whole federation, and the action taken at these very large and truly representative meetings has become a far-reaching influence of national importance.

The club movement was first started by women nearly fifty years ago for self-culture. In America there is great beauty of scenery but very little beauty of art, and almost no historical antiquities. In England such beauty and interest exist everywhere, but in the United States whoever loves classic art can only enjoy it through books or photographs or by leaving the country for travel. It is for this reason that Americans are inveterate travellers, especially the women, whose eagerness for self-culture is almost a religion. In the beginning the women met in clubs for reading or for the exchange of books and of photographs. But of late years they have broadened their outlook beyond their own culture, and have awakened to a consciousness of civic responsibilities to their local communities and to the whole country. In large measure it is owing to the energy and the influence of the club women who work in close sympathy with the men that many of the states have "gone dry," and that the "dry laws" are rigorously enforced.

Since America joined the allies the women have been doing very active work to save food. In March 1918 the scarcity of wheat became so acute in Europe that Mr Hoover called upon all the people of America, asking them voluntarily to abstain from all use of wheat until after the harvest, in order that there might be enough bread for their allies. The response was instantaneous everywhere! The biennial meeting of the federation of women's clubs happened to be then in session and unanimously the delegates voted to give up all use of wheat, not only in their households but in all public eating places.

But the women were not content to give up buying wheat. They ransacked their pantries, and wherever they found wheat held in reserve (the small bagful previously allowed by Mr Hoover as "a patriotic portion"), they sent it at once to the state food administrator requesting that it should be forwarded immediately to the people who needed it here— their friends and their allies. In Arkansas, a state with a very small population, the women sent in a fortnight two and a half million bushels of wheat to the food administrator. Can one wonder that Mr Hoover spoke of the women as "our only police force in our great voluntary campaign for food saving"? Can we wonder that in his report to President Wilson he said, "in assessing the credit for the vast export of food which has been saved for the allies by our people, no one will deny the dominant part of the American women"? Truly it is the women who have been inspiring all the

people with the feeling of self-sacrifice, it is they who are
making of that small commonplace act of food-saving a great
deed of human fellowship.

Third, the labour women. The labour movement in
the United States has less power than in England, for the
wage earners are not as universally unionized. Before the
war only one-tenth of the men and very few women were
organized in trade unions, yet in comparison with the men
more women are organized in unions in America than in
England, and the women have far greater power and influence in the councils of labour. The newspapers give
daily accounts of the work done by women as labour leaders
or as labour agitators. You read of women addressing large
enthusiastic meetings of men, for both sexes are working together in America and helping each other to improve the
conditions of labour. Although an intensely hostile feeling
exists in the ranks of labour towards every other class in the
community, there is no political Labour Party in the United
States. Yet no development of the present time in America is
more interesting to follow than the action of labour—of the
men and the women who work—for they are proving by their
actions that, in spite of the antagonism of class, they realize
their own welfare to be closely bound up with the welfare of
the whole country, that they feel themselves to be an integral
part of the nation.

The Miners' Union, representing the basic industry of the
United States, with a membership of half a million men,
voted quite voluntarily nine months ago that no miner should
be allowed to take more than two days holiday in each month,
and that for every violation of this rule a fine of two dollars
(8s. 4d.) should be paid; since then the miners have voted to
give up all holidays until the end of the war. The Miners'
Union opposed a motion put before them to advise the
government not to draft miners for fear of curtailing the
production of coal, and instead the men adopted unanimously
the following resolution: "The miners inform the govern-

ment that they are ready and anxious to serve the country wherever the government considers that they can be of most use, either in the mines or in the trenches." The shipbuilding trades have voted to give up the usual Saturday half-holidays and Sunday holidays until the end of the war. The Iron, Steel, and Tin Metal Workers' Union, the great seamen's unions, the women workers in many factories and large shops, have voted voluntarily and unanimously, to give up all use of wheat until after the harvest, and to follow loyally the suggestions of the food administrator until the war ends. Truly labour in America is proving itself to be a vital part of the nation's life—the women who labour no less than the men!

Fourth, the rich women, and the poor women. There are two types of women in every country, the rich who have inherited everything, and the poor who have inherited nothing. The rich women of social position in America, with few exceptions, have until recent years taken no interest in political life or in public affairs since the early days of the country. The capacity of these women for public service has been shown by their able organization and administration of the charities, the hospitals, and the many other philanthropies of their local communities. It is to these women of inherited wealth and position that the nation has turned for leadership in the present emergency, and it is they who are successfully organizing all the war relief work throughout the country.

The poor women, the wives of the unskilled workers, the women who are unskilled workers themselves, unlike the poor of other countries, are usually in the United States of foreign birth. These women are often unable to speak English, they keep all their foreign customs and consider their old traditions almost sacred. Their habits are dirty and unsanitary, and they form a serious menace to the community where they live. Moreover the standard of the immigrant with regard to the position of women is usually that of the backward races. The only possibility of influencing the poor and the ignorant women whether native born or foreign, the only way to bridge the great chasm between them and all other women is by inspiring them with the universal American belief in the value of education. The civic and municipal leagues of women which exist everywhere are trying to bring education into the homes of the people by teaching the mothers. The children go to school but the mothers are quite ignorant, and it is absolutely essential for the foreign mothers that they be taught the English language, not merely to enable them to understand American ideals of living, but in order that they may enrich the country with many things brought from their own lands, their manual arts, their folk-lore, their strong ties of parental respect.

Fifth, the municipal league women. A new movement among women that promises to be of fundamental value, and which is already irresistibly advancing their position in public affairs, is the organization of civic or municipal leagues under the leadership of educated women of social position. The Women's Municipal League of Boston is one of the most progressive and typical of these leagues; the women who belong to it are educating themselves to understand what the women have the power to mean in a democracy, what the women have the power to make democracy mean for their country. This league is actually uniting all types of women in the city for work together in the common belief that their city is, in reality, the big house which belongs to all the people, men, women, and children, who live in it together, and that it is upon the women of this great family that the responsibility must lie to make of their common house a clean, healthy, pleasant place to live in, and to give to it the feeling of a home. No one kind of woman can do this for the others, because no one can keep the district where other women live clean and healthy, each one must do her special share of the work.

The annual membership dues of the league are fixed at six-pence in order that every woman and girl who cares to join may be able to do so. Many hundreds of the poorest, the most ignorant women of the crowded districts, even the foreign born immigrants, have become enthusiastic members of the league and are actively doing their share in the common housekeeping and homemaking of their city.

The league has many departments of work. It seeks to secure cleaner streets and markets and better housing conditions, and to prevent infant mortality by the education of the mothers. It aims at the training in citizenship of all the children in school and later placing them in industry and supervising their employment, and opening the school houses in the evening as social centres for the educational recreation of the neighbourhoods. The successful work done by the league in improving the market conditions in Boston and securing greater cleanliness and more sanitary care of the food is typical of all the work done, and is instructive as illustrating the new spirit of democracy in American women—not charity, which means help given to others, but civics, which means self-help for the welfare of all. This modern conception of democracy holds infinite possibilities for the future development of every country, and therefore it may be of interest and value as suggestion to describe in detail the method of work.

The first step taken by the league in Boston was to educate the rich, the middle class, and the college women to understand the dirty conditions of the markets as they actually existed in their own city and to realize the need for better sanitation. It was also necessary to teach these women the importance of working together in order to create an intelligent public opinion which should exert direct influence upon the government of the city.

The second step was to interest the poor and the ignorant women and secure their co-operation, for without their help no permanent result could be achieved. Talks were given at mothers' meetings, and to the utter surprise of the speakers the women responded at once to the thought of the city as *their house* for which they were responsible! Instead of in-

difference or dislike the women showed the keenest enthusiasm, they were overheard whispering to each other
"She's right, we could do that, it would make a difference,"
and after the first meeting they came crowding round the
speaker saying "We always thought it was only the rich and
the educated people who could do anything for the city but
now we see what we can do!" The idea of the city as their
own house was a revelation to these women and an inspiration! They told many stories of dirty conditions in the shops
where they dealt, of which the women in better circumstances
had been totally ignorant. For instance that the food which
they bought, bread, cake, candy, butter and cheese, all things
to be eaten uncooked, were sold to them wrapped up in dirty
newspaper. The dealers, they said, bought from the rag-men
who took it off the filthy dumps, or from the Chinese laundry-
men who obtained it from the wrappings of soiled clothes! The
league made a careful investigation and found these statements true; it was then clearly explained to the women that,
as customers, they held the power of the purse and that if
enough of them would agree not to buy food kept in dirty
conditions the proprietors would be forced in self-defence to
improve their shops.

Three months later the following anecdote was told by a
poor negro woman to an enthusiastic and active member of
the league. She said that one day she bought fish as usual at
the shop where she always dealt, and brought the fish home
wrapped in clean brown paper. A friend who came to visit her
took a fancy to the fish and asked where she bought it and on
receiving the address went to the same shop—but, alas! she
returned with her fish done up in dirty newspaper! Now fish
must be *cooked* before eating, and therefore the paper which
wrapped it was not of importance, but the principle of cleanliness must always be vindicated! The first woman, very angry
at the treatment given to her friend, hurried off to the shop
and asked the dealer what he meant by selling to her friend
fish wrapped in dirty newspaper. The man was quite

startled, and answered that he did not know the other woman belonged to the league; then he added, "I never sell anything done up in dirty paper to anyone who belongs to the Women's Municipal League"! A few weeks later a little girl told her experience; she bought candy in a nice looking shop, but to her disgust she saw the proprietor wrap it in dirty newspaper, she remonstrated with him and pointing to a pile of clean brown paper on the counter asked that her candy might be done up in that paper. The proprietor objected, "I can't do that, because I always keep that clean paper for the members of the Municipal League." "Oh!" answered the child, "but I belong to the Junior League, can't I have clean paper?" and she showed him her badge. "Why, of course," the man exclaimed, "if you belong to the Junior Municipal League, you shall have the clean paper too!"

In all the districts of the city the appearance of the shops improved noticeably as the active interest of the customers increased. One especially dirty shop where the league inspector had been vainly trying for weeks to improve the conditions suddenly became clean and tidy. The inspector asked with much interest what had happened to bring about such an unexpected and rapid improvement and was somewhat amused at the proprietor's reply. He said, "You brought your Junior League organization to the schools in this neighbourhood and hundreds of children came in here every day, and told me, very politely, that they would rather buy their food in a cleaner shop, so of course I had to clean up!" The children had been very carefully told that they must be always polite and not find fault with their elders, and it was pleasing to learn that they followed this instruction.

But the customers cannot do everything that is necessary to ensure sanitary conditions in the markets. Suitable regulations for the storing and the handling of food must be made by the public authorities and these city ordinances must be strictly enforced, for democracy, if it is to succeed as a form of government, cannot be wholly dependent on private initiative.

Yet, since in democracy public opinion is the final arbiter, the league decided to create a public opinion for greater cleanliness in markets, not among women only, but among the city officials as well. For this purpose it was thought necessary to secure the help of the girl students at Radcliffe College. The professor of government at Radcliffe, who was a member of the faculty of Harvard University, was very willing that volunteer students should be trained by the league, and taught, under the league supervisors, to make an investigation of the provision shops of the city. He even agreed that the work of these students should count towards their college degree. The investigation produced a mass of facts, which were carefully tabulated, and these statistics were finally submitted to the Boston Board of Health, with a request for the necessary legislation. The members of the board were first surprised, then convinced. They passed suitable regulations which have been carefully enforced, and the city officials have been heard to say that they were willing to listen to suggestions from the league, because of the common sense shown by its actions. The significant fact in this special piece of work, which excuses the detailed description, is the proof it affords that no one type of woman alone could have accomplished the result. The co-operation of all kinds of women was essential to the final success, and the democratic method of work was shown to be fully justified. The truly democratic membership of such a league is the prototype and the best education for the large democracy of universal suffrage.

Sixth, the women school teachers. A very large number of the teachers in American schools are women, a much larger proportion compared to the men than was the case in England before the war, and especially is this true of the free schools which correspond to the elementary and secondary schools here. The younger children, both boys and girls, are entirely taught by women. Even in the older classes the women teachers preponderate and the boys are under the influence of women for a longer period than is entirely wise. But the salary paid to teachers is at present inadequate to attract a sufficient number of men to the profession. In the meantime the women teachers fulfil their duties with a conscientious, self-sacrificing, enthusiastic devotion which is truly remarkable. No type of woman in the community has as great an influence on the future development of the nation as the teachers, for theirs is an unrivalled opportunity for public service.

Today in the United States patriotism, citizenship, have acquired for everyone a deeper meaning, a more vital significance, and in every state of the union both the men and the women teachers realize the urgent necessity of training the children for citizenship, and are giving to this subject a more careful consideration than has ever yet been granted it. Citizenship as usually taught in school has no interest, no power to attract the mind of the child, to fire his imagination, to touch his heart. Civics is to the child a dull arid subject, a mere series of laws devoid of all practical connexion with his own life. Perhaps the real reason for this lack of vitality in the study of civics is that the subject is actually as remote and uninteresting to the mind of the teacher as it is to that of the child. The most interesting training in the knowledge and practice of citizenship, and therefore the training which is proving most useful, can be given to the children by the teachers only in close co-operation with agencies outside the school, which are able to establish the necessary connexion with the home of the child.

The Women's Municipal League has organized junior leagues of children in the free schools of Boston, teaching them practical civics by means of a travelling exhibit which is taken to each school in turn. The exhibit consists of large models of clean and dirty markets, of clean and dirty houses, with a big doll for a baby, and so on. Talks are given to the children in connexion with the exhibit, they are told that the city is in reality their own big house, and that they must learn to be responsible for the care of it. The enthusiasm of the children is kindled at once. It is truly astonishing to watch the eager interest of the boys as well as the girls, they speak of the streets "as the halls and corridors of our house," they call the markets "our larders," and the different places in which they each live are "our own rooms in the great house that belongs to us all." Yes! even civics can strike fire from the imagination and wake into active consciousness every latent ideal, the children have proved it in their junior leagues. The teachers ask the children to write compositions on their civic work; one little girl entitled her composition "The World as a Family" and wrote:

I will not throw my orange peel or anything else into the street, it is the corridor of my own house and I want my house to look nice. I had never thought before of the world as one big family but now I cannot think of anything else, and when I see a man or a woman working I think to myself, they are doing something for somebody else in this big family. It makes the world seem so much more beautiful to think of it thus.

Many of the school teachers are members of the Women's Municipal League and are convinced believers in the junior leagues as an influence of permanent value in the life of the children. These teachers have asked that a text-book for school use be compiled from the actual experience gained by the teaching of practical civics in the junior leagues. Three thousand children belong to these leagues in Boston, and every child would enthusiastically become a member were there only enough women leaders.

The object of the junior leagues is not merely to teach practical citizenship to the children, cleanliness, health, etc. The boys and girls are taught also to grasp the meaning and use of "the rules of our big family," the laws of the city, the state, and the nation, they are made to understand the government in which they live and of which they form a part, they are taught to feel a personal responsibility in the welfare of their own community. But the proof of success lies in success itself, the effect of such teaching must be found in the children. The boys of the junior leagues are actually co-operating intelligently and willingly with the firemen and the police, because for the first time they understand their value —a notable achievement which stands to the credit of women. Between the ages of nine and thirteen both boys and girls have a natural interest in copying their elders, they like to be busy with grown up affairs, they enjoy the feeling that they are helping to make of their city a clean house and happy home for everyone who lives in it. But if these years are allowed to pass without utilizing this instinct of childhood, without forming habits to last all through life, the opportunity can rarely be regained, for later the child's interest in his own life develops, until in adolescence it becomes the dominant pre-occupation.

This detailed account of one experiment with children is an illustration of the work which women are doing everywhere in America, for the women of the United States believe that the responsibility must finally rest upon them to give to every child in the nation a *feeling* of citizenship which shall later lead to a *thought*, the desire which shall fulfil itself in intelligent action. For in all life there must for ever lie behind every thought which is translated into action the dynamic force, the motive power of an emotion. The emotion which is the life of all the public activities of women in America— the spirit which underlies their national position—is their intense belief that democracy must mean for all of us the *feeling* of an abiding fellowship among all people.

As in the individual life men and women are both needed, working side by side together, gaining, keeping the common home of both, so must it also be in the larger life of all humanity. Woman has the power to see one vision, before man sees it, in its very dawning—the vision of a home shining above the whole wide world—then in the light of that radiance she must turn to him and say "Behold my vision! Come, help me! for only *together* can we attain its perfect realization!"

This is the secret of the position of women in America.